D1234129

MUSIC AND THE MIDDLE CLASS

WILLIAM WEBER

Music and the Middle Class

*The Social Structure of Concert Life
in London, Paris and Vienna*

HOLMES & MEIER PUBLISHERS, INC.
NEW YORK

Published in the United States of America 1975
by Holmes & Meier Publishers, Inc.
101 Fifth Avenue, New York, New York 10003

Library of Congress Cataloging in Publication Data

Weber, William, 1940–
    Music and the middle class.

    Bibliography: p.
    Includes index.
    1. Music and society. 2. Concerts——London.
    3. Concerts——Paris. 4. Concerts——Vienna.
    5. Music——History and criticism——19th century.
I. Title
ML3795.W39   780'.07   75-22197

ISBN 0-8419-0218-6

Printed in Great Britain

CONTENTS

PREFACE

Troubled times have come to the classical-music world. Since the middle of the 1960s its exponents in both Europe and the United States have voiced increasing worry—sometimes virtual panic—that its public is dying, that its institutions are near collapse, and that it will soon cease to be the pinnacle of Western musical culture. Nothing will remain, some have predicted, but rock festivals and Lawrence Welk. While the outcome has not been that severe, much clearly has changed. Orchestras, recitalists, and even opera companies do not reign supreme over all musical life as they once did. Fewer young people seem to be learning orchestral instruments than before. Declining attendance figures and unimpressive record sales (a meager four per cent of the market) make it all too obvious that the classical-music business is now more than ever a minority trade. An era has ended.

But what did that era amount to? It is high time that historians started asking what the classical tradition has meant in the lives of its devotees. Despite all that has been written about the music and the people who played it, there is still only fragmentary knowledge of the life surrounding music. Musicologists have been shy to investigate the social dimension of their field; cultural historians have spent little time talking about anything other than master composers and their camp-followers. Perhaps now that the classical scene has lost much of its luster, scholars will approach its history with cooler eyes and greater respect for the mundane side of it all.

This writer should therefore warn the reader that the present volume is not about musical works or personalities except insofar as they have contributed to the development of concert life in worldly ways. The book concerns the people who went to concerts, the groups they came from, the taste publics they formed, and the huge new entertainment world they shaped. It is a social history.

Some people may, of course, bridle at the implication that society influenced musical experience. But however much this study will press that point, it will not hazard any conclusions about the ways in which society affected the creative process itself. Indeed, it will show how—as always—musical taste had its own social structure and operated independently of other areas of society, even as the concert world, seen as a set of institutions, was intimately linked to major social change.

I am deeply indebted to Peter Stearns for his help throughout the course of this project, for his invaluable analytical perspective and pragmatic criticism. I owe much likewise to Grosvenor Cooper for offering that all-too-rare sympathy for work in another field. Thanks are due as well to Karen Johnson, Carol Rojeski, and Gretchen Icenogle for editing and preparation of the manuscript.

Long Beach, California

For William and Jean Weber

My Parents

CHAPTER I

INTRODUCTION

The "Biedermeier" period, they once called it in Central Europe. The burgeoning economic and political activity of the middle class after the mid-point of the nineteenth century impressed writers so much that they looked back at the two decades prior to the Revolution of 1848 with undisguised scorn. The plain, unpretentious furniture of the period provided them with a handy pejorative term for describing the supposedly passive temper of the times. But historians now see many tendencies of a very different sort among the middle class — dynamic, assertive tendencies which foreshadowed the more open and successful actions of the class after the mid-century. During that time mechanized light industry was initiated in France and Germany and consolidated in Britain; nationalist movements forged many of the intellectual and political tools they were to use later in the century; and the publishing industry emerged in its modern form throughout Europe. The middle class was trying its hand at new things, and even though some of its efforts were fumbling or abortive, they afforded strong evidence of what was to come.

The history of concert life exhibited the intense social energies of the middle class even more dramatically than most such developments. The concert world as we know it now began during the period. The numbers of concerts proliferated throughout Europe, and their customs and design took on characteristically modern forms. With them came a giddying social atmosphere among the middle class and the aristocracy, eager trips to concert halls, ravenous consumption of sheet music and periodicals, passionate support of performers and musical styles, and a shrewd use of all this toward self-advancement. Music fans may have lounged in Biedermeier furniture while talking about these matters, but their behavior certainly did not resemble its stolid tone.

The period of the 30s and 40s is therefore ideal for studying both the development of the concert world and the middle class in general. The two problems are so closely intertwined that this book will treat them with equal seriousness. Analysis of social structure in the two areas involves the same sociological factors — social classes, professional groups, taste publics, institutions, men and women, and the family. The term social structure thus does not stand in the title idly, for it provides the key concept through which we will approach our subject.

There is similar logic and feasibility for studying London, Paris, and Vienna together. As the three most important national capitals of the time, they had great similarities in their social

1

structure which derived from the functions of capital-city life.
Indeed, we will argue that because of their political and social roles
they resembled each other in significant ways more than other cities in
their respective countries. The period of 1830 to 1848 was also chosen
for purposes of breadth. Because that era brought so many modernizing
tendencies to musical life, it can be used to study the evolution of
concerts from its start in the late seventeenth century to its
culmination about 1870. While we will concentrate our attention
upon the two decades prior to the Revolution of 1848, we will often look
before and after that time, especially to the period of consolidation
in concert life after mid-century.

The centrality of the period in the development of concert life is
revealed through the unusually fine sources available. Many new concert
organizations were founded at the time which left many kinds of records:
membership lists, minutes of directors' meetings, and official letters.
Most important of all, the membership lists have provided revealing
information about the occupations and social status of the societies'
constituents. The expansion of the press and the book industry during
the period also furnishes many valuable published works: periodicals,
satirical writings, travel guides and letters, memoirs, and multifarious
books and pamphlets on city life. Because concerts were such a fad
among the middle class, reviewers and columnists talked extensively
about the social fabric of the new events and particularly about the
status levels of audiences. Travel guides and handbooks on city life
likewise always sketched out that hierarchy. The many satirical pieces
which appeared in newspapers, magazines, and books provided even more
probing commentary upon the role of musical activities in the lives
of specific social groups.

Qualitative sources such as these do, of course, present
problems of inaccuracy and vague language. Music critics had their own
axes to grind and often received payoffs from musicians whose concerts
they reviewed. Authors of travel letters or books on city life often
over-generalized about currents in musical life. But such errors can be
identified with surprising ease. While reviewers felt free to flatter
concerts as "brilliant" or "dazzling", they were much more precise
in their descriptions of the status of audiences. Few instances are
found of flagrantly contradictory estimations of the social background
of particular concerts. Furthermore, the great variety of published
sources made possible comparison of the relative merits of each one.
The most powerful critics indicated most clearly where taste was moving
but the information they provided on the composition of audiences was
not as deep or concrete as that of less prominent reviewers or non-musical
journalists.

The directions in which this study will go emerge clearly from a brief exploration of the prior history of the concert world from its beginnings in the late seventeenth century. The history of concerts in London, Paris, and Vienna falls into five periods: 1) 1680-1750, the scattered appearance of concerts; 2) 1750-1790, the growth of frequent events in all three cities; 3) 1790-1813, a hiatus in presentations; 4) 1813-1848, the rapid explosion in their number and significance; and 5) 1848-1870, the consolidation of the concert world in its modern form.

As this periodization suggests, the concert is a relatively recent cultural phenomenon. Prior to the late seventeenth century there had existed virtually no formal and independent settings whose central purpose was the performance of music. Musical activities had been attached to many other institutions and social locales — courts, taverns, the Church, markets, and families — and for the most part served their social and cultural needs. The rise of concerts, the opera, and musical societies during the seventeenth and eighteenth centuries therefore constituted a fundamental reordering of the social structure of musical life. From that time on the pursuit of music evolved into a world of its own, with purposes, etiquette, and social organization specific to it. Opera developed the most rapidly, for by the early eighteenth century there were large, highly formalized companies in all parts of Europe. Concerts grew more sporadically. During the late seventeenth century a few occurred in London, and after the turn of the century they began in Paris. But their number was not considerable until after 1750.[1]

It was only during the eighteenth— and in some respects not until well into the nineteenth—century that the new musical world acquired anything more than a rough approximation of the stable, tightly organized institutions and customs of the contemporary era. Concerts especially remained tied to other social spheres and continued to be subordinate to their activities. Held in taverns, theaters, parks, and homes, they did not differ greatly in their social manners from the other kinds of socializing and entertainment which took place in those locales. Their programmes had an indiscriminate mix of symphonies, dance music, opera selections, operetta songs, sacred choral pieces, serious chamber music, virtuosic numbers, and even poetry readings. The demeanor of their audiences was also quite free. As the heroine of Fanny Burney's late eighteenth-century novel *Evelina* remarked, "indeed I am quite astonished to find how little music is attended to in silence; for though everybody seems to admire, hardly anybody listens."[2]

The growth of concerts during the seventeenth and eighteenth centuries differed in the three cities in ways that influenced later development significantly. In London the events grew earlier and more numerously than in Paris or Vienna. The initial concerts held during the 1680s were presentations by the clientele of taverns, probably

3

members of the lower middle class.[3] By the 1720s these events had largely disappeared, and concerts for the nobility and upper-middle class had replaced them. Between 1750 and 1790 their number increased greatly, producing the closest parallels to the professional recitals and orchestral concerts of the nineteenth century. Concert-going became a central part of the aristocracy's high social season, for musicians planned their concerts with the assistance of their aristocratic patrons. One series, the Concerts of Ancient Music, was directed (and to some extent performed) by the highest noblemen, and became so prestigious that the King often attended. Some wealthy members of the middle class went to the concerts but had no leadership role within them. Several private middle-class performing clubs appeared, but they had little prominence in the city's social life.[4] During the crisis of the '90s concerts disappeared almost completely.[5] But despite their collapse, the intense activities of the preceding decades laid down social precedents which greatly affected the revival of concerts in the next century. The nobility had established itself as the controlling class in the new concert world.

In Paris concerts had a promising but frustrated development during the eighteenth century. In 1725 the state opera began giving what it called "Concerts Spirituels" on the thirty-five holy days during the year when religious laws prohibited operatic performances. By the middle of the century their repertoire had changed from sacred to secular music. It is probable that the concerts had the same kind of audience as the opera theater, that is, a combination of the nobility and a substantial minority from the upper-middle class.[6] But the state officials and prominent aristocrats who managed the opera excluded the middle class from leadership there and in other kinds of concerts. During the second half of the century a few professional musicians began putting on concerts, but the government restricted their frequency severely, to protect the opera and to prevent an independent musical world from emerging. Several groups of wealthy amateurs and hired musicians conducted private performances, but the state denied them licences for public concerts. Had the government not restricted the numbers of events, Paris would certainly have had a concert world almost as active as that in London. The revolutionary regime ended the Concerts Spirituels in 1791, and few concerts other than nationalistic celebrations took place in the following three decades.[7]

The differences in the development of concerts in London and Paris were governed by the contrasting relationships which were emerging between the nobility and the state in the two countries. The rise of centralized monarchy in the seventeenth century forced the nobility to accept new kinds of public responsibility, but in each country the class took a different path in solving the problem.[8] In England it acknowledged the central authority of the state with no major qualifications and involved itself extensively in the state's affairs. In return the Crown granted the nobility autonomy in its cultural life and interfered only when governmental controls were profitable for both parties. The class accordingly shifted its main social life from its estates to London during the spring and developed wide-ranging artistic activities to accompany it. Concert life flourished in this setting, for it provided a casual kind of social intercourse which was ideal for the needs of the season.

In France the state and the aristocracy failed to establish such a working relationship. Bitter infighting continued between the government and the nobility and within the class itself until the Revolution. The Royal House maintained tight controls over all artistic institutions as a means of limiting the power of the aristocracy. While in some fields such as publishing and the opera state controls weakened considerably during the second half of the century, in concert life there was no such change. Even though noblemen supported musicians for performances in their homes, they were not able to develop patronal or dilettante activities within public concerts such as occurred in London. These differences in the roles of the nobility in public concert life in the two cities were to have powerful effects upon the structure of the new concert world of the next century.

In Vienna concerts developed later than in the other two cities and with the greatest involvement of the middle class. Formal concerts first appeared during the 1750s but did not become frequent until the 1780s. They did not decrease much between 1790 and 1813, in contrast to the situation in London and Paris. Concerts developed late because the city had become a major capital only during the middle of the century. The nobility had not yet built up the same large capital-city social life that the English and French aristocracies had maintained since the late seventeenth century, and while its families lived in Vienna part of the year for political reasons, they did not sponsor public concerts or even attend them more than sporadically. Since the middle class was less wealthy and sophisticated than in London or Paris, most of the city's concerts were small-scale affairs staffed by middle-class amateurs, resembling the events of most provincial cities. For the middle class as well as the aristocracy the central setting of musical life remained informal private gatherings.[9]

Despite the differences in the roles of the two leading classes in eighteenth-century concert life in the three capitals, one can still make certain generalizations about the influence and leadership of the middle class. The reckoning must be almost entirely negative. In the first place, the class had minimal formal authority over concerts. Only in Vienna did it control more than a few minor concerts, and there they were unstable and insignificant compared to aristocratic salons. In the second place, the middle class exercised little influence over musical taste. Since performance in aristocratic households was the goal of all ambitious musicians, even in a place like Vienna where the middle class dominated the organization of concert life the nobility held sway in matters of taste. In the third place, professional musicians as yet exerted little entrepreneurial leadership. While a few performers began impressive but short-lived commercial operations in London, virtually all musicians acted either as private retainers or as civic employees who had scant control over their professional opportunities. Finally, the middle class did not yet wield much power in musical life through communications media. Neither magazines nor newspapers played powerful roles in the concert world, such as they were to achieve by the middle of the nineteenth century.

But after the end of the Napoleonic wars a new era began in the history of the concert world, one in which the middle class began taking on dramatic new roles. The most fundamental fact underlying the growth of concerts was the good health and stability of the capitals' economies. After the period of rapid economic expansion and rising prices in the second half of the eighteenth century and the wild price fluctuations during the wars, prices levelled off and economic growth resumed at an even pace. In London and Paris the prices of basic goods and services declined somewhat, and the same was undoubtedly true in Vienna.[10] The middle class thereby gained a rising standard of living and, thanks to the continuing peace, had little worry over general economic crisis.

These conditions affected musical life initially by stimulating a boom in the sale of instruments and publications. Musical activities in the home, though common previously, were rapidly becoming almost standard within substantial middle-class households. Publishing and instrument manufacture had grown steadily since the middle of the eighteenth century, but as home musical activities increased, their production and sales picked up speed rapidly. The dynamism of the two industries derived in large part from other creative energies within the middle class. Technological advance had opened up mass-production of instruments and printed music, and new methods of promotion and sales enabled successful distribution of the products.[11]

But public concerts grew more slowly than home activities and musical commerce. The dates at which the frequency of concerts began increasing significantly differed in the three cities. In Vienna, where concerts had not had a hiatus such as occurred in London and Paris, they grew at a swift rate from the middle of the 1810s on. In 1813 an

organization intended to formalize and centralize amateur performing
was founded in the Society of the Friends of Music (Gesellschaft der
Musikfreunde). During the same year another major institution was
begun in the English capital — the London Philharmonic Society —
but the number of concerts did not begin to rise greatly there until
the middle of the 1820s. In Paris their number did not increase
significantly until 1830.[12]

But in the early 1830s the concert life of all three capitals
exhibited similar dramatic growth, and by 1848 a commercial concert
world had emerged in each city, over which the middle class exerted
powerful, if not dominant, control. After 1848 concert life underwent
the final period in its development which consolidated the innovations
of the previous two decades. Concert institutions became more stable
and better managed; commercial practices took on greater clarity and
regularity; and patterns of taste settled into a more ordered, less
volatile condition. By 1870 there was little in the new concert world
which would seem anachronistic today.[13]

The turbulent events between 1830 and 1848 brought, then, an
independent artistic field such as had never been known in Western
music history. The institutions and customs established during that
time persisted unshaken and unchanged throughout the economic crises,
wartime disasters, and social upheavals of the next hundred years.
By investigating the social structure of the concert public during
that key period we can gain perspective upon the extraordinary stability
which concert life achieved.

Five problems will concern us in this book. The first is big,
potentially very messy, but quite unavoidable: the unity of the middle
class. The simplest way to put it is whether there was one "middle
class", or two, or several. We will contend that in cultural life two
classes were beginning to emerge from the middle stratum of society,
but that their emergence remained ambiguous during the period itself.
Let us go directly to the historical culminating-point of the problem.
By some time in the first half of the twentieth century — probably by
the 1920s in Western and Central Europe — the aristocracy and the
upper-middle class had become so closely fused in all aspects of their
social structure that they ceased to function as separate classes.
Europe now had a single elite, an "upper class". But the starting-point
of the change is very much still in question. Historians used to agree
that the French July Monarchy brought a combined bourgeois and aristocratic
ruling class, but intensive quantitative study of contemporary politics
has shown that the upper-middle class had no such status during the
era.[14] Adéline Daumard's study of the Parisian middle class and
André-Jean Tudesq's work on the national landed elite showed that the
wealthy upper-middle class still did not often intermarry with the

aristocracy.[15] David Spring's study of the English aristocracy has demonstrated that in that country as well the nobility was a dynamic, independent group much farther into the century than had been believed.

Nevertheless, it is clear that the relations between the middle class and the nobility changed in significant ways before the merger of the upper-middle class with the nobility. Historians of the nineteenth century face the intricate task of isolating the stages through which the change evolved. An early key point in the development, one which took place in many areas around the turn of the century, occurred when the upper-middle class became a "second elite", that is, the time when it was recognized to hold an elevated status through its acquisition of key controlling roles in many areas of society. As a second elite, it remained distinct from the aristocracy but held social roles and prestige which made it, while not fully equal, at least comparable in status to the nobility. Before this time, members of only a few specific middle-class professions — primarily bankers in England and judges in France — held elite roles, and most of them were on their way to being assimilated into the lower nobility. From the early part of the century onwards, the acquisition of a title ceased to be the only way to get elite status.[17]

Wealth and professional functions now began to provide an alternative channel — but only one, alas, since wealth was always necessary to it. The growing capital and economic empires of business-men had reached such a point that they no longer acted simply as agents for the monarchy and the aristocracy, but rather as independent entrepreneurs. Men in the liberal professions were building powerful new roles and considerable property which made them, or at least the most successful (or well-married) among them, part of the elite. The families of these men could now live in a style which resembled that of the nobility closely enough that they became part of the cities' high society. In fact, it became common in the three capitals to refer to a "bourgeois aristocracy", a "financial nobility", or a "second high society".[18]

What is more, a limited form of merger may have begun between the two classes at the same time in some social spheres. It must be assumed that the change could not have come about all at once throughout society, since variations in different areas would create quite different rates of change. Too few historians have yet realized that politics would logically have been among the last settings in which integration took place, and for that reason the explosion of the myth of the Orleanist "bourgeois monarchy" does not mean as much as some might think. By the same token, it is probable that the worlds of casual socializing and cultural activities allowed more rapid development of the merger because change within them did not demand

8

as far-reaching a transformation as in politics, economics, or kinship. After all, a concession by the aristocracy toward more intimate social life with the upper-middle class could easily be reversed if events demanded it. The chances of integration of the two classes seem particularly high in concert life. The sudden growth of concert life during the 1830s suggest that the social scene had a high degree of malleability to accommodate such new social needs.

How, then, can we test the hypothesis that the two classes merged into a single public in concert life between 1830 and 1848? For one thing, we must look for the development of a sense of common identity between the two classes. The wealthy middle class had mingled to some extent with the nobility for centuries in all three capitals, and their simple attendance at concerts therefore means nothing. Union between them would come only through the formation of a distinct high-status social world found in both public and private settings. Involved, too, would be a less concrete phenomenon, an awareness among their numbers of belonging to a special milieu, a privileged elite within the concert public. We must also look for sharper and more rigid differentiation between the upper and lower levels of the middle class. Only by determinedly casting off ties to the rest of the middle class could the bourgeois elite hope to take up close and more permanent relations with the aristocracy. Of particular interest, therefore, will be any evidence of conflict between the strata within the middle class.

The second of the five problems involves analysis of particular aspects within the social structure of the concert public, ones which are less easy to grasp than basic class structure in the cultural sphere. Did individual groups and institutions fulfill distinctive functions within the rising middle class? We will examine four areas: the professions, the roles of men and women, the family, and the fabric of casual socializing. This analysis relates closely to that of social class, for the evolution of class structure has come about in large part as the sum of events within such groups. Even — or perhaps especially — during a time of acute status consciousness such as this one, shifts in class structure have taken place within the context of social groups where people experienced change in their daily lives.

One of the main breakthroughs towards a more sophisticated understanding of social classes in modern history has been the discovery that different occupational groups play different roles in certain areas of society. Lenore O'Boyle has shown that in the first half of the nineteenth century the liberal professions took a much more active part in politics than the economic professions.[19] The history of concert life provides an excellent opportunity to see whether the same groups also had significantly different social values, life styles, or artistic tastes. Although a rigid contrast between them seems unlikely, the strong differences in political and economic roles held by them suggests that their members' ways of life may show the same distinctiveness.

The roles of men and women in concert life require a similar comparative treatment. Conventional wisdom has it that Victorian women were passive, subservient creatures, but also — an odd contradiction — that they dominated cultural life. Concert life alone was so large and varied that it is doubtful that women held sway throughout it. Discussion of sex roles leads immediately to consideration of the place of the family in concert life. Most recent research into the history of the family has focused on the internal life in the home and has stressed the isolation of the middle-class family from larger social life.[20] But it is hard to believe that families had no part in the dynamic social and cultural activities of the middle class during the nineteenth century. The importance of music-making in the home offers a fine opportunity to see if such activities had any relationship to public life.

For one area of middle-class society which has received little consideration is the fabric of casual social life, the daily come-and-go in parks, cafés, home gatherings, and the various entertainment worlds. It is important to understand how formal events such as concerts related to the larger framework of socializing in the three capitals, and this can illuminate the lives of key subgroups, including women, and the nature of family life. How much had the street and the gathering places attached to it declined as the focus of urban life? At some point in the last two hundred years most middle-class people shifted the focus of their daily lives from the street into the home and specialized institutions, and it will be vital to find out how far that change had gone by the middle of the nineteenth century. We must also realise, as against the puritanic image of the middle class in early industrialisation, that segments of the middle class were avid for new kinds of recreation, ready to begin their pioneering efforts toward a new leisure ethic.

The third problem is the social structure of musical taste within the concert world. Historians have spent much time showing how artistic taste have sprung from social attitudes, but they have rarely analysed with any conceptual clarity how social groups have formed around currents of taste. We shall use the term "taste publics" for that social phenomenon. By treating these groups as a dimension of social structure like any other, it is possible to ascertain the social background held by supporters of different styles and the settings (institutions, meeting-places, communications media) within which such groups were active.[21]

Such analysis demands working definitions for two concepts which are central to the problem: high culture and popular culture. If the terms are to take on any precision — such as they still lack in scholarly discussion — they must be understood to denote nothing about social class.[22] Each of the two kinds of culture has usually had wide class bases, and in some instances (one of which we will point out later) popular culture has had more prestigious support than high culture. The terms designate rather a distinction in cultural orientations which many societies have applied to many art forms. Popular culture is always assumed to be contemporaneous and non-esoteric; people take for granted that they do not have to know anything special to appreciate it. High culture is the opposite: focused upon classical forms, it is assumed to require some kind of knowledge for its comprehension, and thereby receives an elevated cultural standing. The definitions should not, however, be pressed too far, for in the end their meaning and their application are simply whatever the members of a society (or even just some of them) say they are — and that can change fast.

The development of the musical profession is the fourth problem. During the early nineteenth century musicians underwent that critical change which sociologists have called "professionalization".[23] Before the turn of the century performers had little ability to control the institutions and the activities within which they worked. The social roles of the amateur and the professional were not defined at all clearly, for many players held other jobs, and those who had patronal positions with wealthy families usually played alongside their employers without any sense of illogicality. During the expansion of the concert public in the first half of the century musicians became independent operators in an open commercial market and thereby played a role in musical life much like that of industrial entrepreneurs in the manufacturing field. They developed new methods for the management and promotion of concerts and diversified the functions of their profession in many new areas such as publication, teaching, and the control of performing halls. They also sharpened the distinction between the amateur and the professional.

The final problem we will examine concerns the similarities and differences among the three cities studied. The functions which the three capital cities all performed made the social structure of the middle class within them similar in many respects. First, all three were the key commercial centers for their national economies. Their upper-middle class included the most wealthy and powerful commercial and banking families in each country. Quite different kinds of middle-class society existed in cities with industrial production or small-scale localised commerce. Secondly, the capitals' roles in politics made them the only cities with a resident aristocracy. This shaped the life of the middle class

11

profoundly, for while the wealthy merchants and professional people of a provincial city were an independent ruling class, those in the capitals always lived in the shadow — that long shadow — of Europe's traditional elite. Third, the cities' roles in governmental administration and cultural life brought to them many professional people, who were much less numerous in provincial cities. The increasing centralisation of affairs in most professions made the capitals the drawing-point for ambitious individuals in all fields. The social and institutional structure of cultural life within them was therefore much more competitive and fragmented than in provincial cities. Finally, the growing functions of the cities and their wealthy elites stimulated a large lower-middle class of shopkeepers, clerks, and lower-level professionals. However surprising it may sound, census records suggest that the proportionate size of the middle class as a whole was not radically different in the three cities. Its proportion of the total population was no smaller than fifteen per cent in Vienna and no larger than twenty-five per cent (and probably a lot closer to twenty per cent) in London and Paris.[24]

Yet the three cities obviously manifested deep social differences. In assessing the contrasts among them the main question must be whether the affected the form or simply the degree of development in concert life. Tha is, were the cities moving in fundamentally different directions, or did they share similar social tendencies contrasting in extent of change? The most pertinent question of all is whether London and Paris shared common directions of change with Vienna, a city which most historians consider to have stood outside the mainstream of historical development in nineteenth-century Europe.[25]

Two differences between society in London, Paris, and Vienna deserve particular mention. One was the intensity of social change at the turn of the nineteenth century. After about 1750 London enjoyed relatively strong historical continuity compared with the other two cities. By contrast, the sudden rise of Vienna as a capital city during the eighteenth century brought a rapid social transformation in all areas of society and thereby gave its life an unsettled condition comparable to that of post-revolutionary Paris. The second difference was the readiness of the upper-middle class for union with aristocracy. This was no simple thing, for the achievement of strong social and political roles by that group did not necessarily lead to closer relations with the nobility (as was true in Paris), nor did it bring full equality if such interaction were possible (as was the case in London). To spell out these differences fully we must look at the capitals separately.

In London during the early nineteenth century the upper-middle class had a much more firmly established social position than in either of the other two cities. During the previous centuries London had developed more rapidly than any other European city in the expansion of its population and the modernisation of its urban life.[26] Within its businesses — trading and banking firms unrivalled anywhere in the West — a stable and highly wealthy upper-middle class emerged which a publicist of the 1840s described as "an aristocracy of trade, whose honors and revenues descend from generation to generation by the strictest entail".[27] Nevertheless, the English aristocracy weathered the storms of the revolutionary era without experiencing a direct challenge by the wealthy middle class. Since trading firms held charters granted by the monarchy and banks dealt largely in the affairs of aristocratic estates, the city's bourgeois families depended closely upon that class. They socialised extensively in aristocratic circles, but by virtue of that did not maintain a high degree of independence or separate identity.

Nevertheless, the upper-middle class showed more self-assertive tendencies during the first half of the nineteenth century. Speculative enterprises, particularly joint-stock companies, sprang up to challenge established firms and departed from the traditional function of serving aristocratic interests. Many wealthy manufacturers moved to London from the industrial cities of the North to be in closer touch with English politics and to dramatise their success by gaining entry into elite social life.[28] The wave of discontent which culminated in the reform legislation of the 1830s disturbed the relations between the two elite groups, and the attacks upon aristocratic privilege brought closer ties between the upper and lower levels of the middle class.

In Paris the bourgeois elite had less stability but greater independence than its counterpart in London. The challenge to the aristocracy during the Revolution gave the class greater self-consciousness as an elite than was found among the group anywhere in Europe. In Paris more than anywhere else in France class lines and deference to rank became weaker and more fluid during the first half of the new century.[29] But the Revolution also brought a sharp discontinuity in the social roles of the middle class and in the constitution of its members. From the '90s on there sprang up a whole new set of families, few of whom had been established in the city before 1789, and during the first half of the century they underwent a slow process of consolidation both individually and as a class.[30] The newness of the group posed great uncertainties for all its members both economically and socially and created a sharp competitive atmosphere among them. Their struggles for power gave them a distinctive dynamism and aggressiveness such as was not found among comparable groups in London and Vienna.

The successive crises concerning the Bourbon aristocracy had drawn the battle lines between the classes so firmly that extensive socializing among them became difficult. After the Revolution of 1830 members of the Legitimist nobility retired from both politics and social life outside

13

its own ranks. While they gradually filtered back into public life during the period, the upper-middle class had little contact with them and kept company instead with the Orleanist nobility (most of whom had obtained their titles during the Napoleonic period).[31] The conflict with the old nobility also accentuated the group's ties with the rest of the middle class.

The character of the Viennese middle class derived from the late date at which Vienna became a major national capital. The expansion of the city's political and economic roles during the eighteenth century stimulat the growth of a new wealthy upper-middle class, largely of German extraction, first in the bureaucracy and then in the businesses which controlled trade between Germany and the Balkans.[32] By the 1830s it was considered a second elite much as in London and Paris. The city's rapid development gave it a highly unstable society during the first half of the nineteenth century, resembling the situation in Paris much more than that of London. As in Paris, the recent development of the upper-mi class muddied the definition of class lines and instilled in its members an intense self-consciousness concerning status. The sudden break with the traditional life of the old city also created a sharp dislocation in social attitudes — both snobbery and nostalgia — toward that past, such as was not found in either of the other two capitals.

The Viennese upper-middle class differed even more from its counterpa in Paris and London in its lesser readiness for union with the aristocracy. Because the class was so new and as yet only moderately wealthy, it did not have the lavish life-style or the well-groomed sophistication necessary for close interaction with aristocratic circles. Furthermore, the Austrian high nobility had prevented the formation of a lesser landed elite like the English gentry or the French Orleanist nobility, and the absence of such an intermediary group made socialising between the two elites even more difficult. The Viennese upper-middle class therefore remained closer to the rest of the middle class than it did in the other two capitals. Nevertheless, we must inquire whether concert life may have provided anything of an exception to this condition. Even a society with the most rigid class lines will often have curious chinks in its stony social walls, and this may well have been true in Vienna.

We must not let ourselves get lost in the contrasts between the cities. Social structure comprises places as well as people and therefore betrays certain basic types among locales just as it does among classes or professional groups. We will not follow the social nominalism which dominates so much of urban history but will rather sho the many ways in which the three capital cities were their own kind of place. Historians tend to forget that, then as much as now, Paris was not France and London was not England. Indeed, anyone who uses the wo "Austrian" in the title of a book on Viennese cultural life (and

14

there have been several) should go to Salzburg and hear what people say about *that*.

This study will therefore not be divided into separate sections on each city. Its organization will be based instead upon the different publics created by taste and social class. The following chapter will provide an overview of the leading social and cultural tendencies within the concerts between 1830 and 1848 and examine what patterns ticket prices, that prosaic basis of the new musical world, suggest about the concert world as a whole. Chapter III will treat the most significant concert area which developed during the period: the popular-music world among the elite public. Discussion of developments in the high-status classical-music public will follow in Chapter IV. Chapter V will investigate the emerging public among the rest of the middle class and the artisanry.

This brief introduction should suggest how much the study of musical life can show about other historical areas. Through examining its relations with the many interstices of society it touched one can see social structure with both breadth and marvellous concreteness. Inquiry into class structure has particularly much to gain from it. To understand shifts in macrocosmic social relations such as these it is necessary to look at them close up, deep in the experience from which they came, and then to pull back to see them in a larger framework. By examining the musical world during the first half of the nineteenth century we can see how new hierarchical groups came about in real places, in salons and concert halls, and gain perspective upon how they interacted with other definable social groups like the professions and the family. And on an even broader plane, the study of musical life can make the study of daily life more than just a collection of interesting anecdotes. Because the musical world had a clearly defined power structure, we can with its help see the muscles of authority and influence within the quaint customs of the past.

CHAPTER II

THE CULTURAL EXPLOSION: AN OVERVIEW

The sudden increase in the phenomenon of concerts in London, Paris, and Vienna during the 1830s and '40s amounted to a real cultural explosion. This chapter will first discuss their growth, their principal types, and the cultural divisions they manifested. It will then look into the prices charged for admission to see what this suggests about the class structure within concert life. The chapter is, then, an overview of how the concert became an institution of major importance.

Nothing demonstrates the explosion of concert life better than the increase in the number of concerts during the period (see Table 3). The detailed reporting of presentations in newspapers and magazines in all three cities allows an accurate enumeration of the concerts presented in the two seasons (September through August) of 1826-1827 and 1845- The figures include only formal public concerts. Performances held in private homes have been added only if they were formally announced in press or were presented as a regular series open to the public. Informal concerts held in parks or dance halls are excluded here but will be considered in rough numerical form in Chapter V.

The figures are impressive. Between the two seasons concerts increased in London from 125 to 381 (305 per cent), in Paris from 78 to 383 (491 per cent), and in Vienna from 111 to 163 (47 per cent). And that was not all. The number in London was greater than is shown here, for the concerts held in the many new suburbs of the metropolis often did not appear in the newspapers. In addition, the rate of increase in Vienna is somewhat misleading. Since concerts began growing in the Austrian capital so much earlier than elsewhere, their cumulative increase between 1813 and 1848 must have been threefold. The ratios of concerts to population indeed indicate the growing similarities among the three capitals (see Table 4). Defined as one concert per 100,000 persons, the proportions in the earlier season were eight in London, eleven in Paris, and twenty-eight in Vienna. By the later season Paris and Vienna stood much closer with ratios of 37 and 39 respectively; London lay below them at 22, though the suburban concerts would no doubt narrow the gap somewhat.

No other cultural area experienced so remarkable a history during the first half of the century. While the opera generated interest through its popular composers (Rossini and the rest), no new musical theaters were established in any of the capitals. The dramatic theater had neither such popular new personalities nor an increase in its institutions. The closest parallel to the expansion of concert life was in the growth of the publishing industry, for the steam press was making possible much

16

greater production and sales then ever before. Yet because music was so much more easily diffused, concerts spread more widely and rapidly than books.

They also became more prominent. In 1846 a London journalist stated that many families were putting on concerts in their homes and driving their children to become virtuosi, with the result that "in families the piano has extinguished conversation and the love of books."[2] Not long before that a Parisian newspaperman announced that "music has taken first rank in the distractions and pleasures of high society".[3] A personal illustration came from Mrs Harriet Grote, the wife of the renowned English businessman and historian George Grote, who wrote in her memoirs that during the mid-'40s "the musical superseded the literary world, for a space" — no small achievement in her intellectual circle — because of enthusiasm for the music of Felix Mendelssohn and the singing of Jenny Lind.[4]

In the culturally volatile 1970s such comments may seem bland, but when seen in the context of early nineteenth-century middle-class life they are highly significant. In few areas of life did middle-class people have means of participating actively in matters which concerned the community around them. Politics was the province only of small groups within the cities' elites, and few other people could take part in such affairs. Formal associations of the kind so numerous today were still uncommon. Middle-class institutions for social welfare, hobbies, and cultural activities had only begun to appear. Finally, the tight control of the opera and the theater by cliques of aristocrats allowed middle-class audiences participation of only a limited order. While operetta theaters had opened an exciting arena of middle-class cultural leadership in the late eighteenth century, by the 1820s they had lost their former vitality.

The institutional structure of concerts explains in part why they grew to such an unusual extent. The opera and the theater required extremely large, complex, and expensive organisations, and the governments of the three capitals protected the central "legitimate" halls through tight monopolistic controls. Concerts had no such obstacles. By this time state regulations demanded only modest fees and imposed almost no limits upon the number of events.[5] Their make-up was flexible and inexpensive; sponsors could put them on as individual operations and repeat them as often as was practical. Musicians could obtain performers from among their colleagues and recruit amateurs from among their students to fill lesser accompanying positions. Concerts accordingly proved responsive to many social and cultural needs. They served a wide variety of purposes: economic gain, professional recognition, charity fund-raising, celebration of events, product publicity, and indeed simple entertainment among amateurs. Sponsorship likewise had diverse origins: individual musicians, formal and informal groups of performers, cultural societies, music magazines, charity organisations, theaters, and music publishers; and though this list could quickly become tedious, we cannot end it without mentioning government agencies, pensi organisations, and even a few fledgling concert managers (see Table 1). In none of the cities did concerts grow from a central organisation. That was true in the provinces but not in the capitals. The founders of the Viennese Society of the Friends of Music had that kind of organisation in mind but quickly discovered that it was impossible in the highly fragmented and competitive cultural life of the Austrian capital.

There were three principal types of concert. The most common was the "benefit" concert. Always sponsored by an individual musician for his or her "benefit", it was not a charity affair as its title might suggest (though charity organisations did adapt the form to their own purposes). During the season 1845-1846, between 45 and 66 per cent of all concerts were of this kind. Most were given by local musicians as annual events to maintain their reputations; some were put on by travelling virtuosi. In both instances, however, the sponsoring musician performed only a part of the program, for the concerts presented anywhere from ten to thirty numbers played mostly by fellow musicians who would return the service for each other. As we shall show in Chapter III the audiences were made up principally of persons for whom the sponsor had taught or played at a salon. Out-of-town musicians obtained similar performers and listeners through their contacts in the capitals, for no one just wandered into cities like these and put on a concert.

The second type of event was that presented by a permanent organisat of professional musicians. Composed primarily of orchestral ensembles, these institutions laid the groundwork for the famous symphony orchestr of the next hundred years. Their events differed from benefit concerts not only in their formal organisation but also in their usual requirement that listeners buy subscriptions for a complete season and obtain approval from a board of musicians or amateurs. Before mid-century, however, there were only a few such societies in each city, and their number did not come close to that of benefit concerts since symphony orchestras had not yet become the central institutions in concert life.

The third type of concert involved the presentations of amateur musica organisations. Each city had at least one orchestral and one choral society staffed wholly or in part by amateurs. By 1848 the clubs ranked second only to benefit concerts in the frequency of their events. Most had only a limited commercial orientation and performed chiefly to the families and friends of their members, though some did attempt (albeit with only occasional success) to attain broader publics and wider renown. Virtually all had lower class bases than the other two types of concerts.

To understand the differences among the various kinds of concerts, we must look at developments in European musical taste. As the musicolo

Edward Lowinsky has observed, major musical styles have almost always developed with a distinct geographical identity, entered into competition with other styles, and finally been absorbed into general international usage.[6] Several instances of the process were under way in this period. During the 1810s Giacomo Rossini created a distinctive but widely applicable operatic style which quickly rose to prominence throughout the European operatic world and underwent adaptation by Germans such as Meyerbeer. And at the same time instrumentalists developed a revitalized virtuosic style out of various national sources and with it built an international idiom which dominated European concert life during the first half of the nineteenth century, culminating in the dramatic, unprecedented fame of Franz Liszt and Eduard Thalberg. The two currents became closely linked in the concert world due to the regular performance of operatic selections in benefit concerts. A third style stood far distant from them: the German classical style led by Haydn, Mozart, Beethoven, and Schubert. In its early form during the late eighteenth century it had commanded considerable popularity, but with the wartime lapse in concert life it lost most of its public and was slow to regain popularity. By 1830 it was still little known in Paris, had a weak base in Vienna, and enjoyed a small though prestigious public in London. During the next two decades it began its rise to become the central component of the concert repertoire, but did not accomplish that until well after mid-century.[7]

Conflict between the German classical style and its two competitors permeated all concert life during the first half of the century. The episode had a broader meaning than a simple rivalry between musical styles, for it amounted to an unusually strong dispute between forms of high culture and popular culture. Before the turn of the century European music had had little division between the two kinds of art such as was so strong in literature and the fine arts. The vast majority of composers had written in a highly contemporaneous manner, with little sense that they wrote in a "high" form for which their listeners needed some special training. A few musical genres — particularly religious music and pedagogic exercises — had strong classical frameworks, but they never added up to an integral high culture. The main exception to this had occurred in late seventeenth-century France, when Louis XIV elevated the music of Jean Baptiste Lully to the status of a classical art, but by the middle of the eighteenth century his school had come into considerable disrepute.[8]

From the first decade of the next century, however, both musicians and concert-goers increasingly came to understand that the music of the German classical school was, like it or not, high art and the other two schools distinctively popular in their orientation. Indeed, discussion of the differences between them took on a characteristically modern

19

cast; reading an article comparing Thalberg and Beethoven one might think that it had been written a hundred years later, but setting Elvis Presley against the German master. Members of the public joined forces behind each of the two camps. The division between them became more than just an esthetic dispute of the kind which had been common during the previous century, for the two worlds had distinct publics and institutions and pursued radically different musical activities.

The keynote of the popular-music public was novelty. The technical development of instruments had made possible far greater performing skills and more dazzling new effects than even before, and the virtuosi used them to their full advantage. As is usually true of popular culture, the concerts were concerned more with performance than with the music itself, for the virtuosi became famous less as composers than as skilled players who could use their instruments so dexterously in contexts of high showmanship. Benefit concerts emerged from the entrepreneurial activities of these musicians, providing the institutional flexibility and personal spotlight which the players needed. The listeners, for their part, threw themselves into performances of virtuosic pieces in editions modified to suit their limited abilities. Salons — the cocktail parties of the time — gave them a place to shine. An enormous commercial establishment grew up around the virtuosi and their listeners to exploit the many fads which the new musical world generated. Concerts, publishing music schools, and music journalism became some of the most dramatic "growth" industries of their time.

The classical-music scene — as it was called even then — developed within orchestral and chamber-music concerts.[9] The events rarely presented virtuosi and did not even perform much new music by composers who were influenced by the German style. Their public had a highly ascetic attitude towards music and much antagonism toward the commerce of the other musical scene. A program of the London Musical Union, for example, articulated this point of view (along with a hearty dash of anti-semitism) when it complained that "individual speculations do nothing for art" and denounced those concerts which "fill the pockets of shopkeepers and Jew speculators".[10] All forms of self-display by performers or intense admiration for them by listeners drew hostile comments from this public. In 1846 a Viennese journalist attacked the recent crazes for Jenny Lind and Franz Liszt as "a crude hyper-enthusiasm and lamented that "it is a truly deplorable state of the public when one receives such unedifying nourishment."[11] Proponents of the popular-music scene hit back with charges of comparable acidity that classical-music lovers were purists. A Parisian journalist put their disdain into verse:

Then if music be dead
Ah well! Let us inter it!
Crying tra deri deri!
Crying tra deri deri![12]

The one other leading kind of taste which was not associated with
either of the two scenes was that of choral music. During the period
amateur choruses developed in each city for the performance of the
oratorios of Handel, Haydn, and Mendelssohn, and a few contemporary
composers. Composed largely of people from the lower-middle class, the
choruses did not have a strong orientation to fashion and new music as
did the popular-music public, and in some instances (particularly in
Vienna) their concerts had direct links with the classical-music world.
Still, this public did not have any esoteric or elitist values and
exhibited instead various kinds of religious and nationalistic tendencies.

The classical- and popular-music publics were not equally matched,
in either their numbers or their power within the musical world. In all
three cities popular-music concerts considerably outnumbered classical-music
concerts (see Table 2). During the season 1845-1846 presentations which had
a strict classical-music orientation accounted for eight per cent of all
high-status concerts in Paris, thirteen per cent in Vienna, and twenty
per cent in London. The numbers reflect the minority role of the public
and demonstrate also its contrasting extents of growth in the different
cities (though not so much, as one can see in the Parisian case, its
popularity). Certain other concerts bordered upon the classical-music
world (see Table 2). A few musicians, some of whom were influenced by
the German school, focused their benefit concerts upon composition
more than performance; these events generally had mixed programs of
classical music, new works in various styles, and virtuosic numbers.
During the season 1845-1846 there appeared twenty such concerts in Paris,
fourteen in Vienna, and four in London (few in the latter case because
such performers put on chamber-music concerts there).[13] In addition,
a number of non-benefit concerts had varied programs — that season about
thirty in Paris, fifteen in London, and seven in Vienna. While neither
of the two kinds of events could be considered distinctively classical
in orientation, they made the number of concerts at least related to
that taste substantial — twenty-nine per cent in London, twenty-three
per cent in Paris, and twenty-seven per cent in Vienna. Some normal benefit
concerts did, of course, open with a movement from a classical symphony,
but that practice did not reflect any wider interplay between the publics.
A German visitor to Paris noted that it was intended only "to give the
public time to quiet down", and a Viennese journalist dismissed it as
"a necessary evil" which existed simply because "one must, after all,
begin with something!"[14]

The people who went to the two major kinds of concerts made up disti
taste publics. The differences between them stemmed not only from their
contrasting musical preferences, but also from a broad division in tastes
and life-styles. The rise in the standard of living within the middle
class made possible much more lavish and showy ways of living than befor
and the propriety of self-display and adherence to fashion logically
enough became an intense source of tension within all three cities. The
dispute did not take place between different social strata, for within
each segment of the aristocracy as well as the middle class a significant
portion of families did not approve of the modish quality of life they
saw growing around them. Traditional values of thrift and social reserve
reinforced their feeling. Two observers of the time described the problem
in specific terms. The wife of the Parisian newspaper magnate Emile
Girardin asserted that in the French capital there existed "two
quite distinct worlds, two societies as different as two sects, as
separated as two enemy factions". One, she said, was "the gay
world" which followed all currents of fashion, the other "the
serious world" which acted as "trustee for the old virtues".[15]
A reviewer for a London music magazine stated that "the English
population is divided into two classes which never mingle, which
nothing can unite, and which appear to form two separate nations".[16]
He demonstrated how each of the two milieux drew people from widely
separated social levels; craftsmen and artists, he said, could become
closely involved with the wealthy families they served.

But the two commentators clearly exaggerated the gulf between the
two worlds to a degree, and some people must have gone to both kinds of
concerts. The famous artists who appeared in each world certainly drew
listeners from their opposing camps, and all listeners most likely did not
take the esthetic conflict with complete seriousness. The French writer
Emile Deschamps put the problem in balanced perspective in a comment
he made in his diary in 1835. He noted that the "mutual injustice [of
the two publics] is explained by the difference in their points of view
toward art and by the rivalry between them" and that "they are too
different in this respect and too equally matched to be able to understand
each other". He then qualified his point with the quip that some
Frenchmen "swoon in the morning with Beethoven and in the evening wi
Rossini" and conceded that "there is a fair number of fanatics of the
Conservatory [the site of the city's main classical-music concerts] who
treat themselves in most cavalier fashion at the Opéra-Italien."[17]
Such eclectic music fans were, however, particularly numerous in Paris
because the Conservatory concerts became more prestigious than classical-
music events in either of the other cities. By comparison, a London
journalist stated that he had rarely seen the subscribers to the events of
the Philharmonic Society at other kinds of concerts.[18]

It was these more than any other social phenomena which defined the quality of life in the three capitals. The cities had no tight unitary ruling class which could control musical institutions and guide aesthetic tastes as was true in most provincial cities. Its elite had strong internal divisions both socially and culturally, and musical institutions were consequently highly disunified and torn by conflict. The rising composer and journalist Robert Schumann said this often in letters home to Leipzig during his stay in Vienna during 1838. He remarked to a colleague that "you would hardly believe the petty factions, coteries, etc., that there are here, and to gain strong footing requires serpentine maneuvers."[19] He wrote to his wife Clara similarly that "Vienna has a richness as has no other city; but it lacks a leader such as Mendelssohn who might blend its parts and rule over them."[20]

Let us proceed to the most fundamental division in the three cities: social class. However much middle-class people had more money to spend than before, all but the most prosperous of them had such strict limits upon their expenditure that ticket prices created a finely-graded hierarchy of concerts and listeners. Status-consciousness reinforced the social ladder by ascribing special prestige to events costing above certain amounts. There evolved sharply defined brackets in the cost of tickets which provide a useful means of detecting the social levels of different concerts and — our present task — of surveying the largest divisions in the concert public.

In each city prices fell into three main areas which we shall call the lower, middle, and upper brackets (see Table 5). While the kinds of concert found in each one differed in the three places (in Vienna most of all), the social standing of people who could afford them corresponded closely. If we apply information about average family budgets to the incomes of segments of the concert public, we find that the persons who purchased tickets in the three brackets were similar in the different places. Several discussions of typical middle-class budgets indicate that less prosperous families would rarely spend more than two per cent and in most cases closer to one per cent of their income on entertainment. An English and an Austrian source each stated that persons with a modest clerical salary (£250 and 400 fl.) would spend about three per cent upon medicine and incidentals (especially tobacco and beer) as well as trips to concerts or the theater.[21] That the same English writer said families on the threshold of the upper-middle class (£1,000) would sink two per cent into entertainment alone indicates that lesser ones would put but one per cent into it.

The mathematics of all this can be suggestive if not totally precise. A particularly well-off artisan who earned 400 fl. a year could spend his 4 fl. of entertainment money (one per cent) on twenty-four tickets to hear Johann Strauss (costing 10 kr. each).[22] But he could not have afforded concerts priced in the middle bracket of 1 fl. and up. His colleague in London who earned £70 annually could not have been any more able to spend his 15s. on occasional 5s. (middle-bracket) tickets, and since most prices in that area lay closer to 10s. he would more likely have gone to choral or promenade concerts with tickets in the lower bracket.[23] The Parisian artisan would likewise not squander his 30 fr. of yearly entertainment money (out of 3,000 fr. income) on tickets costing over five francs.[24] Clerks and shopkeepers, however, had earnings several steps higher than most artisans by the time they reached their late thirties and could therefore buy tickets in the middle range at least occasionally. Nevertheless, the main component of people buying these tickets were undoubtedly retailers, middle-level civil servants, and most members of the liberal professions.

The gap between the middle and upper brackets had even clearer meaning for it comprised the dividing-line between the modest middle class and the bourgeois elite. The Londoner earning £1,000 a year would have about £20 (two per cent) a year for entertainment and could therefore buy upper-bracket tickets at 10s. 6d. with some ease — forty, to be exact.[25] Likewise, a Parisian wholesaler who made 25,000 fr. a year (the supposed starting-point of income for the city's elite) could purchase fifty ten-franc tickets with his 500 fr. a year.[26] Finally, the high-ranking Viennese wholesale merchant who earned an average of 10,000 fl. a year could obtain over sixty tickets at the upper-bracket price of 3 fl.[27]

Some concerts did, of course, deviate from these norms. Those by amateur musicians which could not compete with professional presentation often charged prices lower than their audiences would normally pay (most commonly in the lower instead of the middle bracket). Likewise, many concerts of classical music had strikingly low prices considering the relatively high status of their audiences (in the middle or even bottom bracket). We can thus see that the anti-commercialism of that public's values took real effect in its concert life. But even in these two kinds of concert the usual practices often held sway. What is more, the consistency of prices among benefit concerts shows how powerfully status considerations operated in this area. Deviations by individual concert-goers, however, are more difficult to estimate. Some people undoubtedly bought tickets occasionally at prices above their usual range because the events were especially popular or had unusually great meaning for their lives. Two musical instrument-makers who bought subscriptions to the London Philharmonic in 1830, for example, must certainly have had to pinch their pennies to afford the six guineas for this luxury, though it surely afforded them contact with many potential clients.[28] Downward crossover, on the other hand, was restrained by fear of social shame. A novel about Vienna during the period illustrated such pressure when it depicted the famous Baron

Salomon Rothschild upbraiding a young man visiting his home for sitting in a cheap seat at the opera.[29]

The increasing significance of the division between the middle and upper brackets was a powerful force which shaped much of concert life during the period. The concerts or seats priced in the elite bracket did not belong to any tiny group. In London and Vienna (though regrettably not in Paris) enough concerts advertised their prices in the press to allow a quantitative reckoning of the distribution of ticket prices in the various brackets (see Tables 5-10). The tabulation of all price settings during the season 1845-1846 (Table 7) shows that in both cities over one-quarter of the settings lay in the upper bracket (in London 28 per cent and in Vienna 29 per cent). The tabulation of top prices (Table 8) indicates this as well, for in London 39 per cent and in Vienna 48 per cent of all concerts had prices in that region. Indeed, the price charged most frequently in the upper bracket in all three cities lay in its bottom range: in London half-a-guinea, in Paris 10 fr., and in Vienna 3 fl. Unfortunately there is no information as to the proportion of tickets sold at different prices. There is, however, no indication that the high-priced seats were small in number.

The prestige of tickets priced in the upper bracket became much stronger during the period because concert sponsors made an important innovation in concert management during that time: reserved seats. Previously seats had rarely been set aside for specific persons. All tickets were sold as general admission, and if a concert was a popular one people either sent their servants to occupy seats ahead of time or went early themselves. But during the first seasons of the 1830s a few concert sponsors began setting aside reserved seats priced only in the upper bracket, and by 1840 the practice was almost universal in all three capitals.[30] The special tickets therefore afforded people a strong sense of social distinction. Not only did they keep less affluent people from getting the best seats, they also defined high status in a more rigid manner than before. The policy formalised the division of the middle class into two parts and stimulated social tensions between them.

The most immediate reason why the practice was adopted was a practical one. The increase in the sizes of audiences made concert sponsors eager to avoid confusion when their crowds entered the halls. Another one was economic: the device provided musicians with a good means of charging higher prices. But a deeper reason lay in the growing status self-consciousness of the middle class. Social standing was no longer a simple thing obvious to all. It now had much more ambiguous bases than before and therefore needed proving before the general public. The growth in the size of the cities and the middle class intensified the problem because it diluted common knowledge about who was who and

made people resort to conspicuous means of displaying their status. The factor operated with particular strength in concert life, for with the sudden expansion of the public large numbers of people began attending concerts who had not been known there before.

The line between the middle and lower price brackets was also an important one. The chief columnist in London's leading music magazin indicated the difference between them most explicitly in 1845. He said that while he welcomed the growth of concerts with prices below 10s. 6d., he could not approve of concerts given for less than 5s. "The art must not be degraded", he warned, for "to play the finest music to an audience which has been admitted at a shilling apiece, is what I can never give my consent to." "I am a liberal," he concluded soberly, "but I have good sense to guide me."[31] The line between the two brackets was sharp, for the amount of overlap between them during the season of 1845-1846 was actually less than between the upper and middle brackets. To be sure, as the tabulation of total overlapping (Table 10) indicates, in Vienna two-and-a-half times as many concerts had tickets in both of the lower two brackets than did in the upper two. In London much the same was true, for 52 of the 88 concerts whose highest price lay in the middle bracket had a top price of only 5s. and therefore were not far out of the lower one. But the kinds of concert which charged prices principally in the lower bracket had a quite different nature from those in the higher two brackets In all three cities formal concerts given by professional musicians in the main concert halls almost never charged prices below the middle bracket. Those in the lower one had weak status in the concert world due to the composition of their audience or the low level of their performing standards. These concerts usually took place in halls which did not present prestigious events; many were informal occasions which resembled amusement halls more than seated concerts.

The gap between the two brackets shows that the middle-class public was not simply divided between the upper-middle class and the rest of the class. Between the elite and its poorer and less prestigious population lay a group which was less sharply defined than either of the other two but which nonetheless played a role of its own. Its members chiefly attended concerts directed toward the lower-middle class public, but because of their greater affluence went to a few high-status concerts and therefore had some relations with the upper-middle class.

Such are the main patterns of prices in London, Paris, and Vienna. How much, then, did prices differ in the three cities? One problem is the relative expense of concert tickets. Direct comparison is impossible because the cost of living is so difficult to estimate quantitatively. But much the same kind of answer can be obtained from comparison of th

26

spread of concert prices in the cities. The tabulation of the lengths of the price brackets (Table 6) shows strong contrasts among the cities in the distance between the lowest- and highest-priced concerts. In London that range was twice as long as in Vienna and almost one-third as long as in Paris. This meant that most tickets, those in the upper brackets especially, cost a significant amount more in London that in Vienna and somewhat more than in Paris. The lowest-priced tickets in the middle bracket, for instance, were twice as expensive in London as in Vienna. Likewise, prices in the upper bracket went much higher in London and Paris than in Vienna. The figures parallel the differences in the economic development and financial resources of the middle class in the capitals. Just as Vienna's commerce and banking were still limited compared to London's, so its concerts had a smaller scale economically.

The differences in the spread of prices also produced contrasts in the isolation of levels of the public. In London the wide range of prices in all brackets meant that concert-goers were less likely than elsewhere to purchase tickets outside their customary level. This factor helped make levels of the concert public more separate from each other in London than in the other two cities. As we shall see in Chapter V, formal concerts charging prices only in the lower bracket appeared much more numerously and independently in London than in either other city.

The tabulation of prices for the season 1845-1846 shows the same difference in the isolation of publics in the three cities. In London high-status concerts charging prices in the upper bracket were much more cut off from the rest of the concert world than in Vienna or even in Paris. The tabulation of base prices (Table 9) shows that whereas in London 28 per cent of all concerts had prices only in the upper bracket, in Vienna no concerts were isolated in that fashion, for all concerts with prices in the upper bracket also had prices below it. Furthermore, the tabulation of top prices (Table 8) indicates that Vienna had more concerts with their highest price in the upper bracket (48 per cent as opposed to 39 per cent in London) and thus had much greater contact between its publics. The location of concerts in the cities reinforced the difference. In London almost all of the high-status concerts with prices only in the upper bracket took place in private homes or in two concert halls where concerts with broader publics rarely took place. In Vienna one-half of the city's concerts occurred in a central concert hall.

Paris stood between London and Vienna in the degree of isolation of its publics. As in the Austrian capital, its prestigious concerts generally had tickets priced in the middle bracket. Yet the overlap was not as common as in Vienna and usually included only the upper region of the city's middle bracket. As in London the spread of prices in the middle and upper brackets must have somewhat limited crossovers between them. The city compared to London and Vienna similarly in respect of concert locations. Paris had an even greater proliferation of new locales than London, but none of them emerged as strictly high-status concert halls. The different publics therefore had no separate halls as in London, but they did not mingle as closely in a central locale as in Vienna.

Low-priced concerts also had greater segregation in London than in Paris and Vienna. Of all the concerts in the season of 1845-1846 only 11 per cent of the Viennese concerts had prices exclusively in the lower bracket, while 23 per cent of London's concerts had such (Table 8). Many more cheap concerts with lower-middle class audiences developed there than in the other cities. The proportion of total price settings in the lower bracket during the season 1845-1846 (Table 7) was 21 per cent in Vienna and 27 per cent in London. Almost half (54 out of 120) of the concerts with prices in the lower bracket in London had no prices in higher brackets (Tables 8 & 9). In Vienna the equivalent proportion was less than a third (9 out of 28), and even at that some of these concerts were prestigious classical-music concerts with the abnormally low prices such events often charged. Among all the concerts that season only 11 per cent of the Viennese concerts had prices only in the lower bracket, compared to 23 per cent in London. Thus in London the lowest social level in the concert world stood farther apart from the rest of the public than in Vienna. Paris resembled Vienna in this respect. While its medium-priced concerts often had prices in the lower bracket, few concerts had prices only in the lower bracket.

The patterns of prices thus indicate some important points about differences between the cities. The evidence of prices is not the final word on the question, but it does show that in regard to the overall segregation of publics the separation of the upper-middle class from the rest of the middle class had gone farthest in London and least far in Vienna. In addition, it indicates the particularly strong differentiation of the low-status public in London.

Yet the contrasts between the cities have less significance when seen in light of the evolution of prices during the first half of the nineteenth century. In both Paris and Vienna the weak development of concerts during the eighteenth century had kept prices low, but after 1815 they began rising toward the level of London's prices. Before 1815 the usual price of concerts in Vienna was 40 kr., and the highest 1 fl. 20 kr. After the war the new generation of virtuosi began raising the prices of benefit concerts. The change contrasted sharply with the general economic trends of the period, since the prices of most goods declined gradually after the end of the war. By 1830 the

28

conventional range of prices at benefit concerts had risen to between one and two florins, and by 1840 to between one and three florins. Not only did the range of prices increase, but also the isolation of the brackets. Now some concerts appeared with prices only in the lower bracket (particularly the informal concerts of Johann Strauss), and the most fashionable concerts charged at least 3 fl. for reserved seats. The same process occurred in Paris. During the 1820s prices lay principally in the middle range of 5 to 10 fr. After 1830 they went up sharply, and by 1840 the price for general admission was at least 6 fr. and that for reserved seats 10 to 20 fr.

Thus, in Paris and Vienna concerts were moving toward the same patterns as in London: higher prices and more isolated publics. While neither city had gone as far as the English capital in either respect, they were following in the same historical path. What is more, prices declined somewhat in London, bringing them closer to those of Paris and Vienna. Tickets had reached their highest price level early in the century; by 1815 the conventional price for benefit concerts was 10s. 6d., and the price remained the dividing line between high- and low-status concerts. But during the late 1830s, as the city's low-status concerts began to grow so dynamically, some musicians began charging 7s. for general admission and the usual half-a-guinea for reserved seats. As a result, the isolation of the upper bracket diminished slightly and the level of the city's prices moved closer to that of Paris and Vienna.

Overall, the patterns of prices in London, Paris, and Vienna suggest that the upper-middle class was moving away from the rest of the middle class in concert life to form a new "high-status" public with the aristocracy. What had before been a loose association between the groups now, with the inauguration of reserved seats, became a formally defined social union.

CHAPTER III

THE HIGH-STATUS POPULAR-MUSIC PUBLIC

The world of prestigious popular-music concerts developed in London, Paris, and Vienna with considerably more similarity than any other area of concert life during the 1830s and 40s. Its main components were the same in all three cities: an institutional structure of salons and benefit concerts, entrepreneurship of professional musicians, a growing public from the aristocracy and the upper-middle class, and active leadership by key elements of the two classes. The fragmented cultural life of the capitals needed just such a decentralized base for its new concert world, and these events therefore flourished like no others. They provided the cities' two elites a place where they could get to know each other as they never had before, as virtually equal partners at the top of a rapidly changing hierarchy. Within them we can see the first traces of a unified upper class.

Our discussion will begin, however, on a more mundane level. We will first examine the social groups which were the leading actors in the daily experience of concert life: the family, occupational groups, men and women, and professional musicians. We will then look more broadly at what changes their activities brought to class structure. Finally, we will evaluate the significance of differences between the developments in the three cities.

Investigating what the family meant to concert life discloses an important conclusion about each of them. Quite unlike the isolated social unit as which it is often portrayed, the upper-middle class family in all three capitals took powerful roles in public life, and did so particularly in the musical world. Conversely, formal public concerts were not impersonal events as they seem when viewed superficially, for they were intimately linked with the life of the family.

We will not recount all that Arthur Loesser has shown so well about the centrality of music-making in bourgeois homes, but will only sketch out the main functions it served there.[1] For one thing, musical pursuits provided a means for the socialization of children. The watchword of middle-class values was discipline, and musical training helped instill it in young people. For girls especially, learning the piano was virtually a puberty rite, since it was conceived not as a hobby but rather as a social obligation integral to their upbringing. In the second place, music provided activities which members of the family could pursue together, something people were taking more seriously during the early nineteenth century than ever before. An English teenage girl left a glimpse of this life in a letter to a friend:

> The amusements of the evening were our each reading and
> translating a poem of Uhland's, [performing] the
> overture to the Midsummer Night's Dream by Mendelssohn,
> Beethoven's March, looking at books — and supper — in
> imagination and heaps of nonsense and there you have us.[2]

But family musical life went far beyond that. The gradations
between activities in the home — performances in the domestic circle,
those in salons, and in private concerts — were so fine that it is
difficult to see where the family stopped and larger society began.
The great majority of salons within the upper-middle class and
the aristocracy had musical performances. In 1846 a Parisian
journalist estimated that during the previous season about 850 salons
had substantial enough musical interludes that they could be called
private concerts.[3] A London performer indicated much the same
frequency when he claimed that, like so many of his colleagues, he
would appear at about three homes every night during the three-month
spring social season.[4] In some cases the gatherings were planned
explicitly as formal concerts. In London more than anywhere else
prominent performers put on their annual benefit concerts in the
homes of their main supporters and advertised the events in the press.

Salon performances served several basic needs of the family.
Status-seeking was an obvious one. A London journalist, for instance,
said a typical social phenomenon of his time was the woman he knew
who put on "soirées musicales" twice a week "believing them to
create no small sensation in the world of fashion."[5] Another
was more concrete. Families often presented their children in
performance to obtain marriage partners for them. A Parisian journalist
stated that giving young people impressive musical skills was "a
means of shining in the salons, and, who knows? of arriving at a good
marriage."[6] Individuals whose families could not do that also
used the gatherings to that end if they played well. An Englishwoman
wrote to a London music magazine that on the advice of her friends
she had taken up singing for the sole purpose of marrying into a
wealthy family, and had accomplished her goal in a short time.[7]
Men likewise used performing to further their careers. A
correspondent to a Leipzig music magazine reported that in Vienna
young men took up chamber music in order to gain access to the salons
of highly-placed families through whom they might get good jobs.[8]

The role of the family in musical life did not stop at salons.
Public concerts grew directly from the domestic occasions. Most
of the paying customers at benefit concerts had engaged the
sponsoring performer to play at a salon or teach members of the
family. Any such service carried with it the obligation to buy

31

tickets to the musician's annual benefit concert, and few families shirked the duty.[9] Frequent complaints in the press about the pressure of musicians upon their clients show how strong the requirement was. Some writers called it a tax, as did a Parisian reviewer who termed it a "corvée" which functioned "as a kind of contribution levied against amateurs."[10] Others depicted listener at benefit concerts as unwilling victims of voracious professional manipulation by musicians.[11] The many public concerts which appeared at the time thus did not come out of nowhere. Far from being intended for their own purposes, they served the needs of another institution, the family, as musical activities had done for so long. Despite the proliferation of formal events in musical life, casual gatherings designed for rather different ends remained the focus of musical life.

All this does not mean, however, that concerts had only a devious social meaning. If anything, it helps clear them of the charge that concert-goers only went to be seen. The public events had become too large to meet others or even be observed by them; salons provided the place where such gamesmanship took place. As a Viennese satirist put it, salons were dominated by "that affected Vampyrism of the Parisian lions" of the men and "imitation of the George-Sand-like goddess" by the women.[12] Given the extraordinary enthusiasm for the virtuosi of the time, one can only presume that, complaints against pushy musicians aside, people did go because they liked the music. It would even seem that the performances at salons gave the assembled company a psychological respite from the competitive atmosphere they had generated. A Parisian journalist said as much when he noted that hostesses needed to have performances at their gatherings because their guests needed a breather. Conversation had died as the salons' main activity, he said, because the gatherings were too large and their mood too tense — "in default of the old dialogue a bond is needed, and that bond is music."[13]

What is more, public concert life came to exert much more sway over home music-making. While most music published in the eighteenth century for domestic use had had its own small forms, that of the new era was primarily transcriptions of virtuosic or operatic pieces for amateurs. The whole conception of private playing changed from a simple pastime to a means of self-advancement. The Parisian writer Sophie Gay said that during the previous century families had presented their children only singing little songs or performing on the tiny clavecin, but by the 1830s they got them to do full opera arias and virtuosic numbers on the grand piano.[14] The burgeoning publishing industry also intensified the public orientation of domestic musical life. By 1840 virtually all newspapers and magazines had extensive coverage of concert events, and in each city at least one specialized music magazine had appeared. As a Viennese journalist remarked, "if one doesn't go to concerts, one reads reviews, and by that means becomes musical."[15]

So anyone who thinks that upper-middle class people in the three capitals sought refuge from society in their families should just think a moment about the many hours children sat in front of the keyboard and remember all that meant socially. It may be true that the home had taken on an internal life of its own such as it had not had before and that adults used it as a moralizing force upon their offspring. But let us not delude ourselves that the family was a shelter from the world. It was functioning as a link between the individual and society and in so doing manipulated individuals to do many things society wished.

Occupational groups also played central roles in the new concert world. There are unfortunately no quantitative sources of information on this problem for the popular-music public such as those so plentiful for the classical-music public. But the evidence makes clear that business families provided the most powerful leadership in this area of musical life. Contemporaries mentioned them frequently in letters and articles. In London the main upper-middle class salon sponsors, a music magazine reported, were wealthy merchants, chiefly the most prosperous wholesalers.[16] The most prestigious bourgeois salons were at the homes of Jewish banking magnates, many of whom were related to families in Paris and Vienna.[17] Likewise in Paris, three men of high social standing who published diaries of their travels cited business families as the most important salon hosts.[18] A journalistic sketch of the typical high-status salon (set in the home of a retired stockbroker) confirmed their claim.[19] In Vienna business families had possibly the most overriding importance in popular-music life compared with their colleagues in the other two cities, since they were the only families whose salons were attended by the aristocracy.[20] Another contemporary reported that persons from business counted much more numerously among the guests at prestigious salons than people from the bureaucracy or the liberal professions.[21]

Business families dominated the popular-music scene because of the central position they held in the middle-class society of the time. Wholesaling and finance had not yet become separate professions, and their members consequently constituted a massive tightly-knit economic force. Not as many lawyers, doctors, or artists had gone as far in developing powerful professional activities as had businessmen; more specifically, fewer of them had amassed the wealth which was necessary for recognition among the leading bourgeois families in the capitals. Most business families accordingly had a self-confident, ostentatious life-style and valued cultural pursuits of the same order. They looked to the famous virtuosi for an exaggerated picture of the success and glamour they saw in themselves. In reporting a dinner in honor of the popular operatist Giacomo Meyerbeer, a Viennese journalist reported that the musician was

> a prey for the notability-hunters, for Viennese self-display. They will make a lot of him, and want to lift some of his world fame off for themselves. There will be much hully-bully back and forth between the aristocracy and commerce; the stock speculators also will want to get their part as on a five-percent note.[22]

These people also projected values for achievement and progress into musical life. A Parisian journalist described their attitudes in a sketch of the typical prosperous businessman, the "Bourgeois." Much impressed by the new musical instruments of his time, such a gentleman would see in them an affirmation of his belief in the advances of civilization. He would, said the writer, disparage street musicians — as persons of his ilk had not done a few decades before — "since he has heard it said that taste for such music is bad form, incompatible with universal progress."[23] A strong anti-intellectual streak also lay in the attitudes of wealthy business families. While they valued musical skill, they looked down on any form of erudition in musical activities. A Viennese satirist who championed popular-music taste chided certain families (obviously those active in classical-music life) for their "philosophical mania" toward "higher" music" and their snobbish name-dropping of Goethe and Schiller.[24]

We can here see in concrete form how popular-music idioms provided an escape from contemporary anxieties. Despite the stable prosperity of the era, business failures were commonplace, and members of every family worried that this might happen to them. A Parisian music magazine characterized the public at benefit concerts as one which had little interest in artistic finesse but rather wanted distraction "so that it might be able to forget budgets and bankruptcies."[25] The Viennese actor Franz Anschütz likewise described the affluent theater public of the time as people who used the theater "only to inform themselves anxiously of such topics as 'the French', 'the Americans', and 'credit'."[26]

But obviously not all major salon sponsors, and certainly not all people at benefit concerts, were from business families. Their significance in the popular-music scene lay in the strong leadership they exerted over the tastes and social atmosphere of that world. Some people from the liberal professions were also prominent salon sponsors. The most important one was Jean Orfila, the Dean of the Medical School in Paris, who during the 1840s held a salon where many of the most promising performers made their debuts in the city.[27] Yet the function of his gatherings set them apart from the salons of business families, for Orfila acted primarily as a connoisseur rather than as a social host and therefore played a different role than salon sponsors among business families. As we shall show in Chapter IV, it corresponded to the one usually found among people from the liberal professions.

Another leading component of the popular-music public was women. Just as was the case in the professional area, the importance of women in this musical scene lay more in leadership than in overall numerical predominance. Some benefit concerts, of course, particularly those held at noon, did have disproportionate numbers of women.[28] But one should not exaggerate this tendency, since the great majority of journalists gave no such impression and the many comments about men at popular-music concerts show that they attended in great numbers. After all, the working hours of upper-middle class gentlemen were quite flexible, and they could even attend midday concerts without any great difficulty. Nor is there evidence that men went to concerts simply because their wives demanded it.

Women exerted vigorous leadership in the popular-music scene rather because the family figured so centrally in that world. Girls were the main performers in home music-making; married women often continued to perform and supervised their children's musical training. Women managed the salons, for by tradition the wife of the household presided over the gatherings, introducing guests and leading the conversation. Women controlled the directions in which fashions were moving. A Parisian journalist contended that "the piano today shares popular favor with singing, and that is true because, though I do not wish to offend other instruments, the two specialties are exclusively the province of women."[29] The sketch of the "bourgeois" stated likewise that he left purchases of music to the discretion of his wife and daughters.[30] A comment on dress styles showed how seriously women regarded concert life. A Parisian clothing magazine reported in 1846 that while ballroom dresses were designed to appear simple, those for concerts had no such pretensions of modesty. "Their allures are more frank," it said, "and their scrutiny is approved of more."[31] Logically enough, the most popular virtuosi had special techniques to excite the women in their audience. Liszt had the best such act; he would arrive early at the concert hall,

chat with women there, and play with the grandest showmanship.
He demonstrated his power over women best in Vienna, where his
entry into the hall would stimulate loud cries — a gesture reserved
otherwise only for royalty.[32]

The leadership of women in the popular-music scene suggests
that a deep social restlessness was at work among upper-middle
class women in the three capitals. Though it had no political
direction and was inarticulate as to its goals, it manifested
strong stirrings which prefigured the feminist movement of the
late nineteenth century. Social change had dislodged the traditional
roles of men and women from their moorings and caused both groups
to jockey for new social positions. The liberal Parisian Marquis
de Custine described the turmoil in Paris:

> Paris has a kind of women who aspire to become
> what one would call socially preponderant persons
> seeing the world only as their booty, taking part
> in the movement of society only to amass from it what
> they can.[33]

In Vienna female activism in cultural life provoked even
more open conflict between men and women. Political repression
by the Habsburg Monarchy had limited what upper-middle class
men could do in public life, thereby affording women far more
opportunity for social leadership. During the political ferment
of the 1840s a backlash of male resentment broke out against
the dominance of women in salons and cultural life. A progressive
magazine claimed that men were either staying away from salons
or starting their own clubs, and satirised the tendency with
the announcement that an "Anti-Women Society" had been formed.[34]

However, women achieved power only of an unstable, weakly-defined
order. At salons they were still ultimately subordinate to their husbands.
Men were becoming more active in the salons as the growth of
middle-class professions made the gatherings increasingly important
for their affairs. The growth of the press diminished somewhat the
importance of salons generally, for written communication
was superseding oral communication in middle-class life, and
the women thereby lost much of their traditional power. Finally,
the role of women in the popular-music scene brought them no
formal recognition such as men received in music societies. The
annual report for 1847 of a Parisian honorary society for painters
and musicians admitted as much indirectly when it ominously predicted
that women would soon demand membership because they had accomplished
so much as performers and composers during the previous decades.[35]

A third major group which brought about the new popular-music
world was professional musicians. The careers virtuosi

36

launched during the period transformed not only the commercial aspect of concert life but also its class structure. In making concert life a commercial field of the modern kind, they eroded the traditional power of the aristocracy in musical life and forced it to accept the upper-middle class on a more equal basis.

Musicians no longer acted as employees or small-scale enterprisers but rather as powerful independent entrepreneurs. Just like commerce and industry, their profession found new opportunities for actively controlling the market in which they worked. The flamboyant performing skills for which they are so famous was only the most visible of the techniques they developed. One device was shrewd programming. They would schedule long programs with a wide variety of pieces and announce appearances by many famous performers — often fraudulently.[36] Another device was manipulation of the press. Most newspapers and magazines printed short notices about future concerts and the comings and goings of noted performers. A skillful operator would send in his own copy and thereby make his name known widely at little cost.[37]

Musicians also began diversifying their careers. Concerts did not provide anything near a living wage, for competition was so stiff that few made a profit.[38] But the events were excellent channels for developing other lucrative activites. They helped musicians gain entry into the most wealthy households for teaching or salon performances and did much to publicise the sheet-music editions they wrote for amateurs. Some musicians even began building their own businesses. The French violinist Henri Herz founded a publishing firm and a concert hall; a number of musicians in London became the managers of musical and theatrical auditoriums. In London several musicians made the first known experiments in commercialised concert management by undertaking the organisation of other performers' concerts.[39] Specialised, professional concert management was not, however, to emerge until the last decades of the century.

The professionalisation of musical life also sharpened the definition of performing roles. The European aristocracy had always regarded the arts as gentlemen's pursuits, and professional musicians had functioned chiefly to assist laymen in this artistic avocation. Entrepreneurial virtuosi ended this tradition. By 1848 amateurs might perform at salons, but not in public concert halls; they might present concerts in their homes but had to acknowledge that performances in public were the central events in concert life. The professional now had unchallenged authority in his field.

Musicians thereby made a profound change in the relative power of the aristocracy and the upper-middle class within musical life, for while musicians still solicited the support of the nobility, they ran their careers on their own. Even though musicians were not accepted on an equal social plane by their sponsors, they had more to gain from independent commercial relationships with them than from equality in status. They accordingly came and went from prestigious households in brisk, business-like fashion, preferring to play their market for as many profitable contacts as possible rather than settle into tight relationships with one or two families. Madame d'Agoult, for instance, remarked in her memoirs how surprised she and people of the nobility were at the distance even Franz Liszt kept from them, for he would often depart as soon as he had finished performing.[40] Furthermore, some musicians even passed up good chances for profitable careers of the traditional kind in order to experiment with new kinds of musical commerce. The famous English singer John Braham, for instance, disengaged himself from a highly successful career at the opera (and all the salon appearances that brought him) to manage a concert hall.

Behind the new independence of professional musicians lay the enormous commercial potential of the middle-class concert public. This market lay principally in the provinces, not in the capitals. Because performers did not compete as intensively there, concerts yielded enough profit to support even little-known virtuosi, and most ambitious concert performers therefore spent most of the time on long tours. Only because provincial cities provided such return did public concerts become a stable entertainment medium in London, Paris, and Vienna. The capital-city middle class thus became a dominant force in musical life only through the support of the broader national middle class. There were close parallels to this in political and economic affairs. In the long run middle-class economic power grew in industrial cities, and throughout the nineteenth century its political base (revolutionary action aside) lay in provincial cities. Indeed, interaction between the complementary assets of the middle class in capitals and provincial cities was a key to much of the bourgeois dynamism of the period.

The vigorous leadership which musicians and elements of the upper-middle class exerted in popular-music concerts brought a crisis to their relations with the aristocracy. After a short period of uncertainty or conflict in each city, a new integrated high-status public emerged. While the end-product of the process was the same everywhere, its circumstances displayed modest differences in the three capitals.

The crisis was sharpest in London because the nobility had established so strong a hold over concerts there during the previous century. By the early 1820s public concerts by fashionable virtuosi had attracted so much attention that aristocratic families saw them as a serious threat to their role in musical life. They immediately expanded their salons into large-scale private concerts featuring the most popular musicians around and emphasised the exclusiveness of the gatherings as much as possible. "The higher classes are fast gliding away from the support of public concerts," reported a music magazine, claiming that the aristocracy was deriding public occasions as plebeian entertainment.[41] But by that time opera singers — the main attractions at the salons — demanded so much for performances that the families could not afford to hire them often enough to overshadow public concerts. During the second half of the decade they gradually ended their large-scale salons.[42] While some musicians still presented their benefit concerts in aristocratic homes, they always advertised the events in the press and opened the events to the general public. By 1830 formal concerts — and, by that means, middle-class leadership — dominated musical life.

In Paris the process involved less direct conflict than in London. Concerts had developed so little during the previous century that neither class had a tight grip upon them, and the Bourbon aristocracy withdrew from public life for several years after the Revolution of 1830. The Orleanist lower nobility and the upper-middle class suddenly found themselves with an open field for social leadership and united as the base of the prestigious new concert world. A personification of the ties between them was the Prince de la Moscowa, one of the main amateurs in the popular-music scene, who married the daughter of the prominent banker Ferdinand Laffitte.[43] By 1840 the Orleanist regime had consolidated its position so firmly that the high nobility had little choice but to return to public affairs and reappeared in concert life slowly and quietly. In 1843 the writer Victor de Balabine noted in his diary that for a few years the Legitimist families had been attending more salons outside their clan and inviting Orleanists to their own.[44] In a review of a concert held in 1842 a music critic said with some relief that Legitimist and Orleanist aristocrats had been able to mingle without any trouble. His comments are enlightening as to how the city's different elites seized upon musical activities as a setting in which they could coexist:

Music has become a respectable and indeed a distinguished

juste milieu, as an art of reconciliation between all the classes of society. When one listens, no discussions, no disputes are possible. Music stimulates goodwill.[45]

In Vienna the crisis was as intense as in London because one group — here the middle class — controlled concert life. During the seventeenth and eighteenth centuries aristocratic families had maintained enormous musical enclaves, even opera companies, on their estates and in their Viennese town houses, but by 1800 their weakening economic situation forced them to end the practice. While they continued to invite musicians for salon performances, they did not act as patrons to them.[46] Concerts therefore developed entirely under middle-class auspices and drew aristocrats only on rare occasions. By the late 1820s, however, the growth in the number of public concerts made noblemen think again about their standoffish behaviour and ultimately forced them to join the concert public. The first instance of strong attendance by them came when Paganini visited the city in 1828. In a dramatic show of professional independence, he refused to play in salons but still drew a massive titled audience at his concerts.[47] Liszt and Thalberg got the same response (but appeared at salons) when they came in 1836, and thenceforward the nobility was a permanent component of the public.[48] During the 1840s aristocrats attended all kinds of benefit concerts, not just those of the most famous artists.[49]

What came about in the course of these episodes in the three capitals was far more than just greater attendance together by the two classes. A unified "high-status" public had emerged whose structure betrayed itself in a number of ways. In the first place, the social barriers between the bourgeois elite and the rest of the middle class became more substantial and acquired formal definition. The introduction of reserved seats made the change explicit and stimulated resentment from the lesser middle-class public. Such conflict was the most intense in Vienna, where the low price of tickets had unified the different levels of concert-goers. As the charge of three gulden became normal for reserved seats, the usually docile Viennese press objected vehemently. In 1846 the chief music critic of the *Theaterzeitung,* the city's most widely read newspaper, condemned the price of reserved seats as "another form of social discrimation" and exhorted "the two-gulden public" (the middle segment of the middle class) to protest its exclusion from "the three-gulden public".[50] These were fighting words in a society with so little political freedom, and the class consciousness implicit in them suggests how deeply divided the city's middle class had become.

Musicians intensified the division of the middle-class public. Many performers — not just the most high-ranking virtuosi — now shook off ties to their less affluent supporters. A French writer claimed that many artists (painters as well as musicians) he knew had begun snubbing their friends and consorted only with wealthy businessmen, aristocrats, and journalists.[51] Franz Liszt particularly drew criticism for such behavior.[52]

In the second place, the bourgeois and aristocratic elites now played the same kinds of leadership roles in concert life. Bourgeois salons had become so prominent that the remaining difference in the status of their sponsors was less significant than the similarity in their power within the concert world. In Paris especially the most promising performers made their debuts at upper-middle class salons. What is more, the new commercial values of musical life worked to the advantage of bourgeois gatherings. In London, for example, aristocratic hosts drew ridicule for paying performers so much to obtain what upper-middle class households got for much less. "They are the 'order'," said a journalist, "not to enquire too curiously into the amount of return for their liberality."[53]

In the third place, the bourgeois elite now exercised as powerful an influence over taste as did the nobility. It is indeed difficult to perceive any significant difference between the musical predilections of the two classes. The new cosmopolitan instrumental style had grown from both aristocratic taste for virtuosity and bourgeois ideals of achievement, and the two elements had become so fully fused that people were no longer aware of their contrasting origins. The type of event which displayed the union of the classes in popular taste most dramatically was the massive concerts — called "monster" concerts in London — which were presented by the journalist M. G. Saphir in Vienna and the pianist Jules Benedict in the English capital. Though similar to benefit concerts in their basic form, they had scale and prestige of an extreme order since their sponsors managed to obtain the most fashionable musicians in the two cities and attract the most concentrated elite audiences of any events during any season. Blending aristocratic elegance with bourgeois commercialism, they lasted over four hours (offering thirty to forty pieces) and consistently drew crowds of 1,200 in London and 2,000 in Vienna.[54]

Finally, the sense of a common identity was apparent among the two classes. Though yet superficial in its meaning and fragile in its structure, the feeling pervaded the frenetic comings and goings of the period. A Parisian journalist sketched it out in remarkably perceptive fashion. He told how at a salon concert

> the elegant composer drew together the five corners of
> the world, the three aristocracies of birth, of
> industry, and of talent. All of this world, separated
> by interests and reunited by pleasure, submitted to the
> irresistible influence of beauty and music.[55]

Thus did the art provide not only escape from worldly anxieties but
also re-entry into a new social whole. Another Parisian reviewer
commented similarly that since traditional privileges had disappeared

> the arts are the only point of cohesion possible
> between so many persons of varied rank and different wealth,
> who find themselves at the same gatherings and
> carry there the same desire to distinguish themselves.[56]

We should also recall the statement by the Viennese journalist who
predicted much "hully-bully back and forth between the aristocracy
and commerce" at a dinner for Meyerbeer.

The union between the classes was as yet superficial, but
that was the very reason why it came about. Casual social life
such as this acted as the initial stage in their merger because
it involved so little commitment or substantive concession. Intermarriage or political coalition demanded far more and therefore
had to wait. Benefit concerts provided an ideal setting for the
flirtation between the classes because they were *ad hoc* affairs,
not permanent institutions, and therefore allowed either party
to withdraw to whatever extent it wished if the other asked for
too much. Moreover, the musicians served as skillful intermediaries
in it all. The two elites were not about to take on new kinds
of ties on their own; some other group was necessary to match
them up, and the virtuosi played that part to perfection.

The fragmented institutional structure of benefit concerts
did, however, limit the development of the new public. Concerts
of this kind could never become the main base for a tightly-
knit elite public such as symphony orchestras provided later
in the century. Since the managerial authority over the concerts
was diffused among a larger number of musicians and salon sponsors,
competition among them weakened all their efforts. For virtuosi
to maintain their reputations and generate exciting social atmosphere
at their concerts they had to draw large crowds from the upper
classes, but the events were proliferating so widely that it
was difficult to obtain full halls from paying customers. Obligations
deriving from salon appearances and teaching positions were usually
not sufficient to do that, and even the most famous performers
sometimes had a small turn-out. In London in 1831, for instance,
the dean of virtuosi, Johann Nepomuk Hummel, attracted only

some 120 people to a concert.[57]

Most sponsors of benefit concerts therefore handed out many tickets either free or at reduced rates. In London the high price of tickets made the problem particularly bad. The *Musical World* estimated in 1845 that an artist who did not yet have a strong reputation normally gave away up to 400 of the 500 tickets to his benefit concert and that even famous artists might sell only half of the seats at a concert.[58] Musicians naturally tried to get as many of the free tickets as possible into the hands of prestigious persons. The list of persons to whom Hector Berlioz once gave free tickets (totalling 280 out of 1,000 seats), comprised mostly famous artists and wealthy amateurs.[59] Likewise, when virtuosi went on tours they generally sent tickets to friends who could distribute them to noted persons. An English musician who visited Vienna for a concert in 1839 sent a bundle of tickets to an eminent piano teacher with the request that they be given to his students — many of whom were presumably from high families.[60]

But few musicians had such good contacts as Berlioz, and as a result most of the free tickets went to persons outside of the cities' elites. One journalist termed them derisively "a certain number of hangers-on at concerts"; another stated that concert sponsors dispensed tickets "in the servants' hall, in the family, and in the office corridor."[61] As the latter suggested, at concerts of aspiring musicians the families and friends of the performer made up a large portion of the free-ticket holders. A Parisian journalist remarked more bluntly that "each shows himself surrounded by his parents, by his friends, by a coterie."[62] But other people who got in free stood even farther from the upper-middle class. A London amateur mentioned in his memoirs that he had known an elderly widow born into an impoverished aristocratic family who clung to the elite world by obtaining tickets from milliners in the service of opera singers.[63] Some musicians even recruited claques of people to fill the hall and stimulate applause. A London critic once stated that a musician had planted in his audience a claque made up of "profligate persons", undoubtedly the young clerks and apprentices who had regular nightly employment for such duty at the opera.[64]

The free-ticket public thus diluted the prestige of the popular-music public. Because large crowds were so necessary for the maintenance of the concerts the upper-middle class was not able to move fully away from the rest of the middle class. Frequent hostile comments about the free ticket practice in music magazines show the resentment felt toward it by the wealthy bourgeois who constituted the main readership of such periodicals.[65] Even though the persons using free tickets did not occupy reserved seats with the high-status public, they brought discredit to the concerts and thus weakened the union between the two elites.

Benefit concerts consequently did not provide a viable permanent base for the new high-status public. After the middle of the century formal concert series, principally those of symphony orchestras, became the most important foundation for the unified elite within musical life. Such organisations were able to separate the high-status public much more sharply from the lesser middle-class public and bestow upon it full formal standing as an elite. But because they presented much greater organisational problems than benefit concerts they developed only in the classical-music world, and even there in a rather limited form.

Furthermore, even during the 1830s and 1840s the potential for developing a high-status public differed to a moderate extent in the three cities. The Austrian capital had without question the weakest such development. Viennese society posed far greater obstacles to the integration of the aristocracy and the upper-middle class than were present in either Paris or London. The most concrete barrier to the formation of the new public there was the exclusiveness of the salons of the high aristocracy. Not only were the number and the variety of middle-class persons invited to them strictly limited, but also custom dictated that only the men of the wealthy middle class received such invitations and, conversely, only the male members of the nobility visited bourgeois salons.[66] Because women figured so centrally in salons throughout Europe the discrimination against them put a formidable limitation upon the leadership of the middle class in concert life.

This limitation was in turn a very sensitive point among the bourgeois elite. The journalist who reported a concert of Franz Liszt in 1838 had it in mind when he stated that "at this concert the Musikvereinsaal [Vienna's main concert hall] resembled a large salon in which the elite of the nobility and the public gathered to bestow the tribute of their wonderment upon the genial, outstanding virtuoso."[67] In such a fashion would the Viennese upper-middle class fantasize closer relations with their social superiors. Beneath that exclusiveness lay the unusual sharpness of the line between the Austrian middle class and nobility and the high degree of deference that it produced. People still mimicked aristocratic habits with a flagrancy no longer found in the other capitals. They would, for example, address each other with the aristocratic *von,* thus blurring the lines within the middle class.[68]

The high-status popular-music public therefore could not become as unified as elsewhere. The patterns of prices in the city reflected the continuing unity of the middle class, for as we have seen no concerts had prices accessible only to the high-status public, and the expense of tickets in the upper bracket was not so high that people with a modest income could never think of buying them. The presence of aristocrats at public concerts became a fascination for the middle class that obscured the closer relations of upper-middle class families with them. A journalistic sketch of a day in the life of a countess, for example, depicted all concert-goers (presumably the wealthy bourgeois among them) craning their necks to see her take a seat down front. "People stare at those whom she greets with smiles," it said, "and are envious of those who have the right to be near her."[69] What is more, a custom first appeared during this time which, though uncommon until the 1850s, provided special seating for aristocrats. During a dazzling succession of concerts in 1846 Liszt began giving high-ranking noblewomen seats on stage around his piano. Later called "the circle", the practice set that class apart from the middle class in a manner never found in London or Paris.[70]

Another weak point in the growth of the Viennese elite popular-music public was its commercial base. While individual musicians showed as much independence and ambition as in the other capitals, the musical business did not become as strong or as diversified as in the other capitals. No new concert halls appeared during the period; publishers did not exploit the amateur market as vigorously as elsewhere; and the dynamism of benefit concerts did not stimulate musicians to expand their horizons to commercial opportunities in the low-status public.

But it is far too easy to write off the Viennese upper-middle class as a mere weakling compared to its counterparts in the other two capitals. An integral high-status public did at least begin to form there during the 1830s and '40s; much the same social processes were taking place in the Austrian as in the French and English capitals, and the difference between them was one of degree rather than direction of change. Since aristocratic families maintained so little direct support of musicians, the absence of close mingling between the two elites in salon concerts was not as significant as it might have been elsewhere. While the "circle" did perpetuate some discrimination between the elites, it was only an anachronism which gave noblewomen no authority in concert life. Far more important was the split between the upper and lower levels of the middle class created by the introduction of high-priced reserved seats. The protest against the practice during this period shows how divided the Viennese middle class had become.

Comparison of the new high-status public in London and Paris is more a matter of apples and oranges—different forms of development—than comparison of the two highly advanced capitals with Vienna. In London the bourgeois and aristocratic elites had close, intimate relations, yet for that reason the new elite had subordinate leadership roles. In Paris they had more limited integration because the Legitimist nobility held itself so aloof from public life, but by that means the upper-middle class achieved much more power in musical life than did its counterpart in London.

The tight fusion of the elites in the English capital grew in large part from the residential habits of the nobility. While aristocratic families were still rooted in their estates, those that had particularly strong social or political ambitions (and plenty of ready cash) spent two or three spring months in London. During this "season" the nation's elites mingled extensively on the neutral ground which the capital provided them. Close interaction between them therefore posed less of a threat to the nobility than in Paris, where titled families lived virtually all the year round. Concerts took on special importance in the season because they were so suitable for its fast-paced social life. While the opera had a fixed number of seats and a firm hierarchical tradition, benefit concerts had an easily expandable institutional structure and allowed the two elites to mingle more freely than in the highly stratified array of opera boxes.

During these months a socially adroit upper-middle class family could potentially gain contact with the very highest levels of the aristocracy and not just with the new Napoleonic nobility as was the case in Paris. Because English society had not undergone as profound an upheaval as in France at the end of the previous century, its most prestigious aristocrats mingled freely in public life. A list of the most notable persons who attended a benefit concert in 1845 (published in the Tory *Morning Post*) named sixty-one aristocrats, among them two duchesses, five marchionnesses, ten countesses, four viscountesses, and five of the many—probably several hundred—untitled listeners.[71] The many high families at whose salons Ignaz Moscheles performed likewise suggests the elevated status of the audiences at his benefit concerts: the Duchess of Kent, the Marquis of Hertford, the Duke of Cambridge, the Marquis of Lansdowne, and none other than the Duke of Wellington.[72] The absence of any formalized leadership by such personages at concerts made the mingling between them and bourgeois families there particularly significant. Both the opera and the city's main ballroom, a private club called Almack's, had by tradition been governed by committees of noblewomen who dealt out boxes and invitations with fine discretion. In both places the practice was abandoned during the 1830s, indicating the powerful trend toward social equality among the city's elites in which benefit concerts were a leading institutional force.[73]

46

But a countervailing tendency worked upon all upper-middle class Europeans: the higher their company the less they could lead it. In London the aristocracy continued the patronal tradition in a new form which, though much attenuated, limited the ability of wealthy bourgeois to guide concert life. Though noblemen no longer kept musicians in their homes, they retained much closer, more lasting relationships with musicians than their colleagues in Paris or Vienna. Moscheles, for example, began his career in Vienna, but found such strong support from aristocratic families in London that he settled there permanently and became so much of a regular at one titled household that he watched the coronation procession of Queen Victoria with its members.[74] The political events of the time undoubtedly lay behind the intense interest of aristocratic families in the popular-music scene. Since the class saw its political power and social privileges declining, it looked to leadership in the concert world as a means of retaining its pre-eminence in the capital's life. The leading aristocratic families still had far greater economic resources than most upper-middle class families and accordingly lavished enormous sums of money upon virtuosi — fees far greater than those paid anywhere in Europe. Parisian musicians found that the concert public was smaller and tighter in London than in Paris and that virtuosi needed much stronger aristocratic support there if they wished to become leading performers.[75]

The persistence of the aristocratic patronal tradition blunted middle-class leadership and made the popular-music scene less dynamic in its personalities and tastes than in Paris or Vienna. A Parisian musician who had recently returned from a concert tour in England in 1846 claimed that, in contrast to other major cities, in London a virtuoso could not become popular until after several yearly visits for concerts and salon performances. He wrote that

rarely does the public of London let itself go with prompt and spontaneous manifestations of its feelings. In general it needs time to prepare and scrutinize its sensations.[76]

The Harmonicon chronicled a leading instance in which the nobility restrained the faddism which was so central to the influence of the upper-middle class in the popular-music scene. When in 1828 Paganini had a tumultuous reception at his first concert in London the magazine predicted that after the initial excitement "then all of a sudden, his very name will cease to be pronounced by persons of *ton*, and, as a matter of course, people not of *ton*—not of the Devonshire circle, not of Almack's—will imitate those who are."[77] In May 1833 it accordingly announced that "the rage is over" and that the leaders of the public had lost their enthusiasm for Paganini.[78]

Another factor which further hampered the upper-middle class in London's popular-music scene was the weak role it accorded women. A French visitor to London remarked with surprise that he found men managing servants and selecting guests for salons. He concluded that the Englishwoman "does not occupy herself with ruling society, with regulating and governing its customs."[79] A nobleman said as well that at salons men huddled together to talk about sports and politics.[80] Salons therefore did not play as central a role in the popular-music scene as in Paris and Vienna. A prominent female pianist of the time described how the subordination of women in musical life dulled the reception of Liszt—and thereby the influence of the upper-middle class as well—in the English capital. Although at first women became as hysterical at his concerts as was to be expected, she said, "it was looked down upon doubtfully by acknowledged authorities, and so died out."[81]

In Paris the upper-middle class faced none of the impediments to obtaining leadership in concert life such as were present in London. The aristocracy had become badly fragmented, and its Orleanist faction was eager to join forces in the social (though not the political) arena with the bourgeois elite. Even better, neither aristocratic camp had developed strong support of musicians in the manner of the English nobility. The Revolution had left musical life in some disarray, and during the Restoration era aristocratic families did nothing more than ask musicians to their homes occasionally; these performances received little public attention and did not serve as international show places for major artists as did salons in London.[82] After the revolution of 1830 the salons of the upper-middle class and the Orleanist nobility suddenly leapt into prominence, and the dynamism they generated made Paris the musical capital of Europe for two decades.

Because the Parisian popular-music scene possessed weak traditions and had lost its aristocratic dominance, middle-class commercialism developed much more fully there than in London or Vienna. The absence of the traditional aristocracy during the 1830s made musical life an intensely competitive one in which musicians operated with much less stable ties to wealthy amateurs than their colleagues in London. The relations between the musician and his supporter were now considered purely as business transactions. A skeptical writer described in verse the new values which governed musical life:

Instead of men united by an intimate commerce
Which strengthens life and gives birth to estime,
One sees in our time only bonds of conspirators,
Of low and vile clients and arrogant patrons,

Or of those joined by thirst for gain alone,
Or of those seditious ones united by hate.[83]

Not only did the Parisian upper-middle class define the values
of the popular-music scene more in Paris than in London, it also
controlled the advancement of musicians more closely. The leading
violin teacher at the city's conservatory, Emile Zimmerman, held a
regular salon which by the late 1830s had become the main place
where performers had debuts in Paris. His salon was so influential
that almost all major virtuosi made their Parisian debuts in his
home.[84] When Zimmerman's health declined in the early 1840s, the
salon of Jean Orfila took its place. In 1845 the city's main music
magazine called his guests "the elite of that choice public which
makes law in musical halls by its musical knowledge and its pure
taste".[85]

But the Parisian elite public had critical limiations in the breadth
and the integration of its members. The Legitimist aristocracy
stayed away from concerts for the better part of the 1830s, and
when it came back it refused to enter fully into social or cultural
life. The astute Madame Girardin scoffed at those who said that
France no longer had a high aristocracy. "It has lost its privileges,"
she said, "but has kept all its prejudices."[86] Bourbon families
stayed in their own world in the Faubourg Saint-Germain and invited
only a few upper-middle class people to their salons.[87] The
banker Jacob Rothschild was one of them, but only because he had
purchased a baronetcy and held aloof from the leading Orleanist circles.
Called "an exclusive", he gave small, unostentatious salons which
resembled those of the Legitimists more than the flashy bourgeois
households.[88] Indeed, the distance which the old families kept
from upper-middle class life made them not unlike the Viennese high
aristocratic families in their relationship to the new concert
world. We can thus see how much the Orleanist nobility—a social
stratum without parallel in Vienna—did to benefit the Parisian
upper-middle class.

The relations between that titled group and the bourgeois elite
themselves were not totally stable, however, for the salons of the
period were notorious for their deviously competitive atmosphere.
The Marquis de Custine noted that while in London one good contact
opened all doors,

in Paris this work must be recommened every day and in every
salon; no one recognizes the authority of anyone else; success
of yesterday does not spare you trouble today; the man who is
fashionable in one household is unknown on the other side of
the street.[89]

Because of these social and political uncertainties the elite music public retreated into salons for its main diversions. Whereas in London public and private concerts had equal prominence in musical life, in Paris salons were the central events. The most famous virtuosi, all of whom held frequent concerts in the English capital, followed suit and rarely appeared outside salons while in Paris. Liszt appeared in public only a few times; Luigi Giraldi, one of the most popular singers of the time, did not do so even once.[90] For the same reason no highly fashionable "monster" concerts emerged in Paris such as were so powerful in London and Vienna. In 1838 an entrepreneur attempted to establish concerts of that kind in a building containing a restaurant, a ballroom, and a concert hall. He hired Paganini to appear there three times a week—though sometimes only to stroll through the garden—and named the place the "Casino de Paganini". But it went bankrupt after a short season, and a music magazine concluded that "the rich gather only among themselves" and suggested that "it is the middle class which must make for the success of a public casino."[91]

Comparison of the popular-music scene in the French and English capitals shows, then, how both traditional and modern social tendencies interacted closely in the development of the new concert world. In London public concerts had become the center of musical life, but a remnant of the patronal system continued through the strong aristocratic leadership there. In Paris concerts emerged in a more commercialised form, but informal private concerts continued to be the focus of the popular-music scene.

In both cities, however, and Vienna as well, benefit concerts acted as a key transitional institution in the modernization of musical life. Having grown out of salons and patronally-supported formal concerts, they established a new commercial order in the concert world and prepared the way for the modern recital. That social form appeared after the middle of the century, as the upper-middle class and aristocracy began to coalesce in other fields as well. By about 1870 musicians had built up an upper-class public stable enough that they did not need to go to such extraordinary lengths to attract (or indeed coerce) people to attend in substantial numbers. Since professionals now had unrivaled authority in concert life, they focused their events upon their performance and did not need to present as many pieces or as many players as before. Orchestras, groups of musicians, and eventually concert managers founded season-long series of concerts, and the number of entrepreneurial individual presentations accordingly declined.

The recital brought greater coherence to concert programming. The variety of solo instruments formerly presented in benefit concerts thinned out as the piano and the violin became predominant.[92] The kinds of ensemble in any one type of concert underwent specialisation as small orchestras gradually disappeared from recitals and singers (particularly opera stars) began giving recitals on their own. Yet the repertoire of recitals became broader through the addition to it of music from the German classical style. After the middle of century changes in the direction of new music, particularly the rise of Richard Wagner as the main trend-setter in the field, made the earlier issues of taste moot. Classical ideals won out but took on a wider definition, since music of both the virtuosic and German schools—both Liszt and Schubert—now came under the rubric of "serious" music in the concert world. A Viennese journalist noted in 1866 that "individual concert-givers scarcely dare any longer present themselves to the public without Beethoven, Chopin, and Schumann." "It is not long since we endeavored to show", he said, "what a change had taken place there during the last ten years."[93]

In such rapid fashion does a society readjust its conceptions of high and popular culture. Explanation of how and why this came about would require yet another study, but we can speculate that the lofty ideals of the classical-music scene replaced the giddy mood of before because they were more compatible with the greater stability and seriousness which came about in musical life during its period of consolidation. After all, one can push novelty only so far. More specifically, classical values suited the needs of virtuosi to glorify their new social standing and provided a solid standard of taste for the elite public that was now firmly established. Opera, however, remained something of a popular genre, despite all that Wagner did to change that. At the same time cafés and singing-halls—early forms of the modern nightclub—were appearing in which popular idioms of a more distinctive nature grew up.[94]

Tendencies toward these developments were indeed apparent before 1848. By the middle of the 1840s many concert-goers had become quite out of patience with musicians' manipulative tactics and showed signs of fatigue at hearing so much of the flashy virtuosic style. A thoroughly unclassical book on Parisian life published in 1842 suggested that "for some time the musical world has been the monopoly of *coterie* and *savoir-faire*; is it not time that it at last become that of science and genius?"[95] A music journalist from the same city put the point in more specific terms when he said that people were fed up with the excessive length and superficiality of virtuosic concerts.[96] In 1845 the most powerful reviewer in Vienna, a critic who had been a leading exponent of the virtuosic style, stated in carefully chosen words that he saw a trend away from the dominant taste of the previous twenty years and toward solider musical stuff.[97] As we shall see in the following chapter, in all three cities new classical-music concerts appeared at that time which had stronger publics than their predecessors.

People of the time were keenly aware of the transitional nature of their time. "We live truly in a period of upheaval in musical life," said the Vienna *Theaterzeitung* in 1828.[98] A Parisian journalist played upon the metaphor more imaginatively. The musical world had become so powerful, he said, that it would soon have to do battle with "the nonmusical world" and march on the Hôtel de Ville to demand a new "musical" government.[99] Revolution did indeed come, but one much less artistic and far more bloody than he suggested.

CHAPTER IV

THE HIGH-STATUS CLASSICAL-MUSIC PUBLIC

Introduction

For most readers, the classical-music world of about 1830 has a
distinctly contemporary feel. Its concerts were full of the institutional
formality and artistic conservatism people now associate with the
present-day "serious" music scene. The minority status of classical
occasions, too, and their conflict with popular-music events, suggest
much about the make-up of musical life today. Indeed, their sense
of being poor second cousins to the larger musical world seems more
familiar now than the proud mood surrounding symphony orchestras during
the second half of the nineteenth century.

Yet most classical-music concerts still had far to go toward
modernization at the start of our period. As was true of so many areas
of musical life, institutional forms developed faster than the rules
and practices we associate with modernity. The absence of a conductor
facing the orchestra at many of these occasions reminds us that concerts
as we know them now were slow in coming. Developments within
classical-music concerts between 1830 and 1848 did, however, bring
them far along this path.

Classical-music life of that time is blessed with highly
informative quantitative sources—membership lists, most luckily of
all—because the great majority of its concerts had organizational
bases. The events therefore tell far more about musical life than
their small number might suggest, and can help deepen the conclusions
advanced in the last chapter. Since the concert societies in London,
Paris, and Vienna had considerably different institutional structures,
we will first sketch out the similarities among them and then examine
local developments in separate sections.

The new integrated elite public took a formal shape in this
area of the concert world such as it did not in benefit concerts.
In London the series controlled by the aristocracy (the Concerts of
Ancient Music) and the one attended by the upper-middle class (the
Philharmonic concerts) both went into decline and were replaced
by a new unitary high-status series (the Musical Union). In Paris the
Conservatory Concerts brought together all levels of the city's elites
in a similar fashion. In Vienna the Philharmonic Orchestra moved
toward that kind of institution (such as it became during the 1860s)
but before 1848 did not establish itself as firmly or build up as
exclusive an audience as its counterparts in the other two capitals.

The dispute between the two taste publics provided the
historical context within which these new concerts appeared. Although

53

the episode was to pass after mid-century, it generated the social energy for the creation of new social relations in musical life and indeed left its stamp permanently upon concert life. Through its sharp rhetoric the members of the two classes who belonged to each camp took on both a mutual identity and common opponents. The life within the two worlds was so vital and the issues between them so intense that the hierarchical lines between the bourgeois and aristocratic elites lost much of their significance. The unifying effect of the cultural conflict operated with particular strength in the classical-music public. The pride in belonging to music's high culture was such a powerful force that its adherents would attack members of their own class in the other public. The Director of the Musical Union said in his program notes on one occasion that many aristocrats had low musical taste and asked "is it true that they are always as well educated in art as those who look for their patronage have a right to expect?" The audience at his concerts was, he proclaimed, "the happy few" which pursued high art undistracted by the degenerate amusements of the rest of the nobility.[1] But for that reason, of course, the high-status audience was not yet as closely knit as it was to become later in the century. It comprised two separate groups within each of which the two elites became unified.

Further analysis of the merger between the two classes belongs, however, in a discussion of the specific institutions in each capital. The social atmosphere and the broader group structure of the classical-music world are more susceptible of general treatment. Many of the same groups must be examined here as were in the last chapter, but we must ask why this public had so much more conservative an orientation.

The situation in the field of musical composition around 1830 can provide one clue. The death of Ludwig van Beethoven in 1827 had left his followers in a quandary. As the music historian Charles Rosen has pointed out, while Beethoven was recognized as the greatest serious composer of the time, his work indicated few fruitful directions in which the next generation could move. Schumann and Mendelssohn, the most widely recognized composers of that age-group, found his influence more an embarrassment than an inspiration.[2] More important for our interests, the lesser composers who tried to follow in his path produced little more than stilted, over-formalized imitations of the great symphonies and quartets. The academicism of their works did much to alienate contemporary listeners from the classical style and even from the writings of the masters in the tradition. That an artistic turning-point like this occurred in a period of such social ferment did much to hamper the popularity of classical music. For the same reason members of the classical-music public took little interest in new music, including that influenced by Beethoven and Mozart.

The sources of leadership in classical-music life reinforced its conservatism. One such source was men. Customs of sexual discrimination in home musical life dictated that women learn to sing or play the piano but not to take up orchestral instruments. Men were therefore the overwhelming majority of amateurs who performed the instruments central to the classical tradition. They also became the dominant force in the publics of orchestral and chamber-music concerts. Of course, just as many women attended the events as men; fifty-eight per cent of the subscribers to the Musical Union, for example, were women.[3] But men held all of the offices of classical-music societies in every one of the cities. The only exception was a Parisian amateur chorus, the Concerts of Vocal Music, whose female officers were all from the nobility.[4] Women were even denied formal membership in some organizations such as the Viennese Friends of Music, which did not give any formal standing to the female singers in its chorus. Men also made up the most regular and long-standing subscribers to most of these concerts. Among those who held subscriptions to the London Philharmonic in both 1820 and 1830 sixty-eight per cent were men; those who did so in both 1830 and 1840 were seventy-four per cent men.[5]

Another reason why women did not loom large in the classical-music world was that its activities were not tied as closely to family life as popular-music salons and concerts. Since classical music was not often performed at salons, women did not enter into its life as intensively as they did into that of popular music. While families interested in the German school had much music-making within the family, the central role played by orchestral instruments in its musical forms suggests that men dominated such domestic performances. But a deeper source of the difference lay in the basic assumptions about male and female roles in European society. Formal leadership had traditionally been considered as appropriate only to men. Women could achieve strong influence over social life only through informal leadership. Popular-music concerts logically evolved without formal organization because women led their activities. Classical-music concerts merged through musical forms whose instruments were a male domain and therefore became based in organizations run by men.

One might even speculate that the general roles played by men and women had different characters among the families of the two publics. There is little evidence that many households had members strongly interested in both scenes. Two Parisian contemporaries noted that they did not know of any instances in which members of a family conflicted over the issues of taste as had often happened, causing much domestic strife, during the aesthetic controversies of the eighteenth century.6 Thus, in a family whose father was active in the classical-music world the mother probably played a weaker role in their social life than a woman who did not have such a partner and whose domestic musical life was oriented toward salons and the popular-music scene. Besides, the traditional values of the modest life-style of the time most likely tended to induce male dominance in family life.

A second source of leadership in the classical-music world was the liberal professions and the bureaucracy. Membership lists of various concert societies show that the participation of such people extended more into concert attendance than was true of men in the popular-music public. Among the nontitled subscribers to the Concerts of Ancient Music whose occupations were identified, people from business families amount to only three out of seventy-nine in 1830 and eight out of sixty-six in 1848 (see Table 11).7 Similarly, in the Musical Union during the season of 1848 a mere eight out of fifty-one subscribers with known professions were from business (see Table 16).8 The Philharmonic Society had more from the economic professions, sixty-one out of 176 in 1830 (34 per cent) and thirty-two out of 163 in 1848 (19 per cent – see Table 14).9 Many of them, however, had enterprises in the musical world and no doubt attended in part for business purposes; even at that, their proportion was still less than in the middle class as a whole. Finally, in Vienna among the Participating Members of the Friends of Music only thirty-nine out of 184 identified were from business, as were 116 out of 388 Supporting Members (see Table 19).10 The tabulation of the city's leading classical-music dilettantes shows an even smaller proportion – six out of forty-nine (see Table 17).11

While no membership lists remain from the Parisian Conservatory Concerts, two musical directories appeared in 1836 and 1845 which listed the names and addresses of 660 amateurs.12 Since over three-quarters of those on both lists were men and virtually all of them were identified as instrumentalists, the great majority of them were undoubtedly oriented chiefly toward the classical-music scene. Although the two books did not state explicitly the process by which the lists were made, those cited presumably either expressed interest in meeting other amateurs for private music-making or were simply known as proficient performers. Both lists show high over-representation of persons from the liberal professions and the bureaucracy compared to those from economic professions. The city's register of prestigious families can help us isolate members of the upper-middle class.13 Among those in the list of 1836 who were identified occupationally and also appeared in the social register, twenty-one were in the liberal professions, twenty-four in the civil service, and fourteen in business. Those in the list of 1845 were, respectively, twenty-one, eleven, and one. The two directories also indicate the growing rapprochement between the aristocracy and the upper-middle class. Among the 280 names listed in 1836 twenty-six were titled persons, only four of them from the high nobility. Among those cited in 1845 ninety-one out of a total of 380 names were aristocrats, and forty-eight of them had high titles.

Information of the libraries and musical instruments owned by Parisian bourgeois families adds further weight to the contention that occupational groups had different roles in musical life. Adéline Daumard's tabulation of the contents of wills filed between 1815 and 1848 shows that many more families from the liberal professions and the bureaucracy passed libraries between generations than did wholesalers (*négociants*) and far more than shopkeepers. By contrast, the data for musical instruments—in almost all cases the piano—show the wholesalers higher (13.6 per cent) than the members of the liberal professions (9.0 per cent) and the bureaucrats (11.3 per cent).[14] The intensive involvement of business families in the popular-music scene thus induced them to buy pianos more often than the other two groups, who purchased mainly orchestral instruments although somewhat less commonly.

The contrasting occupational functions and social values of the professional groups lay behind the different roles they played in musical life. Even though members of the liberal professions needed significant wealth to be recognized among the bourgeois elite, they nonetheless conceived of their status as arising principally from their skills. Considerable hostility sprang up between the groups during the first half of the nineteenth century, for as titled birth ceased to be the sole avenue to elite status, the exact nature of new bases for such standing became a keen issue. We have already cited a Parisian music critic who differentiated sharply between the "aristocracies" of wealth and talent.[15] The French writer Saint-Marc-Girardin articulated the tension between them in his diary when he objected to the primacy of wealth for high status; even though businessmen had a rightful claim, he said, its true basis was talent.[16]

The different claims to social status took concrete form in the musical activities of the different professions. The popular-music scene was particularly congenial to business families because it suited their role as economic magnates. Through sponsorship of salons and support of virtuosi they could display their wealth and exemplify themselves as bastions of the elite world's musical life. Families in the liberal professions and the bureaucracy, on the other hand, found the classical-music scene useful for exploitation of their intellectual skills. Since most of them had some kind of university or professional education, they were drawn to the proudly esoteric orientation of the scene which put a premium upon their sophistication. They styled themselves connoisseurs, members of the learned elite who could appreciate the high culture of music.

The contrasting musical activities of the professional groups thus adds a further twist to the contrast between them which Lenore O'Boyle found in political life. She claimed that whereas businessmen involved themselves in politics only in limited ways to further their economic goals and enhance their social prestige, those in the other professions were active in politics as a market for their skills.[17] Much the same was true in concert life. Businessmen approached musical activities with broad social interests in mind; lawyers and bureaucrats undertook such pursuits with the more narrowly focused concerns of aficionados. But in concert life the difference applied more to the character of involvement than to its extent. However much businessmen left musical purchases in the hands of their wives and daughters, they did go to salons and concerts and, as we have shown, manifested a sincere appreciation of the virtuosic style. Indeed, the self-interest behind musical participation by the various groups did not obviate real artistic experience. Men and women, doctors and wholesalers went in different directions artistically because they had contrasting values and abilities, and these patterns should not make us cynical about what happened once they got there.[18]

The social origins of the classical-music public had a deep impact upon its concerts. The intensive amateur endeavors of men from the bureaucracy, the liberal professions, and in London from the high nobility as well, held back the professionalization of their musical world. The tradition of gentlemanly dilettantism persisted within this scene as it did not in the popular-music world. At some public classical-music concerts amateurs still performed on an equal basis with professionals. In London and Vienna especially many of them pursued musical interests virtually as full-time avocations, not only as performers, but also as composers, as music critics, and as the administrators of concert organizations. Because they maintained so many powerful positions within the classical-music world they were unwilling to support concerts performed and managed strictly by professional musicians. These dilettantes thereby retarded the formation of an integrated high-status public. The dominance of concerts by an amateur leadership group from one class—in London the high nobility and in Vienna the upper-middle class—prevented members of the other one from attaining equal standing within the events. As we have seen in the popular-music public, a merging of the two classes could come about only when professional musicians seized firm control and gave members of the two groups similar social standing in concert life.

Comparable conservative tendencies pervaded professional as well as amateur classical-music concerts. Many of the orchestras retained highly outdated performing practices. Until the middle of the 1840s virtually all of them still took their conductors by rotation from among their members instead of having a single permanent music director. Moreover, all but the most forward-looking ensembles held no more than one rehearsal for each concert. As a result, most classical-music concerts had low performing standards and could not even approach competition with the events of most virtuosi. Their commercial development also lagged behind that of benefit concerts. Their leaders used few of the new techniques of promotion and management; rarely did they use performances by famous artists to attract listeners. The gentlemanly tradition persisted in professional concerts in strange ways. The London Philharmonic Society, for example, allowed its members to select other (often less skilled) musicians to play for them in the orchestra, since performing there was regarded as a plebeian task which the privileged members sought to avoid.

The controversy between the classical- and popular-music worlds betrayed many aspects of the social bases of the two publics. On the broadest level, its polemic demonstrated the close association of classical-music listeners with the modest social life-style. In all three cities publicists strove to exorcise the demon of fashion from the world around them. A Viennese reviewer, for example, denounced virtuosi for pursuing only "the exercise of modish things", warning sternly that "upon whomever fashion, the most frivolous of goddesses, shines, must come to a rapid death".[19] More concretely, criticism of popular-music concerts indicated the contrasting occupational origins of the two publics in its emphasis upon the value of learning. The more opinionated columnists often insinuated that the fans at those concerts — people from business families who usually did not go to the universities — were ignorant and lacked educated taste. A Parisian journalist shook his head saying that for most people at salon concerts "musical feeling, taste, the study of the great masters, the science of composition are dissonances to their ears that you would be ill advised to pronounce before them."[20] Since professionals such as lawyers and doctors based their social status upon degrees and licences, they proposed extending that practice to musical life. Some writers went so far as to suggest that teachers be required to pass examinations in performing ability and musical taste for a professional certificate.[21] But most specific of all, this hostil commentary sometimes had elements of prejudice toward women—the leaders of the popular-music scene. A French journalist laid all the blame for the popularity of Italian opera within benefit concerts at the feet of fashionable women.[22]

Exponents of the other musical world replied with equally suggestive words. A Viennese satirist ridiculed what he took to be the intellectual snobbery of classical-music lovers, typifying them as an old man who could talk about Beethoven only in garbled classical phrases—"the pride of our German muse—the enlightenment of music—Apollo in its own form—I bathe myself in delight at the anticipation of it".[23] Interestingly enough, he portrayed the more contemporary concert-goer as a young man who declared that such music "is wholly without melody!" and comes from "the pedantic preference for the technical part of a composition over its creative—or in the unnatural predominance of the ground bass over inspiration".[24] A London journalist stressed the same factors of age, hyper-intellectuality and outdated taste:

> Who does not know the enthusiast S——?; the punctual attendant at the Philharmonic Concerts; the worshipper and eulogist of artists; who lives in a dreamy existence, surrounded by the shadows of his beloved ones, to whom he writes sonnets, and drowns them with flowers?[25]

Indeed, a large proportion of the public at the main classical-music concerts in London and Vienna had been attending the events for several decades.[26]

During the 1830s and '40s, however, new leaders among both professionals and amateurs took steps to modernize the policies of classical-music institutions. The amateurs ceded all performing and most directorial roles to professionals and helped upgrade the artistic standards at the concerts. The musicians imposed sharper discipline upon the orchestras, most importantly of all by appointing permanent conductors. Through such reforms integrated elite publics formed within the new concerts which were founded during the period.

The competition between the two musical worlds provided much of the impetus toward professionalisation within each of them. The high technical facility of virtuosi goaded the leaders of classical-music concerts to improve their performing standards. Conversely, the high aesthetic ideals voiced by classical-music writers prodded musicians within the other scene to make their commercialism less flagrantly manipulative. In the process, the difference between the tastes of the two publics began to decrease, suggesting the more eclectic musical climate of the subsequent decades. An episode during Liszt's triumphant twelve-concert visit to Vienna in 1846 showed how the German style was obtaining a broader public base. After his last appearance, the *Theaterzeitung* (which, let us remember, was the most powerful newspaper in the city) published a letter from an amateur entitled "A Challenge to Mr. Franz Liszt" which demanded that he play more works by Beethoven than simply the often-heard "Adelaide".[27] Liszt thereupon returned to present a program which featured two of the composer's piano concerti.

The decline of the dispute between the classical-music and popular-music publics evident by the middle of the 1840s puts the difference between the social bases of the two publics into proper perspective. The affair was a thing of the moment, a "fit of fashion", as Frances Trollope put it, but one which performed a highly significant function in helping to unify the elites of the three capitals.[28] Having answered the needs of that social process, it passed away as soon as the new high-status public became well enough established to be able to continue without such cultural reinforcement. The links between the occupational areas within the nascent upper class proved stronger than the divisions between them in values and life-styles. Indeed, during the 1830s and '40s Parisian families based in business and the most affluent regions of the liberal professions and the bureaucracy intermarried with great frequency and demonstrated close ties by exchanging roles as godparents for their children.[29]

But in analyzing the contrasts between the occupational groups we must distinguish between the brief falling-out in the taste conflict and the more lasting differences in day-to-day musical activities and manners of living. These matters had deeper roots in the existence of upper-middle class families than the musical controversy, for they involved such long-term decisions as what instruments people would learn and the repertoire they would appreciate most. While the various occupational groups certainly went to the same kinds of concerts more often after 1848 than before, they must have maintained significantly different tastes and roles in concert life.

London

The emergence of the new high-status classical-music public in London is the neatest and the most fully documented instance of fusion between the elites in all three cities. During the 1830s both the Concerts of Ancient Music and the Philharmonic Concerts declined in popularity and social standing. In 1848 the aristocracy-dominated concerts collapsed, and by that time the bourgeois series had lost most of its elite public. The Musical Union attracted a public with an unprecedented concentration of prestigious listeners from both classes immediately after its founding in 1845. Its rise as London's center of classical-music concerts ended the tradition of patriarchal aristocratic authority in London's musical world.

The power of the Concerts of Ancient Music within London musical life sprang from the exalted rank of its aristocratic leadership. Its board of Directors was by tradition a tightly-knit group of twenty noblemen of the peerage, who would march into the hall at each concert while a march of honor was played.[1] They were gentlemen of the old school; all had musical training, some composed, and as a group they governed a wide range of musical institutions in the city's musical life. Various of them were officers of the national conservatory (the

Royal Academy of Music), the city's pension organization for musicians (the Royal Society of Musicians), and the Concerts of Ancient Music. They performed occasionally in the concerts of all these institutions, and several had compositions played there. Most of them also met at two private musical clubs—a madrigal society (the Catch Club) and an annual series of private concerts sponsored by Baron Saltoun, the most active of the composers among them.[2]

The Concerts of Ancient Music provided the traditional kind of interaction between the nobility and the upper-middle class in which bourgeois individuals had formal, subordinate status. During the 1820s and '30s between one-fifth and one-third of the subscribers were aristocrats, and generally a third of them had peerage titles (see Table 12). The vast majority of the nontitled subscribers were from professions such as the Church, the law, and medicine, which were closely tied to the nobility because aristocratic families often put their younger sons into such lines of work.[3] Among the fifty nontitled, nongentry subscribers in 1830 whose occupations were identified, forty-one were from such families, and only three were associated with the economic professions into which noble families never sent their children (see Table 11). Those not identified must have been primarily *rentiers*, persons who lived on independent income, many of whom probably had some kind of aristocratic lineage.

The upper-middle class subscribers were, then, from the milieu which accepted, indeed valued, the patriarchal dominance of the high nobility. While ceding all right to leadership in the concerts, they gained the prestige of mingling with the country's highest elite. Tight admission policies guaranteed that these listeners were from select origins. The Directors also ruled that no one could give a ticket to any other person. As a contemporary noted, the series was "the most perniciously exclusive of any other persons than such as had the privilege of belonging to the 'upper ten thousand'."[4]

The political upheaval during the early 1830s was the initial cause of the concerts' decline. By 1833 the total of subscribers had fallen drastically from its normal 650 to 323.[5] That year the Directors made some changes in ticket policies, permitting subscribers to transfer tickets to other persons within the immediate family and allowing outsiders to purchase tickets to individual concerts after gaining the approval of a subscriber and a Director.[6] But the changes had only a limited effect upon the financial health of the series. Although the single tickets sold well during some seasons, by 1848 the number of subscribers had dropped to 220 (far short of the 500 needed to break even) and average attendance, with the singles included, was only 305.

The institution did not die because of any exodus from it by the upper-middle class. Titled persons actually decreased in number the most rapidly, for between 1820 and 1848 their proportion dropped from thirty-one to eighteen per cent (see Table 12). As these figures suggest, the Reform crisis had only a short-term impact upon the series. The high aristocracy, however, remained stable at about six per cent because its members felt an obligation to the series owing to their responsibilities within it.

The reason why the concerts collapsed was rather that their patriarchal structure and conservative tastes no longer fitted the emerging life-style among the city's elites—aristocratic as well as bourgeois. The dilettante tradition was fading within the English nobility, and artistic avocations were giving way to more worldly interests such as politics and agricultural technology.[7] The six Directors of the series in 1848 were well over sixty and were regarded by many of their class as silly old men with eccentric hobbies. A musician recounted a joke then current in aristocratic circles that a foreigner cringed when he heard the first bars of a piece by the Duke of Cambridge, one of the composers among the Directors. "What noise is that?" he exclaimed; "Oh, it's only the Duke," said the person sitting next to him.[8]

The programming of the concerts had a lot to do with their unpopularity. By tradition nothing less than twenty-five years old was performed there. The repertoire was primarily the more sober Eilzabethan madrigals and eighteenth-century sacred music—rather fine stuff to present-day ears, but sheer monotony to classical-music fans of the time who wanted just Beethoven, or more contemporary souls who couldn't stand anything more than a season old. That the Directors refused to allow the piano to be performed until 1837 shows how out of touch with the times they were.[9] Furthermore, the professionalization of concert life had brought a demand for higher musical standards, which the series could not fulfill. As early as 1827 a thirty-year subscriber wrote to the *Morning Post* to complain that its performers were low-caliber musicians who got their positions as favors, and by the early 1830s the series was the laughing-stock of the press.[10] The demise of the series shows better than any other event of the time how a new set of expectations governed musical life. A music magazine expressed these the most sharply when it said that "the public when it pays wants a *quid pro quo*" — which the events did not offer.[11] Attending a concert was no longer thought to be just a social outing; it had to provide its own intrinsic reward. Thus did middle-class commercial values help put concert-going on a more serious plane.

The Philharmonic Society underwent a similar crisis. Its shaky condition during the 1830s and '40s shows how the transformation of European class structure was not a simple "rise of the middle class", but was rather a broad reconstitution of Europe's upper classes. Pre-existing institutions led by separate elites did not provide suitable bases for the formation of an integrated high-status public, and that applied as much to bourgeois as to aristocratic concerts. But while the Philharmonic lost its status as an elite series, it did succeed in adapting to new social needs, which the Concerts of Ancient Music failed to do.

The main stimulus behind the founding of the Philharmonic Society in 1813 was a desire felt both by musicians and concert-goers for greater independence from the nobility. Its leaders had begun their careers under the dominance of the aristocratic dilettantes and wished to build a concert series run by professional musicians where they could play the music of the German classical school. As a journalist reminisced in 1843, "there was no hunting after titled patrons or subscribers—no weak subservience to mere rank."[12] The public they attracted accordingly came almost entirely from the upper-middle class. The proportion of titled subscribers wavered between five and eight per cent (see Table 13), but few of them attended frequently, and none had any formal authority in the Society.[13] Moreover, a large portion of the subscribers were from professions such as journalism, architecture, and the arts which had no ties with the nobility as did the older liberal professions. Only two-fifths of those identified occupationally among its listeners in 1830 were from the more traditional trades, compared with the four-fifths among subscribers to the Concerts of Ancient Music in that season (see Tables 12 and 14).[14] Thus, as a reviewer put it in 1839, the Philharmonic was "a society which is out of fashion with the aristocracy".[15]

By 1830 the Philharmonic displayed much the same internal decay as the older series. Its governing board had become highly ingrown and nepotistic; in 1848 twenty-seven of its ninety-eight members shared a surname with some other member, and others were undoubtedly related.[16] When Berlioz visited London in 1839 he wrote to a friend that the Society's members were "obstinate old men" for whom he had little respect.[17] Because the series had become so renowned as the center of music's high culture in the English capital, it came under the pressure of rising musical standards even more than the Concerts of Ancient Music. By the early 1840s harsh criticism of the concerts was widespread in the press, particularly in the periodicals most identified with the classical-music scene. The issues were wide-ranging: routine programming, weak choices of soloists, poor performing quality, and favoritism in the elections to the Society.[18] A more practical source of discontent was the organization's strict rules against transfer of tickets between people and against the sale of single tickets. The life of the upper-middle class had become too fast-paced for such customs of the old order, and the minutes of the Directing Board during the 1830s are filled with requests for transfers, all of which were denied.[19]

Shrinkage in the Philharmonic's public began well after the political crisis and coincided rather with the appearance of high-status chamber-music concerts. During the early 1830s the number of subscribers dropped by only seventy-five from its normal level of 650, and quickly returned to virtually that number. But from 1836 on the total began falling until it reached a low point of 310 in 1842. In 1841 its Directing Board attempted to remedy the situation by declaring transfers valid without official approval and soon went beyond that to abolish all review of applicants for subscriptions.[20] Tickets for the series and for individual concerts now went on sale openly in music stores, and with that the series lost all of its exclusiveness.

In the meantime the status of its audience had fallen rapidly. By 1848 over a majority of its subscribers were from the middle segment of the middle class. Among those in the law the numbers with the high-status title of barrister and the lesser title of solicitor were in 1830 ten and eleven and in 1848 eleven and one. Likewise, subscribers in wholesaling and finance dropped from thirty-two per cent of all those in economic professions in 1830 to twenty per cent in 1848 (see Table 14). The group which contributed the most of the decline in the public's prestige was professional musicians. The families of members of the Society had always been able to buy season tickets at half price (5s. 3d. per concert); usually between twenty and fifty persons had done so each season. In 1843, however, the Society extended the privilege to all musicians, and by 1846 ninety-seven persons had such subscriptions. Thus in that year twenty-eight per cent of the public were musicians.[21]

The organization at least averted collapse through its reforms. The appointment of a permanent music director in 1845 and the broadening of repertoire he undertook regained some of the concerts' former high reputation. By 1848 the sale of subscriptions and individual tickets brought the average attendance back to 510.[22] But the Philharmonic was no longer an elite institution. The growing social rapport between the aristocracy and the upper-middle class demanded better-disciplined performing in concerts which had no origins in middle-class separatism of the kind which had spawned the Philharmonic.

The Musical Union filled that need. The series developed a public higher in status than even the Concerts of Ancient Music had had in its heyday. In 1848 the 312 subscribers included forty per cent titled persons, one-quarter of whom were from the peerage (see Table 16).[23] The upper-middle class listeners had similar eminence. All three from the law were barristers; none of the businessmen were retailers. A further indication of the prestige of the new series was the large number of its subscribers who were listed in *Boyle's Court Guide,* London's social register (see Table 15). In 1848 the directory cited twenty-seven per cent of the subscribers to the Philharmonic, fifty per cent of those to the Concerts of Ancient Music, and seventy-one per cent of those to the Musical Union.

Yet despite the lofty status of its subscribers, the series had more equalitarian leadership and social policies than the Concerts of Ancient Music. It had a governing committee of twenty amateurs all of whom had the same status; among them were six non-titled persons, seven members of the lower nobility, six members of the peerage, and the Prince Consort.[24] The leadership of the older concerts had had none from the lower nobility, and of course none from the upper-middle class. The Royal Society of Musicians had included several bourgeois men on its board, but they had professional titles ("Honorary Banker" and "Honorary Solicitor") which distinguished them from its aristocratic members.[25] The lists of subscribers which were printed in the programs of all these concerts each season also show the equalisation of the participants. While the Concerts of Ancient Music had listed titled persons separately at the head of the list (themselves according to rank), the Musical Union followed the Philharmonic's practice of citing all subscribers in strict alphabetical order. The series did not draw a wholly new public, since four peers who had been directors of the older series joined it at the start. Its musical director also had the right to invite "a limited number of ladies and gentlemen of musical and literary attainments", demonstrating the growing recognition of an elite of talent.[26] Finally, tickets were transferable without restriction, and single tickets were available from the director without approval by the board.

As was true in all areas of concert life, the rise of the new integrated public went hand-in-hand with the professionalisation of the concerts' management. None of the board's members had any part in the performances. Although they had a voice in the selection of programs, they gave full supervisory authority and a seat on the board to a permanent musical director, John Ella, who had risen to prominence through close ties with high aristocratic families.[27] He ran the series with a tight hand; stories abounded about how he would chastise listeners when they became too noisy. Ella was also responsible for the series' new social policies, for, as he said in his memoirs, he refused to accede to the demand still made by some that

> I ought to conform to the invidious and ridiculous custom of
> accommodating subscriptions by following the exploded fashion of

rating people according to the class to which they belong,
nobility, gentry, and public.[28]
The high artistic standards he maintained reinforced the ties among
these groups, giving them a pride in being the "happy few" in
London's musical life.

The series did not, of course, fail to uphold the other basic
principle of the new public: discrimination between itself and the rest
of the middle class. The board retained from the older series the
authority to be selective among the many applicants for its
subscriptions, and the unvaried high status of its choices indicates
that it took the task most seriously. Indeed, it created a subordinate
concert series in 1847 which formalised the social barrier. After
imposing a limit of 300 subscriptions upon its main concerts,
the board began selling subscriptions to the rehearsal held the day
before each concert. By terming these ticket-holders "Associates",
different from the "Members" who attended the main occasions, it
drove its point home.[29] In most cities in Europe and the United States
orchestras were to adopt the same practice later in the century. By so
doing they could strengthen their financial bases but also enhance the
exclusiveness of their central prestigious public.

The new high-status classical-music public did not, however,
emerge only within the Musical Union. During the late 1830s, well before
the series had been founded, musicians began presenting chamber-music
concerts which attracted an integrated elite public and made the
number of such events far greater than in either Paris or Vienna.[30]
As *ad hoc* occasions presented by individual musicians, they show strong
influence of the entrepreneurial techniques of popular-music benefit
concerts. Some performers held them in their homes, advertising the
events in the press without any restrictions upon admission except
high upper-bracket prices. Others put on series of several concerts
in public halls, but without any formal organisation. During the
season 1845-1846 at least eighteen of the two kinds of concerts
took place.

The public of these chamber-music concerts had a diversity which
shows once again how concerts were able to bring together kinds of
people who did not often mingle socially. Its most prominent
constituent was the elite of the London intelligentsia. England
had a deeply divided intellectual community, for the universities
and serious literary life were dominated by a tightly-knit group of
families—termed by Noel Annan the "intellectual aristocracy"—which
had a limited interest in the arts and harbored much suspicion for
the less austere ("Bohemian") world of professional artists.[31]
The chamber-music concerts provided a neutral meeting-place where
the different groups could meet. A contemporary musician said in his

67

memoirs that the private concerts were "receptions on a grand scale, at which 'society', musicans, painters, and literary people of distinction were wont to foregather". He described the public as "a strange mixture—albeit representative—of the worlds of fashion and of Bohemia, the brightest and best side of the latter being there found."[32] Reports of private concerts sponsored by the leading music critic J. W. Davidson noted in one instance that nineteen of the hundred present were famous in literature or the fine arts and in another that the seventy guests included mainly musicians, painters, literati and journalists in addition to prestigious amateurs.[33] The guests at the domestic concerts of Ignaz Moscheles illustrate a somewhat more conservative mixture. Those from the "intellectual aristocracy" were Sir Walter Scott, the poet Samuel Rogers, the scholar Sir Gardner Wilkinson, the banker and historian George Grote, and the high-ranking civil servant Rowland Hill. Those from the arts were the painters Franz Winterhalter, Edwin Landseer and Johann Hensel, and many foreign musicians.[34]

As was true in the popular-music world, the traditions of patronage and dilettantism persisted within the chamber-music concerts in highly attenuated ways. A private organisation called the Beethoven Quartet Society demonstrates this tendency even more clearly than the *ad hoc* concerts. During the late 1830s a group of amateurs, several of them aristocrats, began meeting in various homes to hear performances of the Beethoven quartets by musicians who shared their interest. In 1841 they constituted themselves as a formal organisation, but limited their membership to fifty men and their wives and never undertook public concerts.[35] The five-guinea fee for the six yearly concerts (thus 17s. 6d. per event) suggests their affluence. The series became the central gathering for the city's most educated amateurs and therefore paralleled closely the private concerts held by Baron Saltoun. But, unlike those events, none of the amateurs performed or wrote music to be played. Moreover, the reverential attitude toward Beethoven gave the gatherings a wholly new social cast, for the romantic cult of genius eliminated any trace of patriarchal dominance by aristocratic amateurs.

This classical-music world of the English capital was the largest and most fully developed of its kind in the three cities. The richness of concert life in London during the eighteenth century had a lot to do with its growth, for it created a world of musicians and amateurs who had the artistic sophistication necessary for the German style to take root. Their educated taste made it possible for chamber music, and the abstract idioms it entailed, to become popular within the city's elites. The institutional flexibility of such concerts accordingly permitted the number of classical-music concerts to increase more rapidly than in Paris or Vienna.

The nature of London society also contributed to the strength of this concert world. The liberal professions had considerably higher status and greater wealth there than elsewhere in Europe because of their close ties with the nobility and the unique economic development the city had undergone. They thus provided the classical-music scene with a stronger potential public than in the other cities. Furthermore, the tradition of gentlemanly dilettantism which the English aristocracy had fostered provided the scene with an active leadership group. The upper-middle class joined its ranks during this period, and the professionalisation of musical life prevented either of them from dominating the classical-music world and thereby hindering the formation of an integrated elite public. But perhaps the simplest reason why these concerts became so powerful in London was the unusually prominent role of men in social life there. The atypically subordinate role played by the women in popular-music life matched the vigorous leadership of men in classical-music concerts.

Paris

No place in Europe of the nineteenth century is so disorienting to historical view as Paris under the July Monarchy. On the surface it seems unabashedly forward-looking, what with the aggressiveness of its upper-middle class social life and the sharp vision of its socialist thinkers. Yet when examined more closely, these tendencies do not yet appear to go very deep into society, and many shadows of the past lie across their activities. By the middle of the 1830s the Concerts of the Conservatory of Paris was the most modern of all concert organisations in Europe. Its strictly professional management and performing practices made its orchestra the best anywhere; its integrated elite public had no parallel in the major capitals until the end of the next decade. There were few other high-status classical-music concerts in Paris, and those had small, narrow audiences. Moreover, the cultural role of the Conservatory Concerts harked all the way back to the royally sponsored classicism of the seventeenth and eighteenth centuries. Thus did the past and the present, currents of growth and retardation, mingle so volatilely in this period of transition.

More than anywhere else in Europe, the evolution of a classical tradition in musical taste was sharply interrupted in France at the end of the eighteenth century. Louis XIV and Jean Baptiste Lully had initiated the first wide-ranging school of self-consciously classical music in secular idioms. Carried on by Jean Philippe Rameau, the style became closely linked with the royal house and officialdom in general. But after 1750 no French composer proved capable of competing effectively with the lighter Italian operatic style or the German classical music of Christoph Willibald Gluck. During the revolutionary and Napoleonic eras Maria Luigi Cherubini quietly maintained the tradition in the Paris Conservatory, but his works were overshadowed by the rising new generation of Italian operatists.

The absence of a strong strain of aristocratic dilettantism in eighteenth-century Paris further weakened the growth of classical-music life. The capital had no parallels with the amateur leadership group in the English high nobility. While learning a musical instrument was part of the normal upbringing of young noblemen, it did not go much beyond that, and the state's restrictions upon public concerts limited the patronal roles of aristocratic music-lovers. Still, at the turn of the century the city did have numerous educated amateurs, both bourgeois and aristocratic, who carried on much music-making in their homes. Beethoven's music first became known there at these gatherings, though only among a small group of people.[1]

During the 1820s Paris therefore had a vacuum of taste and leadership among serious musicians and amateurs. They were hungry for a new kind of classical music but lacked traditions of both amateur sponsorship and musical entrepreneurship. And that is why the Conservatory Concerts went so far so fast. No amateur leadership group stood in the way of professional concerts; no hold-overs from patronal customs limited their modernisation as in the London Philharmonic. In the middle of the decade François Habeneck, the director of the Conservatory and the conductor of the opera, began holding private performances of the symphonies of Beethoven and Mozart in his home. In 1828 he and his players (most of whom came from the opera orchestra) established themselves as the Society of Concerts of the Conservatory. Although a number of wealthy amateurs attended his sessions and helped him obtain a licence, they never had any formal authority in the society. Like John Ella, Habeneck became the permanent conductor of the orchestra and exercised a high degree of control over all of its activities. Participation in the orchestra was required of all members of the society; at least two rehearsals were held for each concert, and attendance at them was obligatory.[2]

Information about the concerts in periodicals, letters, memoirs, however fragmentary it may be, leaves no doubt that their public came strictly from the city's elites. Precisely how the 1100 subscribers were chosen for the eight annual concerts is not known, but social status and personal influence—and chiefly the former—must have governed the process. In 1837 the Parisian correspondent to Leipzig's leading music magazine reported that the possession of a subscription to the series was the highest mark of prestige in the musical world.[3] In 1844 a Parisian music magazine said that some people had tried for years without success to obtain season tickets.[4] The German music journalist Ludwig Rellstab reported after visiting Paris in 1843 that the same families had hung on to subscriptions since the early 1830s.[5] By the late 1850s it was customary to pass subscriptions to the concerts between generations in wills.[6]

The breadth and prestige of the public was extraordinary. The best clue to its eminence is the attendance of the Duchesse de Berry, a member of a leading family in the Legitimist nobility.[7] One would certainly like to know how many of her fellow Bourbon aristocrats also went to the concerts and whether that created any political complications. Since the series became a quasi-official organisation, it is doubtful if many did go, at least during the 1830s. As a woman, she could probably appear there more easily than aristocratic males, but her presence is still indicative of what the institution had become. Members of the Orleanist nobility were understandably quite numerous in the public. The Duke of Montpensier was a regular subscriber; six others of that background gave frequent private concerts of classical music and thus undoubtedly had regular seats.[8] Two bankers, notable exceptions to the usual occupational origins of this public, are likewise known to have given private classical-music concerts and can be presumed to have attended.[9]

Prestigious artists played an even stronger role in the Conservatory Concerts than in the London chamber-music events. A journalistic exponent of the classical style reported that they were "the sanctuary to which the writer, the painter, and all serious artists flock".[10] The most prominent of these who attended were the writers Honoré de Balzac, Victor Hugo, Alfred de Vigny, and Antoine Fontaney, and the painter Eugene Delacroix.[11] Though it is not known whether or not they had full subscriptions, the unusually high standing of artists in the French capital suggests that their status was probably less gratuitous than that of their colleagues at the Musical Union.

This difference aside, the Conservatory Concerts manifested the same exalted values for serious music which bound together the different elites in the English series. One journalist waxed ecstatic over the feelings which united the audience. He found people awaiting the start of the concerts with an eagerness he had never experienced — "what religious silence! what sublime attentiveness!" — and drew upon the Romantic phrases of the time to utter that "for a few seconds there arose among the faithful a remarkable communion of hope and faith, as all souls avidly laid themselves open to receive the sacred word."[12] There was little hierarchical ordering within the public, since all seats were reserved and none of the subscribers had any formal authority. Social competition therefore grew up around the musical expertise which was so highly esteemed in the classical-music world. A German journalist reported cynically that at the concerts "everyone plays the connoisseur and wants his musical knowledge and skills to be recognized".13 These ideals also reinforced the concerts' exclusiveness. Hector Berlioz said in a magazine article that the series owed its success in part to the belief among serious listeners that one should hear classical music only infrequently. As a result, he said, the organization limited its performances to a few each year so that its public might become truly a chosen elite.14

The series' ticket policies were as much in tune with the times as its musical practices. Transfer of tickets was allowed without restriction from the start. Far from weakening the prestige of the public, the policy augmented the social value of holding a subscription, for Berlioz claimed that subscribers would use their tickets to make their friends do favors for them. He remarked that, contrary to the public's high ideals, many went "only to conform to the fashion which obliges them to have a box or a seat there".15

The Conservatory Concerts developed an even more tightly integrated elite public than did the Musical Union. Since it gave no authority to amateurs, it put the aristocratic and bourgeois members of the public on a more equal basis than did the London series. While the English concerts had upper-middle class men on its board, they were outnumbered by aristocrats and suffered under the tradition of aristocratic leadership in music societies. Furthermore, the Society refused to add a second concert series in the manner of the Musical Union until the end of the century. The organisation thereby maintained an even stricter line between its public and the rest of the middle class than the London concerts. As we shall see in Chapter V, when low-priced concerts of classical-music for the modest middle class appeared during the 1830s the leaders of the elite series did all they could to impede their establishment.

Much of the Society's power in musical life came from its revival of the tradition of official classical culture. From the start it had close formal ties to the state and became increasingly identified with it. Even though the Society of Concerts was registered as a private organisation, it required its members to be present or former students or faculty of the national Conservatory.16 In return it received from the government 2,000 fr. a year and the use of the school's concert hall free of charge.17 What is more, the orchestra often performed at state functions—inaugural ceremonies and receptions for visiting diplomats—almost as if it were an agent of the state. As the writer Victor de Balabine said in his diary, the concerts became an equivalent to the Théâtre Français where French classical drama was performed.[18] The state gained from the relationship, for the Orleanist regime needed to legitimise its authority after the overthrow of the Bourbon monarchy. By sanctifying classical music as official high culture, it established a link with a prestigious national heritage. In doing so it was able to claim roots in the older regime without making any substantive concessions to the Legitimist nobility. Paris's most well-known literati did their part in all this, for by putting Beethoven up on an almost unreachable pedestal in their writings they lent an intellectual respectability to the political operation.[19]

Because the German style was so little known in the French capital and the Conservatory Concerts had such monopolistic policies, only a limited number of other classical-music concerts appeared during the 1830s and 40s. Virtually all of them were *ad hoc* concerts presented by individual musicians. In the season of 1845-1846 thirty benefit concerts had programs which included a moderate portion of classical music. Local composers who wrote in the classical tradition also put on concerts with some classical programming. By the 1840s most serious young composers usually wrote a symphony or a quartet on the model of Beethoven, and during the season 1845-1846 twenty composers held such concerts.[20] In addition, the classical-music-oriented *Revue et Gazette Musicale* put on occasional events for its subscribers.

None of these concerts presented strictly chamber-music programs as did the Musical Union and the many other such occasions in London, since the works were considered to be too difficult for most people to appreciate. The chamber-music concerts which took place sporadically during the period had a small, highly specialized public. One journalist called the events "a cult of refuge" for "an elite public"; another said that they "charm a small number of select amateurs, but high society . . . does not know of the pleasures which small concerts procure."[21] A visitor from Vienna found about eighty at one of the concerts.[22]

The one formal organisation for classical-music concerts other than the Conservatory Concerts showed an anomalous mixture of new and old social tendencies. Founded in 1843, the Society of Concerts of Vocal Music performed mostly sacred music of the sixteenth century. It resembled the Concerts of Ancient Music more than the Musical Union in one critical respect: its board of directors was made up entirely of aristocrats, who chose the members of the chorus and the audience. The seventy-two singers in 1845 included fifty-one titled persons, most of them with high titles and thirteen of them with the simple prefix *de*. All the Directors and forty-five of the singers were women.[23] The foreign, chiefly Spanish and Polish, names of the many of the aristocratic members suggest that they were expatriates whose conservative values influenced the organisation's policies. Also among its leaders, however, was the prominent Orleanist Prince de la Moscowa.

The society nonetheless departed in significant ways from the patriarchal model. Even though the noblewomen had formal authority over the series, it resembled the traditional form of dilettantism less than the new kind which was clearly differentiated from professional concerts. In all three cities amateur choruses of this type were conceived as a distinctively middle-class phenomenon, and the organisation's brochure in fact praised the conductor of the city's low-status chorus, William Wilhem.[24] And public performance by aristocrats as a group was something never found in either of the other two capitals.

A review of the differences between the classical-music concerts in London and Paris brings us back to the point we began with: the persistent influence of social tendencies dating from the eighteenth century — especially in Paris. The roles which the various national aristocracies assumed at that time continued to define much of what both elites did in the nineteenth century. From the perspective of London alone the reduction of amateur roles seems primary during this period, but comparison of the English with the French capital shows that the dilettante and patronal traditions had persisted there, though in altered, and rather diluted, form. The cities thus contrasted in similar ways within their classical- as well as their popular-music scenes.

We can see here even more clearly how in Paris the governmental controls over musical life established under the old regime had not disappeared. The state did in Paris what aristocratic amateurs did in London. The continuity with the past seems all the greater in the French capital because the Orleanist Regime returned to the heritage of official classicism in its support of the Conservatory Concerts. Though the direction of its subsidies was different—aimed at noncontemporary, indeed non-French music—the political function of that policy was not. We shall see further instances of state action in cultural life in the next chapter.

The contrasts between the Musical Union and the Conservatory Concerts flowed in large part from these differences. The refusal by the Society of Concerts to establish a subordinate series had firm precedent in the rigid restrictions of Parisian concert life in the eighteenth century. Obviously, England had had its share of monopolistic policies in other economic areas during the previous century, but in London's cultural life the working relationship

74

between the Crown and the nobility had limited such controls. Furthermore, the Society's antagonism toward the lesser segments of the middle-class concert public had the same cause as the support of classical-music culture. The Orleanist nobility needed to shore up its social underpinnings and define itself as a tight ruling elite as the English aristocracy did not need to do. As always, newly established authority was suspicious of its inferiors.

But we must not lose sight of the many wide-ranging similarities between developments in the two capitals. The differences in the rise of an integrated elite public lay in the social materials with which it was crafted, not in the structure which emerged in both places. Whether brought on by the state or by dilettantes, the product was the same: a union between the upper classes of society such as Europe had never seen before.

Vienna

If the German classical style came from any one place in Europe, it came from Vienna, but that city did not recognise it — not during this period, at least. The Austrian capital's popular-music world became professionalised so swiftly and powerfully during the first half of the century that it just blew the classical scene off the map. Virtuosi ruled over Viennese concert halls with a far greater supremacy than in London or Paris and monopolised the city's key business elite. As Frances Trollope put it, "Handel, Mozart, Haydn and the like are banished from 'ears polite'."[1]

All of which does not mean that taste for the German style vanished there altogether during the 1830s and '40s. Robert Schumann said in a letter during his visit in 1838 that "shallowness is at times all too strong" but nevertheless "closer acquaintance with the details of this judgement will lighten much of it".[2] Mrs Trollope noted similarly that despite the dislike for the style people would "utter a very eloquent hymn of praise in honor of their immortal composers". "La reviendra" [it will return], a knowing gentleman murmured to her.[3]

He was certainly right. Changes during the 1830s show that the Viennese classical-music world underwent the very same tendencies of development as those found in London and Paris, but they were simply about a decade or two behind. By 1870 the concerts of the Vienna Philharmonic had become the identical kind of exclusive elite series as the Conservatory Concerts and the Musical Union. It evolved more slowly because the Austrian capital presented more formidable obstacles to the professionalisation of classical-music concerts and the integration of its bourgeois and aristocratic elites.

Some of the obstacles were political. Since the 1810s the German nationalist movement had drawn heavily on musical culture

for its ideological equipment. The instrumental music of Mozart and Beethoven did not figure as centrally in its ideas as choral music, but supporters of the classical style proudly defended their tradition on nationalistic grounds against the Italian operatists and thereby gave it keen political overtones. While one would hardly call the Viennese classical-music fans activists, the expulsion of the state opera's Italian singers in March 1848 manifested the social and nationalistic discontent which had been lingering in the city's musical life.

It was a surprise to nobody that the aristocracy did not favor the German school after the peace of 1815. During the late eighteenth century several of the leading titled families had maintained close relations with educated bourgeois amateurs in the salons where Beethoven got his start.[4] But after three decades of both political and economic crisis the nobility was running scared and, logically enough, shifted to the operatic and virtuosic styles which were lighter and less sensitive to contemporary issues. They did not revive the salons of before and went to classical-music concerts even less often than benefit concerts.[5] While some became Supporting Members of the Friends of Music, that amounted only to philanthropic support of the Society's Conservatory. The upper-middle class amateurs now found themselves wholly cut off from the elite from which they or their fathers had derived much of their artistic sophistication. It was they who built the city's new public classical-music concerts until the aristocracy chose to return to that world.

These dilettantes were themselves an obstacle to the modernisation of this musical world. Nowhere in the three capitals did dilettantes figure as centrally in public concerts. Virtually all the leaders of the Viennese classical-music scene were accomplished, though not necessarily high-calibre performers, and three of them had made concert tours across the Continent.[6] Many were also composers; as a magazine put it in 1830, a "real dilettante" played his own music in public concerts.[7] The same men held most of the offices in the Friends of Music and performed at the city's own Concerts Spirituels. A number of them also acted as music critics in the local press. The bourgeois amateurism in Vienna thus went far beyond the dilettante tradition of London's high nobility. Not only were more men involved in its activities, but also their roles outreached those of English noblemen by a great deal.

The amateur leadership group made an integrated elite public effectively impossible. Attendance at its concerts was inconceivable for all but a few aristocrats, since that would have demanded of them an acceptance of bourgeois authority such as was anathema to their class. The weakening of traditional class structure during the early part of the century prevented interaction even in private quarters between bourgeois and aristocratic amateurs, such as had taken place previously. By comparison, people from the two elites mingled freely in popular-music concerts because the professionalisation of that world had settled the question of authority in a manner which avoided any rivalry between the groups. It is thus ironic that, however little these dilettantes controlled public taste, in the eyes of the nobility they were much too big for their britches.

But just who were they? A total of forty-nine of the city's leading amateurs were identified occupationally (see Table 17).[8] The great majority of them were from the upper-middle class. While two members of the high nobility stood among them, they had special status as the directors of the state's cultural departments.[9] Eleven others had titles in the lower aristocracy, but the only one who lived entirely from independent income was a Belgian emigrant.[10] The rest had middle-class professions and therefore had received their titles either through recent purchase or (much more likely) as a reward for service to the state. Most of the non-titled persons had high-ranking positions in their professions. The six businessmen all owned major enterprises or had high executive positions. The leadership group did, however, include a portion from the middle segments of the middle class. Among them were two teachers, a journalist, a painter, and nine civil servants.

This group dominated a clearly graded hierarchy of classical-music concerts. After the Friends of Music had been in existence only a few years, its leaders saw that many of the members had lower performing standards and a weaker interest in the classical school than they themselves. The gap in abilities was largely a factor of class, since persons from the lower or middle levels of the middle class did not have as much time or money to invest in extensive musical training. In 1819 the more prestigious amateurs set up the Concerts Spirituels to provide concerts with a better orchestra and more sophisticated programs than the "Society Concerts" held by the Friends of Music. Until the founding of the Philharmonic in 1842 it was Vienna's leading classical-music series.[11]

The occupations of the Participating Members of the Friends of Music shows their lesser status compared to that of the Supporting Members who contributed to the organisation (see Table 19).[12] Teachers and musicians accounted for twenty-four of the thirty-four Participating Members but for only seven of the sixty-two Supporting Members who were in the liberal professions. Upper-middle class men from medicine, law, and higher education amounted to twenty-nine of the Supporting Members in that occupational category.

Among those in the economic professions wholesalers and financiers were more numerous as Supporting Members (thirteen per cent). The distribution of people in high-, middle-, and low-status bureaucratic positions showed the same contrast (see Table 18). Members holding high posts amounted to twenty-eight per cent of the Supporting Members but only three per cent of the Participating Members. Conversely, sixteen per cent of the Participating Members had low-status posts compared with two per cent among the Supporting Members.

The Concerts Spirituels drew the prestigious members of the amateur leadership group but nonetheless had a mixed public. The official state newspaper, the *Wiener Zeitung,* termed the audience "the elite of the local friends and connoisseurs of music", but since few of the city's "connoisseurs" were from the high aristocracy or the most powerful business families, that was not saying much.[13] The satirical sketch of different music-lovers discussed earlier made the point more explicitly. When someone asked why people went to the concerts, another replied, "You have to!" because "it has prestige of a sort".[14] The qualification "of a sort" was necessary because the events were open to the public and indeed charged prices in the lower and middle price brackets. Probably half of the audience was from below the bourgeois elite.

The series thus had neither the exclusiveness nor the uniform high status of the Musical Union or the Conservatory Concerts. The top of the social ladder in Vienna's classical-music concerts, however, consisted of private concerts in homes which did have those traits. Almost half the chamber-music concerts held in the season 1845-1846, for example, took place in homes, all but one in the residence of an amateur. The most exclusive and most permanent of them was sponsored by the high civil servant (Hofrat) Raphael Kiesewetter. A talented pianist and one of the main officers of the Friends of Music, he held concerts of pre-classical music in his home every season between 1817 and 1839.[15] When his health declined the publisher Carl Haslinger took his place as the most important sponsor of such gatherings but shifted their repertoire to the German classical style.[16] The events did not, however, have anything like the social prominence of the London chamber-music concerts. They were more cliquish than they were exclusive, for virtually all of their public were from the small leadership group of upper-middle class dilettantes. Schumann wrote home about how ingrown he found the classical-music scene in Vienna, citing the circle around the Haslinger family as the prime example of that tendency.[17]

Amateurism was a fundamental principle in the musical life of this milieu. Although about half of the performers in the Concerts Spirituels were professionals, the dilettantes dominated the series, and the level of the performances (coaxed out of a single rehearsal) reflected it. A Viennese young man who had played in the orchestra came back from France astonished at the high standards he found at the Conservatory Concerts.[18] A reviewer who was sympathetic to the classical school went so far as to say that the unpopularity of the music was justified by the bad performances it always received in Vienna.[19]

Members of the classical-music public in fact valued amateurism so highly that they refused to support concerts by professional musicians. A reviewer in the city's music magazine once said that he saw no need for such events.[20] He and his friends certainly failed to help the opera's conductor, who in 1833 put on a series devoted to classical music and staffed by his orchestra's skilled instrumentalists. The concerts had such poor attendance that they barely lasted two seasons.[21]

We understand better why the Viennese classical-music world had retarded professionalisation if we look more deeply into its predominant occupational base: civil servants. In the Austrian census of 1847 fifteen per cent of the 40,448 Viennese men over twenty with middle-class occupations were in the bureaucracy, though many of them were simple clerks or mailmen.[22] Within the various parts of the classical-music public, however, bureaucrats numbered between forty and eighty per cent. Comparison of the different categories shows a most revealing pattern: the greater the involvement by each one in musical activities, the larger was its proportion of civil servants. The Executive Committee of the Friends of Music had the highest concentration: in 1828 bureaucrats totalled fourteen out of sixteen (eighty-seven per cent) and in 1846 ten out of twelve (eighty-three per cent). The forty-nine men in the leadership group had a somewhat smaller proportion of sixty-one per cent (see Table 17). Continuing down the scale, the Participating Members included forty-eight per cent and the Supporting Members – the group with the least participation – forty-one per cent. Persons from the economic professions show an exactly opposite pattern: eight per cent in the Executive Committee, twelve per cent among the leading amateurs, thirteen per cent among the Participating Members, and thirty per cent among the Supporting Members. Those in the liberal professions had a more consistent representation: eight per cent in the Executive Committee, seventeen per cent among the leadership group, eighteen per cent among the Participating Members, and fifteen among the Supporting Members.

One reason why the bureaucracy figured so prominently in the classical-music public was the extensive university education – usually about four years – which was required to enter the profession.

There bureaucrats acquired distinctive values and avocations which they maintained throughout their lives. A sketch of a high-ranking civil servant suggested the effects of his education upon his ideals in portraying his stream of thought upon arising one morning. It depicted his musing as a stream of abstruse Latin quotations and references to German literature which made little sense other than communicating the pride he felt for his learning and his refinement.[23]

An even more powerful reason why bureaucrats involved themselves so deeply in classical-music life lay in the slippage in their social status. Civil servants had built up high social standing during the eighteenth century while the growing bureaucracy dominated the life of the city, but by 1830 the major wholesaling families had far outdistanced them in income and prestige. The disparity in the status of the two groups had grown so great that many business families refused to marry their children into bureaucratic families.[24] A satirist described their plight in verse:

> Where is gone that good hour
> When our almighty power
> Made clear the way for us?
> When one's office had clear status—
> When no man gave it question
> When we harassed the population?[25]

The classical-music concert thus provided the civil servants a place where they could take leadership roles without having to compete with the wealthy businessmen. Through these activities they were able to display their main asset, their learning, within a world which rewarded it. The larger social values of the classical-music world suited their needs as well. Its elitist theme bolstered their sense of status, and its moral critique of fashion afforded dignity to their modest life-style.[26]

It was the character of the Austrian bureaucracy that enabled them to invest their lives so deeply in musical affairs. During the first half of the century the nation's civil service underwent none of the rationalisation which was taking place in the French and British bureaucracies. Since jobs were distributed randomly because of influence and patronage, many officials had few duties expected of them and had much free time.[27] One observer estimated that most bureacrats spent betwen six and twelve hours a week at their desks. He cited Ignaz Castelli as typical of them, for even though Castelli had a moderately high position he devoted most of his time to editing the *Musikalische Anzieger.*[28] Civil servants dominated many other fields in Vienna's intellectual life.[29] Limited institutional modernization is evident in these fields as in the classical-music scene. The city's newspapers and magazines, Castelli's the most prominently of all, showed few traces of the professional journalism which was developing fast in Paris and London. Similarly, the only Viennese literary society comparable to those in the other capitals before the mid-'40s amounted to little more than a drinking club.[30]

Musical amateurism thus had deep roots in Viennese society. The particular character of the city's bureaucracy, and the intellectual fields associated with it, molded classical-music life and delayed the formation of an integrated elite public. While that profession showed the same tendencies of taste in London and Paris, the professionalisation of those cities' bureaucracies, communications media, and musical institutions had eliminated dilettante leadership of the kind found in Vienna.

But during the 1840s the classical-music scene began moving in the same direction in Vienna as in Paris and London. The changes grew from the social ferment and political discontent that appeared within the middle class during the years prior to the revolution. Formal professional and cultural societies emerged such as the city had never had before: a reading club, a manufacturers' association, a scholarly society, and a literary club. Competition from German newspapers and magazines forced the city's press—even the *Wiener Zeitung*—to update its coverage and format.[31] The liberal professions as a whole began modernizing their practices in comprehensive fashion, with one ultimate consequence—political revolution.

The most important change in the classical-music concerts was a demand for higher performing standards such as had prevailed in London and Paris for some time. The Friends of Music and the Concerts Spirituels came under heavy fire. In 1842, for instance, an amateur who said he had attended the prestigious series for many years wrote in a progressive newspaper that its public had become disenchanted with the venerable institution. Those who still attended, he said, did so "only from an old attachment and tenderness".[32] Several chamber-music concerts presented by professional musicians each season began attracting larger and more enthusiastic crowds than ever before.[33] The challenge to Liszt was the culmination of the growing vitality and public influence of the classical-music scene. An important agent of the current was a new music magazine, the *Allgemeine Musikzeitung.* Founded by a middle-level bureaucrat named Auguste Schmidt, the magazine was modelled upon the professional periodicals in other European cities. Schmidt not only continued the denunciation of popular-music journalism, but also made a running critique of the low standards of the Concerts Spirituels and the Friends of Music.[34]

But the most significant event in the awakening of the classical-music public during the pre-revolutionary years was the founding of the Vienna Philharmonic Orchestra. As was true of the London Musical Union and the Paris Conservatory Concerts, amateurs helped to establish the series but did not wield any authority over it. The members of the orchestra constituted themselves a formal society as in Paris and gave full artistic authority to a permanent music director, Otto Nicholai. The conductor had gained experience in confronting the problems of professional orchestral concerts in Berlin and soon gave the ensemble performing standards far above those of the Concerts Spirituels.[35]

The six main amateurs who assisted in founding the series had a social background significantly different from that of the older Viennese dilettantes. Only one of them had been an officer of the Friends of Music. Only two had bureaucratic positions, and one of them was the energetic journalist Auguste Schmidt. The others—a doctor, a painter, a lawyer, and a journalist—showed the same occupational bases as the classical-music worlds of London and Paris. The group did, however, have a distinctly Viennese origin, for they had known each other as regular visitors to a café (the "zum Amor") which had a clientele of noted amateurs.[36]

While information on the social level of the Philharmonic's public is meager, it does indicate that people from the aristocracy as well as the upper-middle class attended the concerts. One item is a thank-you letter from Nicholai to a high noblewoman for her financial support of the concerts.[37] Two members of the Austrian royal household also contributed to them.[38] Another is a statement—virtually a formal announcement—by a reviewer of the *Wiener Zeitung* that "we can with great pleasure report our observation that it now seems highly prestigious to attend the Philharmonic concerts."[39] By using the customary idiom "zum Ton zu gehören" without any qualifications, he indicated that the concerts' public included at least a few leading members of high nobility. A second reviewer implied the same thing more indirectly when he stated that the hall where the concerts were held was appropriate to its audience because it was so much more elegant than the hall where the Concerts Spirituels took place.[40] Indeed, the middle- and upper-bracket prices (1 and 3 fl.) charged by the Philharmonic stood significantly higher than the lower- and middle-bracket prices (1/2 and 1 fl.) of the older series. But the most substantive piece of evidence is a bureaucratic matter. The state's rules on cultural events prohibited any concerts from occurring at the same hour as opera performances, and for that reason most concerts were held at noon or on Sunday. The Philharmonic's successful appeal for a waiver of the restriction indicates that it had influence in the highest quarters.[41]

The immediate popularity of the concerts demonstrated that amateurism was losing ground in the minds of Viennese classical-music concert-goers. Nicholai set lofty standards for the orchestra, demanding six to ten rehearsals for each concert and refusing to allow its members to introduce substitutes.[42] His original leaflet set the professionalistic tone of the institution: "The time has come when musicians wish no longer just to sleep or fiddle in bed!" He called for concerts which would present "something unusual, something great, something of the highest calibre", with a repertoire which would be "only classical and interesting".[43] Even Ignaz Castelli admitted that by 1846 the concerts raised questions as to the purpose of the Concerts Spirituels.[44]

The Philharmonic did not, however, become nearly as well established as the Musical Union or the Conservatory Concerts. It gave no more than two concerts per season, and its continuance was often in doubt.[45] Tickets were sold without any of the social restrictions which maintained the exclusiveness of the elite concerts in London and Paris. The relations within it between the aristocracy and the upper-middle class were therefore no more than a tenuous association at occasional musical events. The revolution interrupted its development, and while it did not collapse permanently as did the Concerts Spirituels, its concerts were not revived until the middle of the next decade.

The history of classical-music concerts in Vienna shows with particular clarity how much the specific social bases of different kinds of concert molded their character. The Viennese men involved shaped their lives around these concerts more completely than in either of the other two cities through their intensive dilettantism. Even the more limited, informal role of amateurs in the founding of the Philharmonic exhibited the influence of male leadership. We can see, too, how powerfully a single occupational group could act within the cultural milieu. The distinctive tastes and life-style of the Viennese bureaucrats defined the nature of the classical-music world even more than the members of the liberal professions did in London or Paris. Nevertheless, the similarities in the musical interest and activities of these groups in all three capitals indicate how closely the civil service and the liberal professions stood in relationship to each other and how much they differed from the economic professions.

The development of classical-music concerts in Vienna also showed how important public musical occasions were in the growing social leadership of the upper-middle class. Even in a city like Vienna where private interaction between the elites was so limited, events in public halls provided a means by which the class could oblige the aristocracy to accept a measure of social equality with it. The evolution of the Philharmonic Concerts was crucial in this regard, for the series was to emerge as one of the central settings within which the city's elites would mingle in subsequent decades.

As these conclusions suggest, the consolidation of separate nation-states within European society during the middle of the nineteenth century told only part of the story of the times even as far as the ruling classes were concerned. If in 1870 a person had walked into an event each of the Musical Union, the Conservatory Concerts, and the Vienna Philharmonic Orchestra, he would not have found any more than minor differences in the social mood, the class bases, or the artistic tastes of the various audiences. Indeed, a substantial number of people undoubtedly did that, for Europe's capitals were a world of their own within which people came and went in an easy-going manner. Historians who acclaim the supposed integration of European countries today should look back at the cultural life of the nineteenth century and admit that national boundaries have never amounted to much.

CHAPTER V

THE LOW-STATUS CONCERT PUBLIC

Introduction

The history of low-status concerts during the 1830s and 1840s shows the modernization of musical life in even broader terms than the history of elite concerts. During the previous centuries members of lower levels of the middle class maintained many kinds of musical pursuits — domestic music-making, tavern singing, instrumental ensembles, and church choirs. But these activities had only the most limited kinds of formal organization and had virtually no commercial orientation. They comprised no closely-bound musical world and were related less to each other than to the social spheres in which they were based. And they had only the most distant links with the musical life of the nobility and the upper-middle class.

During the first half of the nineteenth century these musical traditions underwent a drastic transformation. Public concerts were established which charged low enough prices to enable even some people from the prosperous artisanry to attend at least a few events each year. While the concerts had a different character from that of high-status concerts, they employed similar commercial techniques. Although many of them did not last more than a few years, they established a wholly new public in the concert world.

The development of concerts for the low-status public had three major resources. One was its enormous potential public. Pre-existing social locales made it easy to attract this public, for just as high-status concerts grew out of salons, so events for the lesser audience evolved from cafés, taverns, parks, dance halls, cultural societies, and churches. A second resource was the strong amateur musical activity within the lower levels of the middle class. Even though people of modest income could not afford many concert tickets or investments in musical instruments, they had strong motivation for musical training and were willing to put what little they could afford into the less expensive kinds of musical activity.[1] The third resource aided exploitation of the other two: the rising income and standard of living among this public. While the change was not nearly as great as among the wealthy middle class, it was still significant, partly owing to more efficient use of income.[2]

Yet there were also strong limitations upon the use of these resources. Obviously, people of modest income could not afford to buy tickets regularly, and sales were therefore erratic and difficult to predict. Most musicians and businessmen were unwilling to face these uncertainties, particularly since the burgeoning new elite public offered such an attractive alternative. Those who did attempt low-status concerts were venturing into a virtually untravelled region of concert management which provided no precedents to learn from such as virtuosi had had in the elite concerts of the eighteenth century.

There were several major types of low-status concerts. The only one which had appeared in all three capitals before 1830 consisted of amateur orchestral concerts. Most of the older societies tried to go commercial and attract a large audience, but all failed. More significant were new, professionally directed ensembles which provided a more viable basis for ongoing amateur activities. Another type was amateur choral societies. A wide variety of such organisations developed out of traditional choral activities and some of them became highly prominent institutions in the capitals' musical life. The third type, professional instrumental concerts, had only mixed success during the period but showed a great potential. In London professional chamber-music concerts became firmly established; in Paris two ventures of orchestral concerts had dramatic, but ultimately abortive histories. The final type was by far the largest in scale and the most successful of all low-status concerts: informal "promenade" concerts. Presented in parks and dance halls, the events permitted the audience to talk, walk, and take refreshments during the performances. Although they were not considered on the same level as formal concerts, they showed the resources of the large middle- to lower-middle class audience the most clearly.

As this list demonstrates, only a few low-status events had direct parallels in the high-status musical world. Neither promenades nor choral societies were matched by any elite concerts. Some amateur orchestras derived from older elite models, but few such organizations remained in high-status concert life by 1830. The cheap orchestral concerts in Paris resembled promenades as much as they did the Conservatory concerts. The only exception was London's chamber-music concerts, but even there the most important such elite occasions were private affairs.

A further difference between the two concert worlds lay in the patterns of taste within them. In the low-status public there was little division between supporters of classical and popular music such as pervaded the life of the high-status musical world. On the contrary, most cheap concerts had repertoire from both kinds of music. While pieces from one of the two schools predominated in most cases, few of the programs were as homogenous as those of high-status concerts. The absence of taste conflict in this public reinforces the contention made earlier that the disputes in elite concerts came from social dynamics peculiar to that world.

The role of the family was also different at the two social levels of concerts. Children functioned less centrally in low- than high-status concerts, for middle-class families of modest income could not afford to give their children all the instruments, lessons, periodicals, and concert tickets which were necessary for close involvement in salons and benefit concerts. Because marital selection was not as crucial an undertaking as in upper-middle class homes, salons and concerts did not have the importance they did in wealthy families. While lower-class families did give their children some musical education, they kept such activities principally within the family circle. As a result, many of the low-status concerts were attended chiefly by single people or by couples without children. Young single men made up a large proportion of the listeners at promenade concerts, and older men many of the performers at amateur orchestral concerts. Eduard Hanslick, Vienna's leading music critic of the late nineteenth century, noted in his memoirs that the people he knew in his youth who attended concerts the most often were primarily couples who had no offspring or whose children were grown up.[3] There were, however, exceptions in cases where tickets had unusually low prices and where the events figured closely in the social life of a distinct community. London's choral concerts, for example, were based upon the tightly-knit Dissenting Community and accordingly upon the families of that sect.

But the broadest line of difference between the low- and high-status concert worlds lay in the role of amateur performing. By 1848 only a few high-status amateur organizations were maintaining concerts; people of such status played in salons but not in public. Indeed, in the public arena amateurism was now becoming a synonym for low-status music-making. The growing professionalism in musical life was creating new class divisions.

The low-status public had three levels: the artisanry, the lower-middle class, and the middle-middle class. No concert had audiences from just one of the three strata. While the proportions of concert-goers can be determined only roughly, there is no doubt that almost all of the concerts had significant representation from two adjoining strata, and some drew heavily from all three. In each city, promenade concerts attracted the widest public, reaching from young artisans to merchants and lawyers, while choral concerts had only slightly more restricted bases.

The attendance of artisans was the most significant element in the class structure of these concerts. Their presence grew the strongest in choral and amateur orchestral concerts in both London and Paris and in the promenades of all three cities. Their entry into the concert public sprang from the upward and downward movement between them and lower-middle class clerks and shopkeepers. Many artisan were changing from simple craftsmen into retailers, and at the same time some shopkeepers and clerks who had bad fortune were dropping back down into artisanal occupations.[4] The middle-class values which were so closely bound into concert life provided people of both kinds with a handy means of identifying themselves with the bourgeois order and pursuing something akin to a middle-class life-style.

Yet artisans could not have made up a large percentage — no more than a quarter — of the low-status public. In the concert societies in which their number is most definitely known they amounted to no more than a third of all members. Since these organisations had an unusually large number of such people, they must have been less in the low-status public as a whole. In Vienna their attendance was particularly weak.

The uppermost level of the low-status public stood apart from the other two in significant ways. Persons from the middle level of the middle class were able to attend a greater variety of concerts and keep up with events in concert life more actively by buying periodicals and new music. They could also afford the tickets to high-status benefit concerts which lay in the central price range. By so doing they gained some contact with the elite public and thereby straddled the two concert worlds. Yet this fact aside, the line between the high- and low-status publics was sharp, for few people from the upper-middle class (and almost none from the nobility) attended low-status concerts. The main exceptions were in Vienna, where the mix between the publics at promenades and choral concerts gave the middle class greater unity than elsewhere. In the other two cities attendance by the elite public took place only for special reasons. For example, in London some aristocrats and Royalty occasionally attended concerts of the Sacred Harmonic Society as a political gesture toward Dissenters; in Paris high-ranking artists and intellectuals attended cheap orchestral concerts because of the significance of the events in the growth of classical-music taste.[5] Thus, upward movement of people into high-status concerts was more extensive than the reverse. But we must remember that those who did this had to accept the subordinate status of cheap seats or free tickets.

Despite the sharp division between the two concert worlds, the low-status public had only a limited amount of class-consciousness. The concerts created little unity among them, for they had highly diverse musical characters, took place in widely separated locales, and drew contrasting audiences. As a result, they produced little sense of a common social world such as was so strong in each of the elite popular- and classical-music spheres. Furthermore, the concerts, even if they diverged in form, derived their basic social definition and commercial structure from the elite concerts. Capitalism unified the bourgeois world in concert life as elsewhere in society.

But even if the low-status concert public had no strong self-consciousness as a public, conflict did occur between it and the high-status public on a number of occasions. We have already discussed one episode: the establishment of reserved seats in Vienna at prices too high for the modest middle class. A similar controversy occurred in Paris when the officers of the Conservatory Concert attempted to crush a series of cheap orchestral concerts. In London comparable symptoms of class tension appeared in public criticism of the city's old elite societies. The disputes have considerable historical significance, for they indicate incipient class-consciousness among the lower-middle class of the kind which was to break out in Paris and Vienna during the Revolution of 1848. They suggest that the rise of the upper-middle class as a new elite was provoking active dissatisfaction among the rest of the middle class.[6]

Such conflict sprang from the tight control which the high-status concert world exerted over low-status concerts. The increasing professionalization of musical life gave elite concerts and their public a high degree of power over cheap concerts, even those by amateurs. In some instances such control involved explicit institutional authority maintained by high-ranking amateurs and musicians as well as by the government. In other cases it was more indirect, but nonetheless powerful. Young professionals used appearances in low-status concerts as a means to rise into the elite musical world, and the lesser events thereby came to function as steps in the ladder of career advancement in the musical profession.

The elite public controlled the low-status musical world as well by going to the concerts occasionally, but its attendance differed considerably in the three cities. Just as in benefit concerts, overlap between the two publics was the greatest in Vienna, where the middle class preserved an unusual degree of unity. London had the sharpest separation between the public, for the rise of exclusive elite concerts during the eighteenth century forced low-status concerts to develop independently in the following century. In Paris the concerts emerged without such a tradition, but the fragmentation in the city's middle class presented as extensive a mingling between social levels as in Vienna.

The nature of the concerts also differed greatly in London, Paris, and Vienna. The proportions of formal and informal concerts contrasted significantly. London had by far the most formal concerts, for neither Paris nor Vienna had as many presentations by choruses, chamber-music ensembles, or cultural societies. Vienna, on the other hand, had the most numerous and the most solidly established promenade concerts. While the city had examples of most kinds of formal concerts, they developed far less size or prominence than in the other cities. Paris stood between the two cities' patterns. Its promenades were more frequent than those in London but less stable than those in Vienna; its formal concerts were small in number but included highly significant orchestral events.

The breakdown of the numbers of low-status concerts for the season 1845-1846 indicates the differences between the capitals (see Table 2). These figures must be construed only as estimates, for the precise number of certain kinds of concerts was not clearly stated in the press, and sometimes the announcements of the less well-known kinds of high-status concerts were difficult to distinguish from those of low-status concerts. The proportions of formal low-status events within the total number of concerts during the season was 42 per cent in London, 18 per cent in Paris, and 15 per cent in Vienna. The average frequency of promenade concerts, on the other hand, was by the mid-'40s 75 in London, 150 in Paris and 400 in Vienna.[7]

The differences between the cities also stemmed from the contrasting extents of urban development within them. Of all European cities London had gone the farthest toward the modern patterns of metropolitan demography. Not only was it over four times as populous as Vienna, and almost twice as populous as Paris, but it also had a low concentration of population in most districts.[8] The city's cultural and governmental institutions were becoming dispersed outside of the old central city. Its low-status concerts were accordingly much more localised than in Paris or Vienna; its choral societies and amateur orchestras had much stronger roots in specific areas than those in the other two cities. For the same reason London's promenades became less numerous than in Paris or Vienna. In Vienna low-status concerts (chiefly promenades) retained the greatest focus within the traditional central area, for its small population and active street life made possible such a framework for the concerts. In Paris the development of cheap concerts was affected more than in the other cities by a different factor of modernization — the state. Many of its institutions were either directed or influenced by governmental programs which induced a centralisation of a new order in musical life.

The low-status concerts in London, Paris, and Vienna thus differed less in the extent of their development than in their character. While elite concerts were evolving in quite similar paths

90

in the three cities, the low-status concerts offered more substantial contrasts in their overall orientation. London's concerts were predominantly localized amateur activities with formal institutional structure. Vienna's were chiefly informal events with strong ties to the city's folk tradition. And the Parisian concerts had some strength in both areas, but particularly in professional concerts and state-sponsored amateur events. Still, in all three cities concerts grew up within the same kind of tight hierarchical structure which was based on capitalistic professional control and was bound to the new class structure emerging in the capitals.

Orchestral and Chamber-Music Concerts

Of all the types of low-status concerts, amateur orchestras had the greatest continuity with earliest musical activities. Semi-formal gatherings of amateur instrumentalists had been one of the central settings in musical life during the seventeenth and eighteenth centuries. Found among both the aristocracy and the middle class, such groups met either in homes or taverns and normally had only the most rudimentary organizational structure. Many presented both professionals and amateurs, and some put on formal concerts.[1]

By 1848, however, such ensembles had become almost entirely the province of people from the lower-middle class and the artisanry. The concerts were of two main types. One derived from the older model of elite dilettantism. Governed by amateurs, these societies retained the traditional collegial framework of their predecessors but in most cases became more commercial and almost semi-professional. They did not, however, have the artistic standards or the financial assets to compete with professional concerts. Because their character did not fit the new roles of the cities' elites, they drew only a few people from that group. The other kind of orchestra provided a base for amateur activity which was more suited to the cities' metropolitan life and to the new commercial order in musical life. These ensembles were directed by professional musicians as entrepreneurial ventures. The musicians had the business skills to give the orchestras stable activities such as amateurs could not, and in return they gained teaching jobs, publicity for their own concerts, and occasionally even some profit. While the concerts generally had little prominence and were attended chiefly by friends and relatives of the performers, they built a solid and enduring basis for amateur performances and developed a new working-class, or more precisely artisanal audience.

Because the development of public concerts was late in Paris, that city's history shows these changes handily within a concise period of time. During the eighteenth century several ensembles of noblemen and wealthy bourgeois had regular sessions in private homes, but the government prohibited them from conducting any public concerts. The Restoration regime did not continue this policy, and immediately after the war amateur concerts were established in a central city park, the Tivoli, under the title of Société des Amateurs. They drew strong representation from the upper-middle class, "personages of high society", as one journalist put it, but ended in 1829.[2] In 1828 a new organization called the Athenée Musical was founded which had a less prestigious public yet a more active commercial orientation. Its orchestra included some professionals, and such notable performers as Henri Herz and Ferdinand Hiller appeared with it as soloists. The government played a powerful role in its affairs, for the Prefect of the Department of the Seine (who was an amateur of some pretension) gave it official sanction and provided use of the City Hall's auditorium free of charge.[3] His support suggests a new interest on the part of the governing elite in controlling middle-class social ambitions through the sponsorship of cultural events. The eleven members of the orchestra identified from its list of sixty-six players in 1836 came almost entirely from the central segment of the middle class. One had a title deriving from the Napoleonic era; the others were four middle-level bureaucrats, three retailers, and three minor textile wholesalers.[4] The concerts closed in 1844, probably due to the rising cost of hiring professionals.

The first of the new professionally-managed organizations for amateur peformance, the Société Philharmonique, had been founded in 1822 upon the traditional model but subsequently came so much under the control of a musician named Loiseau that in 1846 a journalist referred to one of its concerts as "a Loiseau concert".[5] His position as conductor of the orchestra at the prestigious Théâtre-Italien is an instance of direct influence of high-status institutions over low-status concerts. A second ensemble, the Société Bonnet, was likewise named after the musician who directed it. Two others, the Société du Lycée Musical and the Société d'Emulation, appear to have had the same structure.[6] None of the orchestras achieved any prominence in Parisian musical life; only the Philharmonique had public concerts well known enough to be mentioned in the press, and their audience could not have been any broader than the families and friends of the players. The predominant class base of the concerts was far from the city's elite. The membership lists of the four societies show a high number of artisans (see Table 20). Among the 276 members in all four organizations sixty-six non-professionals were identified occupationally, and twenty of them, almost a third, were artisans. Most were from the most highly trained and lucrative trades — tailors, printers, jewellers, engravers — but some were from the more mundane trades — an assembler, a painter, and a varnisher.[7]

There were still other such professionally directed concerts. Music teachers often presented concerts by their students; during the season 1845-46 at least seven such events took place. That year four low-status cultural societies presented ten concerts by their members under the direction of professional musicians. Six music shops also put on concerts directed by music teachers. One took place at a minor piano showroom located in the lower-middle class commercial Faubourg Saint-Dénis — a location which a journalist said "indicates topographically that it [the shop] gives the afternoon concerts of the small property-holders".[8]

Still more evidence for the widespread musical education among artisans is their large number in the band of the National Guard. Among the seventy-two persons in the band in 1845, ten of those identified occupationally were artisans.[9] In neither London nor Vienna did artisans become as numerous in orchestral concerts. Their active role in Paris derived from the stimulus which the revolutionary state had given to new cultural institutions. The National Guard and the mass army built during the 1790s all had musical ensembles which spread musical education within the working class in a rapid and systematic manner. This development shows how powerfully governmental institutions acted in France as a force for changing the traditional life-styles of lower-class people, though without necessarily altering overall class balance. After the end of the war those educated within the military entered public musical life either by starting their own bands or joining the amateur orchestras.[10] In addition, many took employment in promenade and theater orchestras. Two satires of Parisian theater life characterized orchestral players as a retired hosier and as a cook and a barber who had moved out of their trades into full-time performing.[11]

Comparison of the publics in the various Parisian orchestral concerts thus shows a distinct social ladder with rungs consisting of the Conservatory Concerts, the Athenée Musical, and finally the four other amateur orchestras. The numbers of people from the latter two steps who were listed in the city's prestigious directory show the distance between the two social levels. Six persons from the Athenée Musical were in the register, but among all of the four other societies only one person (a *propriétaire* from the Lycée Musical) appeared there.[12]

The lists of orchestral performers show another significant

social tendency: the high representation of people from the liberal professions and the bureaucracy, just as was found in high-status classical-music life. The sixty-six members of the orchestras identified include twenty from the liberal professions, five from the civil service, and only eighteen from all areas of business. The same pattern is apparent among those cited in the two lists of dilettantes which were cited in Chapter III. Among those who did not stand among the city's elites (that is, those who were not named in the prestigious directory), the list published in 1836 showed sixteen in the liberal professions, six in the civil service, and fifteen in business. The list of 1845 showed, respectively, twenty-two, nine, and twenty-six.[13] Indeed, one can see evidence of the same intellectual values in the amateur orchestral concerts as in the high-status concerts, for the organizations' names all connoted pedagogical and classical orientation.

In London the development of amateur orchestras had different antecedents than in Paris but culminated in the same kind of institutions. The unusually early professionalisation of the city's musicians had prevented the rise of high-status amateur orchestras of the semi-formal kind found in Paris during the eighteenth century. One amateur group with a strong high-status public appeared in 1817 but died in 1822; the society which did last then emerged outside the London elites.[14] Begun in 1822 under the title of the City of London Amateur Concerts, it was based in the lower-middle class central commercial district. Initially only a group of friends who met periodically to play together in a tavern, it underwent the same formalization and commercial expansion found in the Athenée Musical. In 1832 its leaders adopted the high-sounding title of Societa Armonica, moved their concerts to the fashionable West End of the city, and began hiring prominent musicians, many of them from the Philharmonic.[15] Thus whereas in Paris amateur orchestral concerts moved down in status, those in London moved up — but to roughly the same level as the Parisian society. While occasionally journalists noted fashionable people in the audience, one stated that its clientele comprised people who did not have the income or the connections to obtain subscriptions to the Philharmonic's concerts.[16]

The orchestra had much the same problems as its Parisian counterpart. Both societies were tied to the musicians' career ladder, for their soloists and first-chair players were young professionals who aimed to move into high-status concerts.[17] The groups' efforts to obtain civic prominence thereby diluted the role of amateurs and increased costs enormously. As in Paris, the expense of the new commercial orientation forced the London series to close in 1845.

At the same time there appeared professionally managed amateur concerts similar to those in Paris. Two violinists began holding sessions of symphonic music for amateur players and small audiences. They first started them about 1830 in a tavern located in the lower-middle class central city and by 1845 had made them weekly gatherings in a public hall.[18] The most important new amateur concerts developed in a type of cultural society which was unique to London and showed how low-status concerts were influenced by the capitals' elites. Called "mechanics' institutes", the organisations were established by aristocratic or upper-middle class patrons to educate (and thereby control) the lower orders. Concerts proved even more successful than the courses for which the institutes were intended (and for which working people had little interest or energy), and in the season 1845-1846 ten societies presented at least forty-eight events. In most instances a professional musician (usually a teacher) directed performances by amateurs (often his students) and a few of his colleagues who were willing to play for a similar service in return.[19]

What made the institute concerts more significant than those of the amateur orchestras was the size of their audiences. The strong roles which the institutes played in local districts made it possible for them to draw between six hundred and a thousand people, double the usual attendance at most high-status concerts.[20] The events were also important because, like those of the Parisian amateur orchestras, they had a substantial number of artisans in their public. While it is true that by 1830 the initial artisanal membership of the institutes had given way to a clientele made up chiefly of clerks and shopkeepers, a considerable minority of artisans remained who indubitably attended concerts more often than educational sessions.[21]

The local roots of the institutes show how London's urban growth gave the city's low-status concert public its strong local bases. Entertainment halls were moving west as members of the elites fled to the suburbs and thus stood far from the less prosperous areas in the central city; the concerts of the mechanics' institutes accordingly took on great importance in the life of that district. Furthermore, as the city swallowed up small towns in outlying areas similar societies developed within them. Greenwich, for example, had an old music hall which still served the town's elite but was too expensive for the many lower-middle class and artisanal families who were moving into the area. A new mechanics' institute therefore became the cultural center for the town's new population.[22] London's sprawl also gave its life much of the impersonality of modern metropolitan experience. In 1845 a dilettante wrote to the

Musical World to complain about it; he said that because of the city's size and fast-moving life he needed help from the magazine to locate other amateur performers.[23]

In Vienna the modernisation of amateur orchestral concerts did not go as far as in London or Paris. During the late eighteenth century many semi-formal amateur concerts took place in parks and taverns of this kind which were common throughout Europe. Formalisation of such gatherings came with the Society of Friends of Music in 1813, and hierarchical differentiation among them developed with the founding of the Concerts Spirituels in 1822. But during the 1830s the Society's concerts did not go commercial as did those of the Athenée Musical and the Societa Armonica. Members of the orchestra stuck to their principles of strict amateurism and held off demands from the press and from officers of the Society that they hire professionals to improve performing standards and attract public attention.[24]

Nor did there appear new kinds of professionally managed amateur concerts such as those in London and Paris. While some music teachers presented concerts by their students, they were not numerous (seven in the season 1845-1846). The only place where amateur performing grew was in benefit concerts. Since audiences expected long, varied programs, concert sponsors usually obtained a small group of amateurs to play a movement or two from a classical symphony at the start of the concert and provide instrumental support as needed.[25] But while the association with professional players was flattering to them, nobody took their performances seriously. Thus in Vienna amateur activity occurred almost entirely in informal home gatherings.[26]

An obvious reason why amateur musical life remained unorganized in Vienna was the near universality of musical training among the middle class. As an English visitor noted, "to play is their pride, and in that consists chiefly the education of the middle class."[27] But there were many amateurs in all three capitals, and to understand the weak development of amateur concerts there we must look at the city's particular urban character. Viennese middle-class society was still small, tightly-knit, and compressed with a central urban area. For that reason organization was largely unnecessary to bring amateurs together; the family and street life took care of the problem. An English visitor noted that

> a gentleman wishing for a quartet or quintet in the evening walks out in the morning for the purpose of inviting any friends he may chance to meet; and as the slightest acquaintance is sufficient, no difficulty occurs.[28]

We should not, however, exaggerate the point. Life was becoming faster and more complex among the middle class in Vienna than in any major European city. Indeed, a writer in a popular magazine said in 1840 that he was having increasing difficulty finding evenings when four of his regular friends were all free to play quartets.[29]

But we must conclude that social modernization proceeded much less far in this area of musical life in Vienna than in London or Paris. The limited development of commercially managed amateur concerts prevented the low-status public from taking independent leadership in musical life as did the participants in the orchestral societies and mechanics' institutes in Paris and London. Furthermore, the city's concerts had no working-class base. The absence of any artisans among the Participating Members of the Friends of Music shows how sharp class lines were in Vienna. While persons from that group certainly took part in informal domestic concerts, they did not enter public musical life.

Much of the same contrast becomes apparent when we examine the history of professional instrumental concerts in the three cities. The development of professional concerts by orchestral or chamber-music ensembles differed in the three capitals according to the condition of elite institutions in each place. They grew the least in Vienna, where elite orchestral concerts were still young; the most in London, where long-established high-status concerts were in crisis; and with the greatest conflict in Paris, where the sudden popularity of classical orchestral music stimulated entrepreneurial activity for the low-status public.

In both London and Paris low-priced professional concerts emerged in contexts of social tension. While they did not spring from social protest movements as did choral concerts, they originated in situations of conflict between the high- and low-status musical worlds. Professional instrumental events had become such powerful bastions of elite musical life that any attempt to extend them into the low-status concert world posed a serious threat to the ruling institutions. Though often abortive in their history, the concerts demonstrate the strong lines of hostility between the bourgeois elite and the broader middle class.

In London cheap classical-musical concerts were a direct by-product of the reconstitution of the city's elite concert world. As the bourgeois and aristocratic publics abandoned their older institutions and reformed as a unified public within new ones, the confusion accompanying the changeover jolted musicians out of their narrow orientation toward the high-status public. Dissatisfaction with the old institutions moved musicians to widen their horizons and establish concerts for the low-status public. Much of the thrust behind the new concerts came from the egalitarian ideals of the Reform era. "The time will come," said one reviewer, "when professors [musicians] will find it their interest to appeal to the public rather than the few."[30] Another sneered that "Lords spiritual and temporal are useful in their proper places, but they are sorry managers of a concert."[31] The bourgeois as well as the aristocratic elite came under fire, for as early as 1822 a music magazine protested the discriminatory admission policies of the Philharmonic, concluding that "the Metropolis now needs a concert of general resort."[32]

The unusually strong development of concerts in London since the early eighteenth century also contributed to the strong growth of low-status concerts because it had built up a large cadre of musicians and induced those who did not succeed in the high-status concert world to look in new directions. Virtually all of the musicians who began low-status concerts did so because of disappointment at failure to advance within elite concerts. The first two series of cheap concerts during the 1830s, called the Society of British Musicians and the Vocal Society, were established by performers or composers who had been denied entry to the Concerts of Ancient Music. Neither series, however, succeeded in attracting significant crowds or establishing itself on a permanent basis.[33]

The concerts which did last grew from conflict within the Philharmonic Society itself. Since the organisation had become increasingly ingrown in its leadership, promising young performers found themselves denied opportunities to play first chair or participate in the chamber-music pieces included in most of the programs. Accordingly, in 1836 a group of four string players set up their own concerts of classical chamber music which had prices limited to the middle bracket. Among them was one of the musicians who had been holding amateur performances in his home. The project was a bold one, for even though the Society was already under critical attack, its membership had not yet begun to drop significantly.[34] The performers also challenged the city's requirement for concert licences, for the fee had limited the establishment of new presentations. They proved that the Office of the Lord Chamberlain had no legal basis for demanding the licences and thereby cleared the way for many other kinds of cheap concerts.[35]

The concerts proved an immediate success, and other musicians soon followed their lead. By the late 1840s low-priced chamber-music concerts were frequent events in the city; during the season 1845-1846 twenty-three such concerts took place. Because the concerts did not require many performers they had lower costs and greater flexibility than benefit concerts or orchestral series, and their sponsors wisely avoided the restrictive ticket policies which the Philharmonic was slowly abandoning. The events brought a new element of listeners to the concert world. As a journalist put it in the patronizing manner of the period, the concerts "afforded an easy acclivity out of the confined and miry way in which the many have been long doomed to wander neglected".36

Yet their sponsors went only part-way in shifting to the new public. They kept their prices in the middle bracket, never below five shillings; as one astute observer pointed out, they thereby excluded all but the most prosperous artisans.37 Furthermore, the musicians used the concerts in large part to spread their reputations in the high-status musical world. They therefore put on the concerts only during the fashionable spring season, even though their listeners were year-round residents of the city.

In Paris professional instrumental concerts had a promising but abortive history during the period. Because music of the German classical school had had little exposure in the French capital the public was not ready for the more abstract chamber music of the style. Orchestral concerts appeared even earlier than in London, but the enormous organizational problems they entailed doomed them to a premature death. The concerts grew from political conflict within the musical world. The Conservatory Concerts had become so powerful so rapidly that by the middle of the decade there were rumblings in the press against the series. The criticisms indicate not only professional jealousy of the expectable sort, but also social hostility toward the bourgeois elite such as was prevalent during the period. In 1835 a writer in a low-priced music magazine claimed that the concerts had become "a veritable musical oligarchy".38 Another journalist attacked the officials of the series for establishing a "monopoly" over classical-music concerts, for obstructing the careers of other musicians, and for refusing use of the Conservatory's hall to other concerts.39 An action which drew particular attack was a set of rulings made in 1838 that students from the school and members of the orchestra could not perform in any other concert without permission.

The first series of concerts met immediate obstruction from the government. Begun in the winter of 1835, it was based in a newly redecorated hall called the Gymnase Musical and presented two to four concerts per week primarily of classical music. The manager had to accept the crippling proviso that no vocal music be performed, a stipulation which no other series had ever been given and which denied to him the many popular numbers from operas and oratorios. The venture lasted only six months.[40]

The second series, the Concerts St Honoré, was more successful. Opened in 1837, it lasted four years (though not continuously) because it had greater flexibility in its locale and its programming. Its hall held almost twice as many people as the Gymnase Musical (2,000 as opposed to 1,200 persons) and accommodated balls as well as concerts through the use of movable seats. Indeed, the large open space in its rear made it a close relative of the promenade concerts; a visitor from Vienna complained that many people — clearly newcomers to concert life — wore hats and walked and talked during the performances.[41] The lower-bracket price of one franc stood below the one-to-three franc levies of the earlier series and the consistent middle-bracket prices at London's chamber-music concerts. Its clear low-status orientation may very well have been the reason why the government did not impose as rigid programming restrictions upon it as upon the earlier series.

No such concerts were even attempted in Vienna. The recently-established Philharmonic Orchestra had not yet become an exclusive series and still charged prices accessible to the larger public. Thus once again we see the greater unity among levels of the middle class there than in the other two capitals. Yet the histories of mass concerts in all three cities during the ensuing decades show that it was an illusory kind of unity. By 1870 the revived Philharmonic had developed a tight, highly exclusive elite public like those of the Conservatory Concerts and the Musical Union. While the Friends of Music shifted to professional concerts (thereby weakening even further low-status amateur presentations), the events maintained relatively high prices and built up no mass public. The lower-middle class remained largely excluded from this area of public musical life until the twentieth century.[42]

In London and Paris, however, large-scale cheap orchestral concerts proliferated during the 1850s and 1860s.[43] In London a new institution (St. James' Hall) was founded in 1859 specifically for chamber-music concerts priced in the lower bracket. By that time the English capital had acquired the most broad-based music public of all three cities. The developments in the two decades before mid-century thus set in motion an unprecedented widening of the concert public in the French and English capitals.

Choral Concerts

During the 1830s and 1840s processes of social modernization took place within choruses which were quite similar to those in amateur orchestras. During the eighteenth century choral singing had been a common pastime among the lower-middle class and the artisanry in taverns, churches, and private choral societies. Such institutions were widespread in all three cities but took almost no part in public concert life.[1] After 1830 large-scale choral organisations suddenly emerged out of the traditional activities which began presenting formal public concerts. By 1848 some of them had established themselves firmly as prominent institutions in musical life. They dramatized mass involvement in musical life — indeed, the very unity of middle-class musical values — better than any other kind of low-status concerts.

A striking similarity in the development of choruses in London, Paris, and Vienna was that in cases it was a product of social discontent. In London and Paris numerous choral societies sprang up during the political upheavals of the early 1830s; in Vienna one came with the pre-revolutionary social ferment of the 1840s. It was the choruses rather than the orchestras which were involved with the protest movements because they required little formal training and could therefore draw upon a much wider range of people for their members. Furthermore, while learning an orchestral instrument was a highly individual activity, acquiring choral skills was an intensive group experience, and those who did it understandably had a sharper interest in contemporary social movements than instrumental players.

The choruses did not, however, continue as sources of political dissent after their early years. The cities' political elites quickly assumed patronal or even administrative control over them, sensing that choral activities could provide a useful means of redirecting the social energies of the populace away from political action. As an article on singing classes published in the *Westminster Review* in 1842 suggested, since "penal measures, and moral exhortations fail to reach the hearts of the people—why not try to act upon them through the medium of their entertainment?"[2] The societies themselves were strongly oriented toward broad middle-class values. Their activities epitomized the bourgeois ideals of self-improvement (through disciplined musical training), moral uprightness (through performance of religious music), and philanthropic benevolence (through the dedication of concerts to charitable purposes).

But however much the choruses lost their political role, undercurrents of tension remained which showed continuing stresses within the middle class. The assumption of active public leadership in musical life by people from the lower-middle class or the artisanry was still considered social presumption by some members of the high-status public, and patronizing compliments about the choruses masked a fear that the clubs could generate new discontent. A long-time member of an upper-middle class singing club in Paris complained that the city's new choruses exhibited

> that continual pretension to treat in scornful terms the
> highest questions—social, moral and religious questions—instead
> of devoting oneself, in the fashion of singers of before, to
> a naive expression of the most natural and the most true
> sentiments. They offer us a symptom of that unfortunate
> tendency which drives so many worthy young people to leave
> their social class.[3]

Moreover, the choruses acted as a rallying-point for people who felt distaste for the modish, status-seeking tendencies in the high-status popular-music world. In London the choristers sang almost entirely religious music and thereby provided a strong moral contrast to the fashion-oriented benefit concerts; in Vienna they sang largely German music whose popularity grew from nationalistic feeling and declining interest in the international virtuosic style.[4] Antagonism to the popular-music concerts among prestigious classical-music listeners brought additional support to the choral concerts. A writer in the high-ranking London *Athenaeum,* for example, denounced "Rank and Fashion" while praising "the 'vulgar crowd' . . . in the congregation whereof there lies a promising feature of our times."[5]

The choral concerts showed much the same differences among the three capitals as were present in the amateur orchestras. In London the societies had strong local roots in the City and the East End, but unlike the city's orchestras grew from a group which was unique to English society, its religious Dissenters. By contrast, in Paris choruses developed under state auspices, through government-subsidised singing classes for both children and adults. In Vienna choral concerts had closer links to the high-status musical world but did not have a significant political role.

In London choral concerts sprang up during the Reform crisis. In 1834 the Crown put on a festival of oratorios by George Frederick Handel in Westminster Abbey. Though the concert was supposedly designed to commemorate the seventy-fifth anniversary of the composer's death, it had the obvious purpose of dramatising royal leadership after the bitter dispute over electoral reform. Its administrators not only restricted admission to a carefully chosen list, but also excluded local church choirs from the chorus, inviting only singers from Anglican churches and predominantly upper-middle class provincial choruses. The discriminatory policies caused a bitter outcry among the city's choirs, and in the fall of the same year several of the groups joined to present an Amateur Music Festival of Handel's oratorios. They continued meeting together and in 1836 constituted themselves as the Sacred Harmonic Society, adopting the name of a small chorus which had been begun in 1832.[6]

Dissenters predominated in the chorus and within the organisation's public.[7] They were the key source of militancy in the dispute, for they brought to it a self-conscious social base and a tradition of protest against discrimination. But the controversy was much more than a religious one, for it manifested a strong need in the low-status middle-class public for involvement in public musical life. There was a great yearning among the chorus's members to appear in public, to be on stage before a multitude of people, and to know that they had played a part in the affairs of the larger world. The Society's records are filled with complaints that choristers would appear at the concerts but not the rehearsals.[8] Experience in public events mattered far more to them than participation in close-knit small groups like the old choirs and tavern singing groups.

The chorus drew its members predominantly from the lower two social strata in the low-status public, the artisanry and the lower-middle class (see Table 21).[9] Among the seventy-three people who belonged to the Society in 1834 whose occupations were identified, thirty-six were artisans and twenty-seven were shopkeepers. By contrast, only five per cent were wholesalers and four were from the liberal professions. Likewise, among the fifty-two members in 1849 who were identified occupationally were twenty-eight artisans, fifteen shopkeepers, three wholesalers, and five from the liberal professions. Many more of the artisans were in mundane trades than in the Parisian amateur orchestras; among them were a glove-cleaner, a plumber, two painters, and a trunkmaker.[10] Once again we see close ties between the artisanry and the lower-middle class, for in addition to the shopkeepers there were undoubtedly many more clerks among the chorus's members since the city directories rarely listed such people. A journalist indicated their number in a rich, Dickensian description of how singing in the chorus could "cheat the toiling man of his thoughts of ledgers, day-books, and all the troubles of bookkeeping, and ease his weary carcass of its remembrances of office desks, high stools, and pen-cramped fingers."[11] There were, however, a few persons from the central segment of the middle class in the chorus. Among them were a surgeon, a solicitor (not a barrister), and a member of the Novello publishing house which pioneered low-priced sheet music.[12]

The Sacred Harmonic Society attracted audiences even larger than those of the mechanics' institutes. By the early 1840s it presented an average of sixteen concerts annually and claimed that the overall attendance for the ten seasons between 1837 and 1846 was 406,670 persons at 160 concerts or an average of 1917 per concert.[13] The religious base of the organisation was the key factor behind its rapid growth, for its Dissenting leadership obtained use of Exeter Hall, the main auditorium and office building of the city's Dissenting community. The concerts became so prominent that by the early 1840s one or two members of the Royal family attended one each season as a political gesture toward Dissenters, even though the visits generated considerable tension in the hall.[14]

But in the process the organisation ceased to act as a source of discontent in musical life. Noblemen and wealthy bourgeois who contributed to it came to wield some influence over its affairs; most important of all, the upper-middle class elders of Exeter Hall exercised tight authority over the concerts' programs in order to prevent the performance of secular music. The culmination of the Society's new role came when it was selected as the main chorus for the opening ceremonies at the Crystal Palace in 1851. Yet the membership retained its original artisanal base. While most mechanics' institutes lost most of their working-class members as they became prominent, the proportion of artisans in the choral society did not change between 1834 and 1849 (see Table 21).

The Sacred Harmonic Society demonstrates once again the strong localisation within London's low-status concert world. The chorus was made up of a number of smaller groups, most of them from Dissenting Chapels, which maintained activities of their own and participated in the central organisation because of its great fame in concert life.[15] Many other choruses also sprang up which were more fully localised. During the season 1845-1846 thirty-seven choral concerts took place in addition to the eighteen of the Sacred Harmonic Society, most of them in the City and East End of the metropolis. One chorus called the Cecilian Society had been in existence since 1785 as a private singing club, but during the early 1840s it began giving a dozen low-priced concerts each year.[16] A new chorus entitled the Melophonic Society gave seven concerts each year in the hall of a piano dealer in the East End.[17] Five mechanics' institutes also presented choral concerts. Two other organisations located in the City did, however, have bases closer to the central segment of the middle class than those groups. Called the London Choral Harmonists and the Abbey Glee Club, they charged the moderately high prices of one guinea a year for singers and two for listeners.[18]

The rapid spread of choral singing came partly from the dynamic entrepreneurship of several music teachers. During the 1830s John Curwen, Joseph Mainzer, and John Hullah began giving low-priced singing lessons to large groups of students; each tried to parley claims for a special system of teaching into a reputation for miraculous pedagogic skill. Their students had the same artisanal and lower-middle class background as the new choruses. They dramatized choral singing even more than the choral societies, for in 1838 a Parliamentary committee held a hearing to discuss state sponsorhip of such classes. While it refused to grant any funds, it gave John Hullah a formal sanction through which he acquired enough financial support by the early 1850s to buy a building for classes and public concerts.[19]

In Paris new choruses grew even more directly from social protest than in London. The city's taverns had a long tradition of informal singing groups based in the artisanry and the middle class, and while they normally had no political orientation, some of them took active roles in the revolutions of 1789 and 1830.[20] During the weeks following the Glorious Days a number of artisanal choral groups roamed the streets singing revolutionary songs and began establishing organisations to present formal concerts. Initially the events were simply local gatherings, but in 1832 twenty clubs joined together for a mass concert of six hundred singers and several of the choruses were subsequently invited to sing at theaters and promenade concerts.[21] Thus, just as in London, the formalisation of choral singing came with a protest movement. Social discontent was the germ for new public involvement in musical life by groups outside the cities' elites.

But in Paris state intervention gave the choruses a larger and more centralized structure than London's amateur societies. Since the clubs were aligned with the radical left, they were suppressed along with all such organizations between 1833 and 1835. During the ensuing decade the state stepped in to organize choral singing. The person who guided this development was the forceful musical entrepreneur William Wilhem. The son of a small Parisian perfume merchant, he began his career as a musician in the Napoleonic army (showing yet another effect of the military bands) and under the Restoration initiated singing classes in a few Parisian schools. His work attracted little attention until after the revolution, when he began large evening classes for adults. In 1836 he received a substantial subsidy from that musical empire-builder, the Prefect of the Seine. A national educational commission then expanded his classes (now called the Orphéon) into a program for adults and children throughout France.[22]

Even though the French and English choruses had different institutional frameworks, their main concerts were ultimately quite similar. The climax in the development of the French singing classes came in 1859 when singers from Orphéon societies performed in the new Palace of Industry in Paris—just as the Sacred Harmonic Society had appeared at the Crystal Palace. Such concerts were to become regular events in the second half of the century. They show how industrial development provided bases for mass musical culture and brought people from the nonaffluent middle class into concert life in a dramatic fashion.

The Orphéon had an even larger artisanal base than London's choruses. One journalist identified the origin of the singers as "the intermediary and even popular classes of society".[23] Another described the singers more colorfully as "adults in overalls" and "true types of the intelligent street urchin in Paris".[24] The teaching assistants Wilhem hired were also artisans, some of whom began choruses of their own for performances in churches and theaters. Yet the role of the state made the choruses' audiences more prestigious and more distant from the low-status public than in London. Unlike the cheap, mass-based concerts at Exeter Hall, the moderately expensive annual concerts of the Orphéon drew few members of the singers' families.[25] In 1844 a reviewer noted that, as was conventional at the events, the listeners included the Royal family, several aristocrats, and a few bourgeois from among "our modern courtesans".[26] Still, it is doubtful that such persons amounted to more than a small part of the audience whose origin was predominantly from the center of the middle class.

In Vienna, finally, the main choral society had a cloaked, but still significant political role. Men's singing clubs had been a key agent of social protest in Germany after the Napoleonic Wars, providing meeting-places for liberals in many cities and helping to spread social discontent throughout Central Europe. In Austria, however, severe government restrictions had prevented the establishment of choruses either in Vienna or provincial cities. But during the early 1840s political ferment became so great within the middle class that the state could no longer stop activities of this kind. In 1843 a Men's Singing Society began giving semi-formal concerts in a tavern and in 1846 received a licence from the city to give regular concerts. It obtained the sanction through the influence of some high-ranking supporters, particularly one who was a teacher in Prince Metternich's household.[27] The club quickly became a powerful force in the musical life. While its officers abstained from performing songs which had controversial texts, any organisation of that kind had a clear political meaning, and no one needed inflammatory songs to recall its heritage. Indeed, in 1848 the Society was the only musical organisation which continued to present concerts, and its events became a rallying-point for the revolution.[28]

106

The members of the Society were not from the prestigious leadership group which dominated the Friends of Music but had higher standing than those in the choruses of London and Paris.[29] The men who began the organisation were almost entirely from the central level of the middle class—an accountant, an officer in a wholesaling firm, and a number of students, music teachers, and middle-level bureaucrats. The only person among them who could have been from the bourgeois elite was a state lawyer; the only one of notoriety was Auguste Schmidt, the editor of the *Allgemeine Musikzeitung*. The membership of the chorus also had few persons from the upper-middle class. The two men in wholesaling and finance did not own large firms; the bureaucrats who had aristocratic titles had obviously obtained them recently for state service; and those from the liberal professions were mostly from the less prosperous and prestigious fields such as teaching and the arts.

But the chorus had strikingly few artisans among its members—only twenty-two (six per cent) out of 358 Participating Members (see Table 22).[30] Furthermore, the society had closer relations with the high-status public than any of the other choruses in Paris and London. While the wealthy supporters of the Sacred Harmonic Society and the Orphéon attended concerts only occasionally, those of the Viennese chorus had the formal status of Supporting Members and seem to have used their free tickets, for newspaper reports indicated that some people of high standing attended regularly.[31] Indeed, by the time the organisation received its state licence it was charging the notorious three-gulden rate for reserved seats.

We find once again that the liberal professions and the bureaucracy were highly overrepresented among the members of the club. The liberal professions accounted for thirty-five per cent of those identified, the civil service for twenty-nine per cent, and the economic professions only twenty per cent. As was the case in the Friends of Music, the Supporting Members included more businessmen, but even there the other two professional areas amounted to forty per cent. The chorus had close links with the classical-music world, for virtually all of the music it performed was by German composers.

The other kind of choral concert held in Vienna also drew together both low and high levels of the middle class. Each season the Friends of Music presented a festival of two to six oratorio performances. They resembled the concerts of the Sacred Harmonic Society and the Orphéon in their repertoire and their scale, for they generally had choruses of at least four hundred and audiences of over a thousand.[32] The festivals were tightly controlled by the officers of the Friends of Music and were put on chiefly to raise money for the music conservatory run by the Society. Even though the choruses were predominantly composed of lower-middle class amateurs, the concerts did not rest upon a mass-based choral organization such as the Sacred Harmonic Society and did not have a larger purpose of spreading musical training within the middle class as did the clubs in London and Paris. Indeed, the city had no singing-school entrepreneurs like Hullah or Wilhem and therefore had no democratically-oriented choral movement such as was strong in both England and France.

A satirical article in a popular magazine illustrates how weak the involvement of lower-middle class people was in concerts such as these. The story concerned a conversation in a café between a butcher—dubbed "a truly respectable bourgeois"—and others of his kind about his visit to one of the Festivals. On hearing of his trip, his friends expressed great surprise, and he immediately protested that it had really only been an oratorio, therefore nothing fancy or pretentious, and added apologetically that "I was only in the second gallery . . . but I heard it all just fine."[33] His response demonstrates how little the Festival or any other Viennese concerts provided the lower-middle class with musical events which were really their own. It shows how much discomfort people like him felt at being associated with concert life and how strong the social stresses had become between levels of the city's middle class.

From a comparative standpoint, the choral music concerts in Paris and Vienna resemble each other because of the direct control exerted over them by the upper-middle class. The difference between them lies only in the agent of control—in Paris the state and in Vienna elite leaders. But when we look at both kinds of amateur concerts, orchestral as well as choral, Vienna seems more the exception, with London and Paris sharing a similar dynamic. What stands out as the most significant difference is the absence in Vienna of the dynamic movement for mass participation in public musical life that was so strong in London and Paris. Because no organisation like the bands and choruses in Paris or the mechanics' institutes in London appeared in the Austrian capital, it experienced no popular movement in musical life comparable to those in the other two capitals.

Promenade Concerts

The low-status concerts which had the strongest indigenous roots in lower-middle class life were promenade concerts. While informal concerts had been central to high-status musical life during the eighteenth century, they had largely disappeared among the cities'

108

elites by 1830. The new concerts grew less from such antecedents than from the traditions of informal music-making among the lower-middle class and the artisanry in taverns, cafés, and parks. During the 1830s and 1840s these locales were undergoing processes of modernisation toward greater specialisation and formalisation. In Vienna, for example, the Prater was declining as the central gathering-place in the city; people now danced in new large ballrooms, took day trips to the country, and patronized specific theaters and concert halls.[1] In all three cities street musicians were beginning to slip into the status of beggars. Taverns and cafés were shifting from such itinerant players to ambitious professionals for their background music.[2] Some such places became virtual concert halls when they engaged a popular player.

Promenade concerts turned the heritage of informal entertainment into a large-scale commercial enterprise. The size of their audience far outreached those of all other concerts, for reports of their crowds ranged from 1,500 to 5,000 with a rough average of about 2,500.[3] The halls where they were held had lavish decor. Sumptuous furniture and exotic potted plants stood along the wall; huge water fountains cooled the air; and gas lights with color filters gave off dazzling, almost psychedelic effects. A spacious open area lay in front of the orchestra in which people could walk at their leisure, and refreshments were always available during the performances.[4] During the summer months similar occasions were held in parks outfitted in comparable ways.

The concerts drew their audiences from all three levels of the low-status public. Artisans were a common but not predominant component of audiences. A sketch of the crowd at the presentations of Johann Strauss stated that "a murderous mustachioed gentleman"—probably a young dandy—would often be seen beside "a slim tailor".[5] The most prominent group among the public was young unmarried clerks and shop attendants, a vivid and gregarious social milieu which set the tone of life at cafés and theaters and in the streets. A description of the public at London's musical events said that "a very numerous class of young men" went to "promenades always, never a good concert, only rarely the gallery at the opera".[6] Momentarily blessed with some spare cash for entertainment (which marriage would soon deny them), they had a strong upward orientation in their tastes which a Viennese journalist said was "after all the latest Parisian magazines—all [that] is modern".[7] Prostitutes were another regular element of this public.[8] But the bulk of the adults in the audiences came from the lower and middle levels of the class, what a Parisian called "small property-holding amateurs" or a London magazine termed "the most respectable of the middle classes".[9]

Some members of the upper-middle class also attended the most famous of the promenades. In Paris the highly successful Musard Concerts attracted what an English visitor called "a quantity of Parisian fashionables", but a journalist reported that this group "does not deign to pay its tribute" to the more mundane concerts at the Turkish Garden.[10] Similarly, in Vienna Johann Strauss drew some people from the bourgeois elite who never went to the events of Joseph Lanner, the initiator of waltz concerts.[11] But for many of these visitors the trip was social slumming, and they neither became a numerous element in the public nor acquired much influence over its social tone.

Unlike most other kinds of low-status concerts, the promenades did not grow from tendencies of social or professional conflict. Since they were rooted in the tradition of informal entertainment and rivaled no high-status events, the cities' elites laid few restrictions upon them and indeed saw them as a useful means of rechanneling the social energies of the lower orders away from protest. The annual report of a noted Parisian artistic society in 1847 complimented the concerts in the Champs Elysées for giving working people "a pleasure which tames their morals and keeps them off the barricades".[12] One of the leading entrepreneurs for such concerts had been a bailiff for the Duc de Berry, one of the leaders of the Legitimist aristocracy.[13] But even he could go only so far. When the businessman proposed a new series in 1843 the Prefect of Police denied the request because of its late hour of closing (11 p.m.), the poor lighting in the area, and the low price of admission (one franc) which, he stated, would attract "nothing but a numerous and ill-tempered population which is always turbulent and difficult to control."[14]

Each of the most successful promenades was focused around a flashy personality who functioned both as conductor and entrepreneur—Johann Strauss in Vienna, Adolphe Jullien in London, and Philippe Musard in Paris. They all toured Europe to conduct each other's orchestras. and Strauss even managed to take his entire ensemble with him to the other capitals. Their sudden fame dramatized the commercial potential and social meaning of the broad middle-class public. While the mass orchestral concerts of the ensuing decades did not grow directly from the promenades, they certainly owed their inception to the abundant evidence they presented that the middle class contained an enormous potential public.

As these international trips suggest, the promenades resembled each other in the three cities more than any other kind of low-status

110

concerts. But the differences among them suggest important contrasts in the nature of the three societies and in the stages of their urban development.

One difference lay in the extent of attendance by the cities' upper-middle class. It turned out the least numerously in London. A French journalist claimed that fewer people from that public attended than in Paris because the low price of tickets at the events exerted a greater social deterrent there.[15] Such snobbism stemmed from the unusually long tradition of concert-going among the English elite during its fashionable spring season and further reinforces the contention that class lines were strongest in the musical life of the English capital. The bourgeois elite went to the informal concerts the most numerously in Vienna, where Johann Strauss built up a large, highly inclusive public. A description of his annual May Day extravaganza reported that shop attendants would arrive when the gates opened at 9 a.m. and "the elegant world" would put in its appearance about noon.[16]

A more basic difference, but one which has even larger implications, is the frequency and stability of the concerts. They were by far the most numerous and stable in Vienna. By 1830 both Strauss and Lanner had performances about three nights a week, and after Lanner died in 1842 a third conductor, Franz Morelli, established a new set of concerts.[17] In Paris, however, they had a brief but dazzling history. The first series began in 1834 with three performances a week during the winter in a ballroom and during the summer on the Champs Elysées. The next year summer concerts began in the Turkish Garden, a park located in a lower-middle class area of northeastern Paris.[18] Musard initiated his series in 1837 as a year-round operation in the central shopping district. But in 1838 and 1840 all three collapsed. Musard dropped out of sight, but the concerts he had directed continued under new auspices on an erratic basis until 1846.[19] In London promenades were less numerous than in Paris but had greater stability. Jullien held a series of nightly concerts for an intense four to six weeks during the winter and spent the rest of the year touring the provincial cities. He maintained his concerts until 1859. Two less prominent series took place during most summers, one in the old Vauxhall amusement park and the other in the Surrey Zoological Garden.[20]

Behind the numerical contrasts in the frequency of informal concerts lay profound differences in the urban social development of the three cities. Vienna and Paris were still highly street-oriented in the fashion of traditional European society. Walking outdoors was an important pastime for all classes. Cafés had diverse roles as entertainment spots, reading rooms; and bases for networks of social relationships.[21] Despite the growth of specialised entertainment, parks still functioned as important centers of casual social life and the new kinds of diversions. In London, however, the impersonality and internal orientation of the modern metropolis was much more prominent. The city had no central park like the Prater or the Champs Elysées. Taverns and cafés had by this time become principally simple refreshment spots.[22] Formal organisations—men's clubs among the prosperous and mechanics' institutes among the poor—played a much more significant role than their parallels in Paris or Vienna. Newspapers had pioneered the development of advertising and thereby outmoded the street posters which still provided the main source of such communication in the more traditional two cities.

The promenade concerts show a similar contrast. In London the weakness of the street tradition kept the concerts from becoming more than occasional spectacles; in Paris and Vienna they flourished in the rich soil of the old casual social life. A contemporary biographer of Musard noted that people welcomed the return of concerts which required no planning.[23] Frances Trollope, one of the most astute social observers of her time, likewise claimed that the many couples she saw meeting without prior arrangement at promenades in Paris confirmed her belief that the city's social life was far freer and less organized than in London.[24]

But Vienna was far closer to the tradition than Paris. Apartments were generally quite small, forcing people into public places; cafés served all ranges of the middle class, not just elements of it as in Paris.[25] A German visitor perceptively reported that in the Austrian capital people would drop by for a call without warning, so different from the strict custom followed in the other capitals of simply leaving a card.[26] In Vienna as in the traditional city, people lived in the street and used the home, while in the more modern cultures people used the street and lived in the home.

The Viennese waltz conductors built their concert empires upon this continuing tradition. Whereas in the other two cities their repertoire of promenades was predominantly international genres of dance and program music, in Vienna it grew directly from the society's folk heritage. Always focused closely upon the waltz, the events differed from those in Paris and London in their union of dancing with listening. The resistance to further specialisation among entertainment forms was not lost upon Strauss or the Viennese, for he always dubbed his presentations by terms other than concert—"reunion" or "musical evening"—and the press bridled at

112

any implication that his gatherings stood on the same footing as normal concerts.[27] By contrast, in the other two cities, where dancing never took place at promenades, the term concert was used conventionally. In London their separation from dancing was complete because the halls in which they were held did not even host balls on alternate nights. Indeed, Jullien often included classical works in his repertoire, something which never happened in the Viennese promenades.

The evolution of waltz nights from Lanner to Strauss nonetheless shows that a particular process of modernisation was taking place. Lanner remained close to the tradition of informal dancing and music-making in the city's taverns and parks and maintained a less sophisticated or prestigious public than Strauss. Lanner called waltzes by the dialect term *Wuadler*; Strauss used the high-German word *Tänze*. The difference in styles and publics is evident in the old custom men followed at Lanner's events of tapping their canes on the floor—a practice regarded as improper of Strauss's events.[28]

But the evolution went no farther. While in London and Paris promenades gave way to mass orchestral concerts during the 1850s, in Vienna the waltz nights remained the one form of mass musical entertainment throughout the century. Thus, while the city's elite public underwent changes in quite the same direction (though at a slower pace) as those found in the other two cities, its low-status public traveled a significantly different path.

Conclusion

We are, of course, close to the full conclusion of its study. But a few brief comments are in order to tie up the many strands in the history of low-status concerts.

One thing that stands out from these many events is that the musical life of the artisanry and the lower-middle class underwent a sudden and profound transformation during this period. Almost all the concerts emerged from informal musical activities or small private associations into formalised undertakings on an impressive scale. The change was not just an organisational one, for it gave these pursuits a wholly new character and thrust them into the center of musical life in the three capitals. As we shall show in the following chapter, these changes constituted that far-reaching process which historians call modernisation.

A second conclusion is that people from the highest level of the working class and from the lower segments of the middle class mingled extensively in concert life. This is particularly true if we modify class by age categories, for single people or young married couples often shared resources and interests that cut across occupational boundaries. Historians have too often assumed that each major social stratum had a cultural world all its own and have therefore failed to look closely at the exact makeup of publics to see if this was true.[1] The overlap between the two classes in low-status concert life makes a great deal of sense, for if modern social analysis has established anything solidly, it is that adjoining social levels have close ties in many areas of activity.[2]

A third conclusion is that the concerts of the lesser public did not show such broad similarities in the three capitals as those of the elite public. The cosmopolitanism which unified the major capitals had some traces in the amateur orchestral and promenade concerts, but even they (the Viennese promenades especially) showed sharp local idiosyncracies. All in all, the cities seemed to move in more distinctively different directions in this area than in the high-status musical world.

A final point is a simple one: the remarkable size of the new low-status concert world. Given the limited income of its listeners and their lack of experience in public activities, it is surprising how many concerts appeared, how many people they attracted, and how many different shapes they took. All this could not have come out of nowhere; it testifies to the strength of traditional musical activities among the modest levels of society in the three cities. The rapidity with which this heritage took modern forms shows the profound readiness for change which lay in so many parts of European society at the turn of the nineteenth century.

CHAPTER VI

CONCLUSION

Fifty years hence the concept of modernization may seem as oversimple as the Enlightenment idea of unlimited progress does now, but for the moment it provides a useful analytical tool. *Something* has come about during the last three centuries deeper than what the political narratives have shown, and the long-range changes which Max Weber and Ferdinand Tönnies originally spelled out have put many of its dimensions into an interesting perspective.[1] We will therefore use the concept to look at the whole of what happened to concerts in London, Paris and Vienna between 1830 and 1848—indeed, since the very origin of concerts.

The thrust of the concept is that a thorough-going rationalization of social and economic relationships and institutions has taken place. Traditions and customs have given way to organizational norms which determine the roles individuals play and the manner in which they get them. Society now codifies what it formerly just did, and the nature of all social activities has changed in the process. As job relationships have become more functional than personal, much social interaction has lost its former polymorphous character and become highly segmented and specialized. Individualism and self-interest have emerged as guiding principles within the new corporate structure of human life. We must not think, however, that these changes were caused by dark, impersonal forces. The use of power and gain have been central to the process; some people have wanted new things, and many times they have gotten them. Indeed, it is astounding how smoothly the upper classes have either guided the transformation or prevented themselves from being hurt by it.

The evolution of concert life shows many of these tendencies. We can see them most explicitly in the development of the musical profession. By 1848 performing roles had taken on a high degree of rationalization: public concerts were now the undisputed province of professionals—the performance of professionals and amateurs together was now confined to the home, and participation by amateurs in public concerts took place only as a cost-cutting device or as a separate sphere designed for them and their families. Self-interest in terms of musical performance was thus expressed in two ways, the economic gain of the professional and the personal self-improvement of the amateur; but it was the former that now dominated public concerts. The roles of concert-goers demonstrated a similar new definition. Among the elite public the traditional patronal relationship had given way to an economic tie based on formal social gatherings controlled by musicians. Benefit concerts afforded virtually impersonal relationships; concert societies established permanent institutions such as had never been known in musical life. Among less affluent amateurs informal music-making became transformed into formalized events governed by professionals. London choir members and Parisian tavern singers found themselves part of nationally prominent musical organizations.

The nuclear family played a central role within these processes. As the home became increasingly separate from the family's occupational base it took on a deeper function of guiding children socially and to a point much later in their lives than before. Learning music instilled in them the discipline and propriety which were necessary in the new world of individual occupational choice; salon concerts provided social settings where that skill could help them in concrete ways. The close links between musical education, salons, and public concerts show how closely the family was bound to the outside world. The home was not just a retreat from the pressures of the rationalized society (though it could certainly act as such if needed), but also prepared its members to deal with those problems—though often in a manipulative way. Indeed, the personal stresses and intense cultural conflict which grew from all this answer the criticism that such an interpretation of how the nuclear family has functioned in society represents a static social analysis.[2] Like so many powerful institutions, the new middle-class nuclear family created as many problems as it solved.

Musical tastes, too, were affected by modernization. The formalization of musical institutions brought a specialization of the genres performed in different settings, and concerts separated out into their modern types of orchestral, virtuosic, operatic, and chamber-music presentations. Furthermore, the differentiation between high and popular culture came into effect in musical life in its peculiar modern form. "Art for art's sake" became the dominant organizing principle of the musical world, ranking genres according to their supposed level of seriousness. The professionalization of musicians had much to do with the process, for the concept provided a useful means whereby the most powerful among them—chiefly those playing in or composing for the major orchestras—dramatized their new social position. Although classical taste was not fully accepted until after the middle of the century, its main cultural slogans were developed in full form before that time.

The variations, indeed the contradictions, among different areas of the new rationalized concert world show the inconsistent manner in which such changes have occurred. The high-status concerts of popular music underwent modernization more rapidly than those of classical music between 1830 and 1848. As in the industrial sphere, individual entrepreneurship provided the most rapid channel for early development, and more impersonal corporate institutions—the large-scale modern orchestras—became established more slowly. But the sudden emergence of the Parisian Conservatory Concerts shows how (as happened in German industry) state support could speed up the evolution of the larger structures in a country which began the development late. Furthermore, the concepts of a musical culture and of the specialization of taste developed initially within a less modernized area of concert life, the classical-music scene. That anti-professionalistic Viennese amateurs articulated these notions the most forcefully of all demonstrates how curiously the new and the old could interact in the process of change.

The wide-ranging similarities in the processes of modernization in the three capitals force us to be as specific as possible in isolating differences between them. Overall, change was slowest in Vienna, most particularly in the areas of classical-music concerts and enterprises related to the elite popular-music world (concert halls and the publishing industry). Still, these lags can too easily be exaggerated, since in that city virtuosi exhibited more vigorous entrepreneurship than their colleagues in London who retained a diluted form of patronal relations with aristocratic families. Likewise, the persistence of amateurism in classical-music concerts in London and Vienna makes the concerts in the two cities resemble each other more than the swiftly professionalized Conservatory Concerts. Even Paris showed limited development in the small size of its classical-music world and the subordination of public concerts to salons. As these examples suggest, it is erroneous to depict modernisation moving across Europe from northwest to southeast in some simple pattern. Each city had its strengths and weaknesses in modernization, and Vienna was deeply involved, if at a slight remove, in the process of change. Forms might vary, but new tastes and the pressures of a new elite were revolutionizing the musical world.

We can look at this problem in an even broader perspective. However small a part concerts occupied in the European economy, their development has significant implications for our concept of the relationship between modernization and industrialization. One is that the location of these events within cities lacking any factory industry reinforces the growing doubt of the interdependence or even the simultaneity of the two processes. While industrial production did assist the growth of home music, its influence was small, for most musical instruments were not yet made in factories. The centrality of family investment within the new concert world confirms rather the theory that rising real income was a crucial prerequisite for modernization and by that means for eventual industrialization. The increasing demand for products—pianos, sheet-music, and so forth—would in time bring about large-scale manufacture of these items. A second implication is that the sudden growth of concerts in cities with such different economic scale weakens further the analysis of modernization and industrialization in terms of standard "stages" of growth. Just as economic historians have shown that few countries followed the English model of development, so we have seen how the tight international framework in musical life not only did not fit the pattern of stages but also cut across national differences in economic change. While in Vienna concert life did not match that of London or Paris in every respect, its elite popular-music concerts and promenades kept pace fully with their parallels in the other two cities. That Johann Strauss made the first international concert tour with a complete orchestra in tow shows that in some areas a country with virtually no industrialization could lead other nations in commercial modernization.

A third implication is that the industries of service and distribution — areas usually thought to come at the end of the process of industrialization — could appear in strong form quite early. While the distribution of goods produced by industrial methods was still primitive and small in scale by 1850, the dissemination of those made with updated traditional methods had gone far by that time. Artisanal production of musical instruments and the commercialization of musical services (teaching and concert-giving) had become highly modernized, extensive industries by the middle of the century. The periodicals of these decades suggest that some musicians and entertainment entrepreneurs had developed much of the commercial expertise of contemporary rock stars and their agents. While concert management had not yet separated out fully from the music profession or become a source of capital accumulation, the basic techniques of the later impresarios were already established. A related modern tendency was equally strong: the demand for consumer protection. By the middle of the 1840s concert-goers were objecting vociferously to the shady practices of some musicians (ineffective teaching, undependable programs, and the fraudulent sale of tickets to nonexistent concerts) and called for the licensing of professionals to ensure better business standards. During the ensuing decades the outcry helped to bring about stricter planning in concert management.

The concept of modernization can provide useful perspective also for the development of class structure in concert life. Rationalization has fundamentally reshaped the ways in which societies (or at least their dominant groups) have justified social hierarchies and ordered individuals on different levels. The merger of the aristocracy and the upper-middle class into a single upper class amounted to a shift from vesting elite status in a hereditary

118

group to defining supposedly rational means for the recruitment of the elite. The high-status concert life of the 1830s and '40s exhibited early traces of the new social ideology. The intense interaction and equality of leadership roles among the two classes implied not simply that society now had a second elite but also that it had a different conception of elite status itself. The vigorous display of individual achievement by musicians gave the aristocracy and the upper-middle class a means by which they could vicariously look at each other in a new way, as holders of elevated status by virtue of what they possessed and what they had done. Every man was his own Franz Liszt, every woman her Jenny Lind.

Concerts and salons complemented each other in providing different ways in which the two elites could take a common identity. At salons amateur performers put the model of the virtuosi explicitly into practice, bargaining their way into prominence by exhibiting their abilities, and those who listened to them applied the same principle of social gamesmanship. In both cases self-assertive individualism broke down traditional class barriers. In the process members of the two elites took their first steps into new social relations in a concrete and conveniently limited manner. The affairs had a vital element of play in their social dynamics: the assembled company could try on new roles as if they were not yet real, and the musical focal point of the gatherings made their game-like quality explicit. Since the activities demanded no permanent commitment as intermarriage or political coalition would, they allowed an easy escape route if the going became rough or if some persons began demanding too much—which is, after all, the nature of play.

Public events, however, ultimately had greater significance, for they had fewer traditional implications than the salons. Within them the two segments of the high-status public could visualize themselves as members of a grand new "high society" whose size and imposing cultural leadership compensated for the loss of the clearer separate elite roles of an earlier day. Concert institutions themselves became ordered upon the principle of achievement in a manner which affected the listeners as well as the musicians. By 1848 a hierarchy was emerging whose social and artistic levels matched each other closely — the better the performers, the more prestigious their public. The ranking was the most sharply graded in the classical-music world, where orchestras with the most wealthy and notable subscribers could easily recruit the most proficient musicians. The exceptions only reinforced the rule. As we have noted, the cheap chamber-music concerts in London acted for their talented sponsors primarily as a means of gaining recognition in the high-status musical world.

The functional subordination of low-status concerts also foreshadowed the social hierarchy which was to emerge throughout Europe during the rest of the century. Just as artisans and clerks were to be forced into wage-earning employment within centralized industry, so during the 1830s and 40s low-priced musical events created tight institutional or professional control by the elite musical world. The attendance of artisans at these concerts shows the close ties which that group was developing with the lower-middle class as the bourgeois elite pulled away from the rest of the middle class. The mingling of the adjoining segments of the artisanry and the lower-middle class in concert life casts doubt upon the recent assertion by Gareth Stedman Jones that an isolated working-class culture developed in London after 1870.[3] While the incomes of the two groups were still unequal, their leisure activities had begun to take on the unity which has been so prominent in popular-music life of the twentieth century.

The social control which the new joint elite exercised over lesser groups in concert life thus had a highly rationalized, and one should add secularized, structure. The far-reaching moral authority which the Church had maintained against potentially disruptive behavior during the early modern period (within which sacred music played no small part) had given way to regulation by both private and governmental institutions. As we have seen in the low-status concerts of London and Paris, the state and formal organizations acted in similar ways as devices through which the elites tried to redirect the lower orders away from protest. This authority was primarily secular, nor moral, both institutionally and intellectually. Histories of Victorian society have taken the social moralists of the time a great deal too seriously, simply because they were so vocal and articulate. Denunciation of cultural locales such as music halls was a minor form of social control compared to the new means of such manipulation — among which the music halls themselves must be included.

But despite all this, that maddening question remains: was there a definable middle class in concert life during the 1830s and '40s?

R. S. Neale has suggested the most prominent alternative model. He has claimed that a "middling class" stood apart from the traditional middle class and from the deferential attitudes of that group toward the aristocracy. Made up of ambitious but frustrated people from many levels (the artisanry as well as professional and clerical milieux), it played a powerful role in challenging privilege and the old social order.[4]

There are certainly interesting parallels here with the present study. The many episodes of discontent found in the early history of low-status concerts resembled the social currents Neale has analyzed in English provincial cities. The musicians who began London's chamber-music concerts acted very much like the Philosophical Radicals, and the people of modest income who attended the professional orchestral concerts in Paris and benefit concerts in Vienna seem like counterparts of the intellectuals' supporters. That these tendencies appeared in concert life, an area where social controversy has not been common, means that they should be seen as highly significant. Still, it is hard to find in them indications of a full new social class, at least as they appeared within musical life. Low-status concerts had so little unity among them that no overt class-consciousness developed among their public as a whole. What is more, the people who began cheap concerts quickly abandoned their protest roles and became reintegrated into the musical world under the control of the high-status public. The appearance of the Sacred Harmonic Society at the Crystal Palace in 1851 exemplifies the shift most concretely of all.

This point leads even further. For all the self-consciousness of the new high-status concert public, the upper-middle class still had strong social and economic ties to the lesser middle-class public which held it apart from the nobility. It was bidding for recognition, not consolidating it, and for that reason had not achieved full union with the nobility. The old elite, for its part, had accepted the commercial redefinition of concert life but was not a purveyor of that new order such as was the wealthy middle class. The pushy professional musicians had, one might say, pulled (conservatives of the time would have said *smuggled*) their bourgeois compatriots into the province of the aristocracy through their dynamic concert and salon performances—and both remained somewhat foreign to the world. Members of the upper-middle class still involved themselves in the battle against aristocratic privilege and thereby retained ties with the rest of their class. Furthermore, however much the high-status music world controlled the other public, it needed the resources of the lower-middle class public in certain important respects. Even the most fashionable performers had to hand out free tickets to people from the lesser public in order to fulfill the commercial requirement for crowded concert halls. Low-status concerts also provided a large reservoir of musical talent on which more powerful institutions needed to draw. The different segments of the middle class thus shared economic interest, continuing social ties, and even some mutual identity.

This argument leaves us, then, with the uncomfortable answer

121

that there-was-but-there-wasn't a single middle class. Yet such was the character of life during that time. The European social hierarchy was undergoing such a drastic reshaping that many people, particularly those in the middle and upper segments of the middle class, did not know whether they were coming or going in their social location. Certainly those who were directly involved in political disputes such as Neale has described had definite orientations. But since few members of any class carried on more than a passing acquaintance with politics (many historians call that apathy; this one just sees it as a norm), such a clear sense of identity could not have been common. Besides, the lives of most energetic middle-class people were becoming splintered into so many parts that they could easily have shown contrasting attitudes in different settings. A prosperous Parisian retailer, for example, might have pinched his pennies to attend a number of fashionable salons and concerts (thereby struggling to gain the prestige of aristocratic contacts) but cursed the nobility while reading about its tax exemptions in the papers — and then tacitly supported the revolutionary regime in March 1848.

Differences among the cities proved greater in the development of the integrated public than in the modernization of concert life. The abrupt terminal-point of our period in revolution suggests a fruitful means of surveying the contrasts between the cities. The development of low-status concerts indicates the varying suitability of the three societies for that spontaneous form of protest. Modernization had robbed London of the social structure necessary for it: the suburbanization of the metropolis spread too thin the ranks of potentially revolutionary groups, and their fragmentation in the social hierarchy hindered union among them. The city's promenade concerts show this best in their narrow class base and short performing season. By comparison, in Paris and Vienna the continuing vitality of traditional interaction in informal concerts depicts the social framework necessary for revolution (after all, when two or three classes are gathered together in one place . . .). We can also discern a major difference in the social bases of the events in the two Continental capitals. The absence of artisans from the Viennese concert public parallels the weak role they played in the uprising and contrasts with the dynamic leadership exerted by their Parisian colleagues both in amateur concerts and in the revolution.[5] Indeed, the modernization of their concerts in Paris matched the modernization of their protest during the revolution and in the strikes of the 1860s.[6]

When we look at the developments in both high- and low-status concerts what stands out most sharply is the unity of the Viennese middle class at both ends. Not only did its upper-middle class remain distinct from the Austrian nobility, but also its lower-middle class established little relationship with the artisanry. When one recalls the strength of working-class participation in the amateur orchestras in London and Paris, one cannot help but think that such people were actively excluded from musical organizations in Vienna. The social division had a crippling effect upon the growth of cheap concerts, for the lower-middle class did not offer a large enough public for mass concerts such as appeared in London and Paris. The wealthy members of the middle class added to the problem, since their frustration at not achieving full social union with the aristocracy made them unwilling to assist lower-middle class concerts or deepen the base of the music public. In the process the city's elites failed to build strong means of social control over the lower orders in concert life such as their colleagues in the other cities constructed so ably — even if, in the Parisian case, with only partial success. Their shyness of such action either through private or public institutions certainly contributed to the rise of anti-governmental nationalistic movements during the late nineteenth century.

The latter half of the "it-was-but-it-wasn't" proposition about the middle class applied more firmly to London and Paris than to Vienna. We can see why this was so concretely within the structure of each elite. The French and English aristocracies both had substantial lesser segments which proved crucial in the union of their class with the upper-middle class. Members of the Orleanist nobility, people like the Prince de la Moscowa and the Comtesse de Merlin, provided key leadership in the popular-music salons and the Conservatory Concerts. Less obvious but equally significant was the activity of the English lower nobility. That members of this group left the Concerts of Ancient Music more quickly than the high aristocracy and joined the Musical Union more numerously than the older series suggests the powerful influence they exerted in the reconstitution of elites in London's musical life.

The main factor contributing to the process within the upper-middle class was balance among its different occupational areas according to wealth and social status. Weakness in these respects within any major occupational group, as was true of the bureaucracy and the liberal professions in Vienna, would make the aristocracy reluctant to form close, lasting ties with any part of the bourgeois elite. The strength of the noneconomic professions in London and Paris gave the bourgeois public a breadth and a grandeur which attracted the nobility to change the orientation of its social life.

Thus, the vigorous, and in many ways so impressive, efforts of Viennese bourgeois to make up for their city's late emergence as a national capital ultimately fell short of success. While the high-status popular-music world achieved a commercial dynamism equal to its counterparts in London and Paris, the rest of their concert life remained smaller and less professionalised, because of the lack of unity among its elite groups. One might speculate that the artistic revolution brought by Arnold Schoenberg and his followers at the turn of the century stemmed in part from the inhibited growth in the city's musical world.

Let us pass on to the other dimensions of middle-class social structure. One showed a novel effect of modernization: the growing tension among adherents of contrasting tastes and manners. Conflict between prominent life-styles has become one of the characteristic social features of the contemporary era, though one not normally studied by social historians. While some such differences existed in the old society, they grew more from individuals' economic condition and social function rather than from any free alternatives in cultural orientation. During the nineteenth century the rise in the real income of the middle class expanded its members' ability to define their lives as they wished and thereby created serious divisions among them over the values they adhered to and the activities they pursued. During the 1830s and '40s there was not yet as much variety in such groups as has come in the twentieth century, and only two of them were apparent. The "modish" and "modest" taste publics, as we have named them, constituted the leading alternatives in general life-style and fitted closely with the similarly inclined popular- and classical-music taste publics in musical life. The division among these groups grew from the long-standing tension in all three capitals over adherence to fashion but gave the issue much greater breadth and intensity than it had had before.

Far from weakening class identity, the conflict between the publics strengthened the nascent merger between the aristocracy and the upper-middle class. Since tastes and life-styles had such strong meaning and immediacy for people of the time, it provided small-group bases within which members of the two classes could learn to know each other better. Because the issue had little origin in hard class differences, it allowed people to flirt with common identities without raising tough economic or political questions. Cultural experience served as an entry-point into a new class.

Modernization also heightened differences between middle-class lines of work. The growth of the European economy stimulated each of the professions to seek out new functions and areas of leadership, and the various directions they took in tastes and cultural activities gave them considerably different life-styles. Families in business became the most prominent in the modish popular-music scene; those in the liberal professions and the bureaucracy predominated in the more austere classical-music world. Both the traditions and new economic roles of the professions helped bring these tendencies about. While wholesalers dramatized their affluence with a gregarious salon life and vigorous support of virtuosi and the Italian opera, lawyers, artists, and civil servants capitalized upon their learning and intellectual skills with intensive involvement in symphonic and chamber-music concerts. The dispute between the two musical camps served the interests of both groups by giving them arenas in which they could show off their various assets, and it has not ended to this day.

This pattern was not confined simply to the elite public. The disproportionate representation of men from the liberal professions among members of the low-status amateur concerts in all three cities shows that specialization of taste was general within all segments of the middle class. We can thus see that differences in fashions within the middle class went deeper than just the musical controversy of the 1830s and '40s. Contrasting artistic orientations were based upon day-to-day musical activities and social values and had close links with occupational groups and taste publics much wider than the concert world. What is more, we can see where that controversy came from. The absence of any serious conflict between popular- and classical-music concerts in the low-status public reinforces the contention that the dispute within the elites sprang from the social needs created by changes in its structure. Although lower-middle class musical life showed much tension over adherence to fashion, the issue did not have a parallel in musical tastes, for most low-status concerts mixed popular and classical forms without any controversy. In Vienna, however, amateurs from the lesser public did take part in the dispute because the city had so much more unity within its middle class than London or Paris.

We should stress the particular significance of the noneconomic professions within musical life of the time. Ever since Alfred Cobban laid bare the roles of lawyers and civil servants in the French Revolution, historians have come to realize how much such men led the development of the middle class.[7] Just as they provided the cutting-edge of political leadership, so they built much of the institutional and intellectual groundwork for the modern concert world. In Paris the doctor Jean Orfila played central roles as a powerful salon host and as a sponsor of the Orphéon; in Vienna the civil servant Auguste Schmidt founded the city's first solidly professional music magazine and helped establish the Men's Singing Society. Their early tendency to specialize in classical music helped propel this world to the fore as concerts became still more institutionalized after 1850. In this area the professionals largely triumphed over the businessmen, which helped compensate for their relative decline in other respects.

But what about women in concert life? The central role of upper-middle class women in the growth of concert life shows that the homilies concerning their passivity and submissiveness did not go very far in practice. They were the key agents during this time in one of the biggest power-plays in Western history: the retention of young people in the home during their teenage years and their segregation as a distinct social group. Musical education — the puberty rite of learning an instrument — was a critical factor in this process, and one governed almost entirely by women. They also took charge of a vital means of self-aggrandisement for upper-middle class families: salons. Their central role in the popular-music world shows in concrete terms how powerfully they functioned in developing the middle class as the principle source of consumption in the European economy.

Here we must return to the differential roles of the professions. Businessmen acted with the same passivity in musical life as in politics; just as they let the lawyers run the parliamentary scene, so they left leadership in salons and benefit concerts to their wives and daughters. Men from the other two professional areas saw so much to be gained from social activism in musical life that women achieved no such power in classical-music life. Males imposed upon this world a lofty intellectual definition through which—thanks to the traditional conception that men were more serious than women—they excluded the other sex from leadership, even though women attended classical-music concerts just as much as men.

The tragedy of all this is that women got so little credit for what they did. As the middle class was opening up new areas of social and economic activity, men and women jockeyed for positions of power within different areas, and while women established some significant lines of influence, they achieved no formal authority. One of the most interesting questions to pursue in study of late-nineteenth century concerts is just when and how women obtained positions on the boards of symphony orchestras.

Thus, three kinds of groups in the fabric of concert audiences — taste publics, occupations, and men and women — exhibited a fascinating overlapping of social patterns. We must remember, of course, that they did not fit all that tidily; social structure is rarely tidy. The people who showed unusual tendencies (the businessmen, for example, who broadened London's classical-music public by going to the events of the Musical Union) themselves contributed much to the growth of concert life. But it was these main groups which generated the dynamic social energies in the concert world during the period when it became a major entertainment medium. As always, musical life served many purposes for many different kinds of people — but with a definite coherence in its social and cultural shape.

This book should alert historians to the wealth of insight which musical life can provide for understanding the most central developments in their fields. In many ways we can better grasp what was happening within the middle class if we look at its members singing, playing, or listening than voting or fighting. Because music touched people's lives at so many points, the history of what they did with it has taken us into many regions of their society and into some of the most critical developments of their day.

And such a time of ferment it was. When this writer looks back at its frenetic doings he sees a strange parallel with the explosion of popular music in Europe and the United States — indeed, worldwide—between 1955 and 1970. During both periods there appeared dynamic new kinds of performers (virtuosi and rock stars), larger publics (the middle class then and hip-minded young people now), and modernized commercial frameworks (the new concert world and the enlarged record industry). These social developments brought with them daring artistic tendencies and sharp conflict among different publics. Both currents emerged within contexts of social and political change but then — as has by now become fully apparent — consolidated into less controversial and more lasting forms. Just as Franz Liszt turned to more serious musical ideas after 1850, so Frank Zappa has sobered up a bit and John Lennon has made himself a rock philosopher. In such a manner can culture cut across national boundaries, break down traditional restraints, and set up whole new realms of social and artistic experience.

APPENDIX A
THE SIZE OF THE MIDDLE CLASS

Adéline Daumard has made several estimates for the Parisian middle class, conceived in varying ways and derived from different sources. Using the occupational census of 1847 she found that if all independent artisans be included in the class, it would comprise about thirty-five per cent of the population. Yet she also shows that these artisans were still marginal to the middle class as their social status was still identified with that of persons performing manual occupations. The breakdown of the cost of rents provides a better index of the size of the class. It shows a clearly distinguishable group of families who held twenty per cent of all rented units. Data of occupations yielded a somewhat higher figure.[1]

The records extant of the Viennese census of 1847 present fragmentary information, but they do suggest that in Vienna the class was not much smaller proportionally than in Paris. The records show that the number of men over 20 in the Church, the bureaucracy, most economic professions, and selected liberal professions was 9.5 per cent of the population (40,348 out of 429,120). Thus the total population in the families of these persons certainly amounted to at least 19 per cent of the city's total production. Even at that, the census did not tabulate several fairly numerous middle-class groups: *rentiers,* technicians, and lawyers.[2]

London's census of this period provides a weaker means of estimating the proportion of the middle class in the city's population. The one indicative figure it cites is that in 1841 fourteen per cent of the men over twenty were "capitalists, bankers, professionals, and other educated men".[3] The size of the number indicates that the London middle class was probably as high as that of the Parisian middle class since it excluded shopkeepers. A population study of England as a whole made in 1881 estimated that the middle class (including clerks but not artisans) made up 21.5 per cent of all employed males.[4] It is dubious whether, four decades before, the class in London had been much larger than that. While the capital city would be expected to have had a larger proportion than the country as a whole, the expansion in the middle class between 1841 and 1881 suggests that the national figure must have been closer to fifteen per cent at the earlier date.

BIBLIOGRAPHY

1. Governmental Archives

Materials in governmental archives on concert life are in almost all cases fragmentary and uninformative. A few records of concert licences, most of them from the 1820s, remain in London (Theater Collection, Public Record Office) and in Vienna (Central Administrative Registry, "Prison Income: Concert-Givers", Archive of the City of Vienna). In Paris the Archives Nationales have some interesting but difficult to interpret tax statistics on entertainments (Minister of the Interior, Bureau of Hospitals, F15 3867) and — much more profitable — Miscellaneous Papers on Shows and Cafés (F21 1038). The Library of the Hôtel de Ville contains similar information in a paper printed in 1849 of "l'Administration générale de l'assistance publique". The Archive of the Seine has a few papers of the Orphéon Society.

2. Records of Musical Institutions

This area is rich in highly informative sources for the period 1830-1848 and would seem to be even better for later in the century. The membership lists in Vienna cite occupations; those in Paris list addresses. Official papers, however, are in some cases (as in the Gesellschaft der Musikfreunde and the Royal Academy of Music) not fully open to scrutiny.

London: The Papers of the Philharmonic Society (British Museum) include Minutes of Directors' Meetings, Official Letters, Minutes of Annual Meetings, and printed lists of *Subscribers to the Philharmonic Concerts* (for the lists between 1843 and 1848, see the Papers of Sir George Smart). Also in the British Museum are the Concert Programs (including membership lists) of the Concerts of Ancient Music and the Musical Union (in the form of the *Musical Record*). The Library of the Royal College of Music holds the records of the Sacred Harmonic Society: Annual Reports of 1832-34 in manuscript (citing all new members) and those of 1839-48 in printed form, together with a *List of Members of the Sacred Harmonic Society in 1848*. The London Museum, the Guildhall Museum, and the Victoria and Albert Museum have extensive collections of concert programs.

Paris: The Bibliothèque Nationale contains principally the papers of Hector Berlioz, the Prince de la Moscowa, the Société Académique des Enfants d'Apollon, the Société des Concerts Vocales, and the Société Philharmonique. The Orchestra of Paris denies that any records remain from the Conservatory Concerts for the period prior to mid-century.

Vienna: The Archive of the Society of the Friends of Music contains manuscript collections of Official Letters, Programs of the Society, miscellaneous concert programs and circulars, and the *Verzeichnisse der Mitglieder der Gesellschaft der Musikfreunde, 1813-1848.* It also has "Materials for the History of the Opera and the Ballet" in the papers of Leopold Sonnleithner. The manuscript Collection of the Austrian National Library holds a collection of miscellaneous letters of musical figures; the Library of the City of Vienna has similar papers, most prominently those of Josef Fischof. The Vienna Philharmonic Orchestra holds a few letters from before 1848, but almost all of them have been published.

3. Periodicals

Magazines and newspapers are unusually informative for musical life during this period because both concerts and the press were undergoing sudden expansion and music journalism had not yet become professionali or focused exclusively upon performance. The list of abbreviations for periodicals indicates the main such sources among the over one hundred consulted for this study (see page 138). Several others had unusual value: in London, the *Penny Satirist* (1841-46), *Punch* (1841-48), *The Town* (1837-42), and *La Belle Assemblée* (1830-32); in Paris, *l'Album de Saint-Cécile* (1845), *Charivari* (1832-46), *Journal des théâtres* (1843-46), and *Mercure des théâtres* (1843-46); in Vienna, *Der Adler* (1833-48) and *Mittheilungen aus Wien* (1832-40). Columns on concerts in foreign capitals make many periodicals useful for more than one city.

4. Bibliographies of Contemporary Books

Research on capital-city life during the first half of the nineteenth century sports several marvellously complete bibliographies: *Bibliographie parisienne, tableaux des moeurs, 1600-1880,* ed. Paul Lacombe (Paris, 1887); *Bibliographie zur Geschichte und Stadtkunde von Wien,* ed. Gustav Gugitz (Vienna, 1947-62, 5 vols.); and *London History and Topography,* Vol. 1 of *Members' Library Catalogue*, London County Council (London, 1939).

5. Books on City Life

The burgeoning book industry of the time turned out a wide variety of works on social life in the capitals: travel guides, city handbooks, satirical sketches, and social tableaux. Since virtually every volume cited in the three city bibliographies between 1830 and 1848 has at least a sentence on musical life, we will list only the most useful of them. Place of publication was in the city in question unless otherwise noted.

London: The Ball or a Glance at Almack's (1829); A. Booth,
The Stranger's Intellectual Guide to London for 1839-1840 (1838);
Charles Dickens, *Scenes of London Life* (1850) and *Sketches in London* (1839); James Grant, *The Great Metropolis* (1838);
Kidd's London Directory and Amusement Guide (n.d.); Lemercher de
Longpré, Baron d'Haussez, *Grande-Bretagne en 1833* (Brussels,
1833); John Fischer Murray, *World of London* (1843); Boleyne Reeves,
Sports and Pastimes in Town and County (1841); Charles Manby Smith,
Curiosities of London Life (1857); Francis Wey, *Les Anglais
chez eux* (Paris, 1856); and N. Whittock, *The New Picture of
London* (1838).

Paris: Honoré de Balzac, *Traité de la vie élégante*
(1853), *Nouveau tableau de Paris* (1845), and *Physiologie de
l'employé* (1841); Adelbert von Bornstedt, *Pariser Silhouetten*
(Leipzig, 1836); Dr. C. G. Carus, *Paris und die Rheingegenden*
(Leipzig, 1836); Edouard Charton, *Guide pour le choix d'une
profession* (1848); Marquis Adolphe Custine, *Ethel* (1839) and
Le Monde comme il est (1835); *Français peints par eux-même*
(7 vols., 1841); James Grant, *Paris and its People* (London, 1844);
Intellectual Guide or How to Live in France (London, 1835);
Edouard Kolloff, *Schilderungen aus Paris* (Hamburg, 1839);
Musée Dantan (1838); *Nouveau tableau de Paris* (1835); *Paris actuel*
(1842); *Tableaux de Paris* (1842); William Thackeray, *The Paris
Sketch Book of Mr. M. A. Titmarsh* (London, 1904); and Frances
Trollope, *Paris and the Parisians in 1835* (London, 1835).

Vienna: Heinrich Adami, ed., *Alt- und Neu-Wien* (1842);
Victor Andrian-Warburg, *Oesterreich und dessen Zukunft* (Hamburg,
1843); Adolf Baüerle, *Wien vor zwanzig Jahren* (1855); Eduard
Bauernfeld, *Ein Buch von uns Wienern* (Leipzig, 1858); Julian
Chownitz, *Moderne Wiener Perspectiven* (Leipzig, 1843); Eduard
Maria Hügel and A. J. Gross-Hoffinger, *Wien wie es ist* (Leipzig,
1833); *Kaiserstädt, Licht- und Schattenseiten* (Leipzig, 1847);
Matthias Koch, *Wien und die Wiener* (Karlsruhe, 1842); Adolphe
Carl Naske, *Wiener Kanzlei-Zustände* (Leipzig, 1846); Johannes
Nordmann, *Briefe aus Wien von einem Eingebornen* (Hamburg, 1844);
August Schilling, *Satyrisch-komische Wiener Skizzen* (1841); Charles
Sealsfield, *Austria As It Is* (London, 1828); Frances Trollope,
Vienna and the Austrians (London, 1838); and Franz Wiest, *Geist,
Witz, und Satyre* (Leipzig, 1847).

6. Memoirs, Letters, and Diaries
These literary forms were at their peak in both volume and social insight
during the first half of the nineteenth century. As in Section 5, the
city bibliographies present such comprehensive listings that we will cite
only the most important of them here. The many works by famous

musicians (Berlioz, Liszt, Schumann, etc.) need no specification, but we should stress the value for study of London and Vienna of *Aus Moscheles' Leben*, ed. Charlotte Moscheles (Leipzig, 1872). Place of publication is city in question unless otherwise noted.

London: John E. Cox, *Musical Recollections of the Last Half-Century* (1872); J. W. Davidson, *From Mendelssohn to Wagner, being the Memoirs of J. W. Davidson* (1912); Alice Mangold Diehl, *Musical Memories* (1897); John Ella, *Musical Sketches*, 3rd. edn (1878); William Gardiner, *Music and Friends, or Pleasant Recollections of a Dilettante* (1853); Wilhelm Kuhe, *My Musical Recollections* (1896); Lord William Lennox, *Story of My Life* (1857); Count Edouard de Melfort, *Impressions of England* (1836); and Rees Howell Gronow, *Reminiscences of Captain Gronow* (1892).

Paris: Adolphe Adam, *Souvenirs d'un musicien* (1860); Victor de Balabine, *Journal, 1842-1847,* ed. Ernest Daudet (1914); Vicomte de Beaumont-Vassy, *Les Salons de Paris sous Louis-Philippe* (1866); Charles Bocher, *Mémoires* (n.d.); Maréchale de Castellane, *Journal, 1804-1862* (1896); Marquis de Custine, *Souvenirs et portraits.* ed. Pierre de Sacretelle (1956); Sophie Gay, *Salons célébres* (1837); Vicomte de Launay, pseud. [Mme. Emile de Girardin], *Lettres parisiennes* (1856); Heinrich Heine, *Lutèce: lettres sur la vie politique et sociale de la France* (1872); Lemerché de Longpré, Baron d'Haussez, *Mémoires* (1896); Comte de Rambuteau, *Souvenirs,* ed. Georges Lequin (1905); Saint-Marc-Girardin, *Souvenirs d'un journaliste* (1859); and Anton Schindler, *Tagebuch aus den Jahren 1841-1843* (Vienna, 1939).

Vienna: Franz Andlaw, *Mein Tagebuch* (Frankfurt am Main, 1862); Heinrich Anschütz, *Erinnerungen aus dessen Leben und Wirken* (1866); J. F. Castelli, *Memoiren meines Lebens,* ed. Josef Bindtner (Munich, 1914); Ludwig August Frankl, *Erinnerungen,* ed. Stefan Kock (Prague, 1910); Karl von Hailbronner, *Cartons aus der Reisemappe eines Touristen* (Stuttgart, 1837); Eduard Hanslick, *Aus meinem Leben* (Berlin, 1894); Moritz Hartmann, *Briefe aus dem Vormärz,* ed. Otto Wittner (Prague, 1910); Wilhelm Christian Müller, *Briefe an deutsche Freunde* (Altona, 1824); Caroline Pichler, *Denkwürdigkeiten aus meinem Leben* (1844); Graf Prokesch von Osten, *Tagebücher, 1830-1834* (1909); Ludwig Rellstab, *Aus meinem Leben* (Berlin, 1861); and *Briefe an die Wiener Philharmoniker,* ed. Wilhelm Jerger (1942).

7. Contemporary Books on Musical Life

London: Thomas Busby, *Concert Rooms and Orchestral Anecdotes* (1825); Frederick Crowest, *Phases of Musical England* (1881); George Hogarth, *Musical History, Biography, and Criticism* (1838); Francis Hueffer, *Half a Century of Music in England, 1837-1887* (1887);

and Joseph Mainzer, *Musical Athenaeum* (1842).

Paris: J. Martin d'Angers, *De l'Avenir de l'Orphéon* (1846); E. Destouches, *Physiologie des barrières et des musicians de Paris* (1842), J. F. Gail, *Réflexions sur le goût musical en France* (1832); Joseph d'Ortigue, *Palin-génésie* (1833) and *De la guerre des dilettanti* (1829); *Paris chez Musard par un habitué* (1857); and V. Scudo, *Critique et litérature musicale* (1859).

Vienna: Denkschrift zur 25-jährigen Jubelfeier der Gesellschaft der Musikfreunde (1840); *Musikalische Geschichts- und Erinnerungs-Kalender* (1842); *Orpheus: musikalisches Taschenbuch* (1840); Gustav Schilling, *Das musikalische Europa* (Speyer, 1842); Sigmund Schlesinger, *Josef Gusikow und dessen Holz- und Strohinstrument* (1836); August Schmidt, "Selbstbiographie", *Der Wiener Männergesangverein* (1868); and Leopold von Sonnleithner, "Musikalische Skizzen aus Alt-Wien", *Recensionen und Mittheilungen über Theater und Musik,* VII (1861), pp. 737-741, 753-757.

8. Social History

The field of social history has not developed as fully for the nineteenth century as it has for the early modern period, but its works have much to offer the history of culture. Indispensable for a survey of social developments and a useful bibliography is Peter N. Stearns, *European Society in Upheaval* (New York, 1967). National histories include Harold J. Perkin, *Origins of English Society, 1780-1880* (London, 1969); Pauline Gregg, *A Social and Economic History of Britain, 1760-1960* (London, 1960); Georges Dupeux, *La Société française, 1789-1960* (Paris, 1964); and appropriate sections of A.J.P. Taylor, *Habsburg Monarchy, 1809-1918* (London, 1948). For specific topics see sections below.

9. Urban History

Still necessary for basic information is Adna Weber, *The Growth of Cities in the Nineteenth Century* (Ithaca, 2nd edn, 1963). For provocative discussion of more theoretical problems, see *The Study of Urban History,* ed. H.J. Dyos (New York, 1968) and Robert E. Dickinson, *The West European City: A Geographical Interpretation* (London, 1951).

The fullest study of one of the capitals is Francis Sheppard, *London, 1808-1870: The Infernal Wen* (Berkeley, 1971). For London see also Asa Briggs, *Victorian Cities* (London, 1963); *London: Aspects of Change* (London, 1964); R. J. Mitchell and M.D.R. Leys, *History of London* (London, 1958); Steen Eiler Rasmussen, *London: the Unique City* (London, 1937). For a brilliant article on the earlier period, see E. H. Wrigely, "A Simple Model of London's Importance in Changing English Society and Economics, 1650-1750",

Past and Present, XXXVII (1967), pp. 44-70.

There is no parallel to Sheppard for Paris. See Louis Chevalier, *La Formation de la population parisienne au XIXe siècle* (Paris, 1950); M. Poëte, *Histoire de Paris* (Paris, 1925); and Charles Simon, *Paris de 1800 à 1900* (Paris, 1900).

For studies on Vienna, see Josef Karl Mayr, *Geschichte der oesterreichischen Staatskanzlei im Zeitalter des Fürsten Metternichs* (Vienna, 1935); Sigmund Mayer, *Handwerk und Grossindustrie in Wien, 1700-1850* (Vienna, 1889); Friedrich Reischl, *Wien zur Biedermeierzeit* (Vienna, 1921); and Ludwig Eisenberg and Richard Croner, *Das geistige Wien* (Vienna, 1889).

10. The European Middle Class

The area of study in nineteenth-century social history which offers the most help to the history of culture is the extensive work done on the middle class. A goldmine of information on its structure in France can be found in Adéline Daumard, *La Bourgeoisie parisienne, 1815-1848* (Paris, 1963) and André-Jean Tudesq, *Les Grands notables en France, 1840-1849* (Paris, 1964). Broader in time but still useful for this period are Roy Lewis and Angus Maude, *The English Middle Classes* (London, 1949) and David Lockwood, *The Blackcoated Worker* (London, 1958). Treatment of the relations between the aristocracy and the middle class lie chiefly in Ernest K. Bramsted, *Aristocracy and the Middle-Classes in Germany* (Chicago, 1964); Franklin Ford, "The Revolutionary-Napoleonic Era: How much of Watershed?", *American Historical Review*, LXIX (1963), pp. 18-29; and M. Reinhard, "Elite et noblesse dans la seconde moitié du XVIIIe siècle", *Revue d'histoire moderne*, III (1956), pp. 5-37. For interesting theoretical discussion, see R Neale, *Class and Ideology in the Nineteenth Century* (London, 1972).

Inquiry into the occupational bases of the middle class produced a flurry of commentary, though less disagreement than was alleged. See Lenore O'Boyle, "The Middle Class in Western History, 1815-1848", *AHR*, LXXI (1966), pp. 826-40; Alfred Cobban, "The 'Middle Class' in France, 1815-1848", *French Historical Studies*, V (1967), pp. 41-53; and O'Boyle's reply, *Ibid.*, pp. 53-46.

Rethinking of the "bourgeois monarchy" under Louis-Philippe has also been productive. See David H. Pinkney, "The Myth of the French Revolution of 1830", *Festschrift for Frederick B. Artz*, ed. Pinkney and Theodore Rabb (Durham, 1964), pp. 52-71; and Patrick L.-R. Higonnet and Trevor B. Higonnet, "Class, Corrpution, and Politics in the French Chamber of Deputies", *French Historical Studies*, V. (1967), pp. 204-24. For works fashioned on the older, more impression model, see Jean Lhomme, *La Grande bourgeoisie au pouvoir, 1830-1870* (Paris, 1960) and Charles Morazé, *Les Bourgeois conquérants* (Paris, 1957).

12. Middle-Class Culture

There is a vast literature on the culture and manners of the middle class. For London see primarily G. M. Young, *Early Victorian England* (London, 1934); Richard D. Altick, *The English Common Reader* (Chicago, 1957); N. G. Annan, "The Intellectual Aristocracy", *Studies in Social History*, ed. J. H. Plumb (London, 1955), pp. 241-87. Other works include E. Beresford Chancellor, *Life in Regency and Early Victorian Times* (London, 1926); R. J. Cruikshank, *Charles Dickens and Early Victorian England* (London, 1949); John W. Dodds, *Age of Paradox: a Biography of England, 1841-1851* (New York, 1952); Jacob Korg, ed., *London in Dicken's Day* (London, 1960); and Maurice Quinlan, *Victorian Prelude: a History of English Manners, 1780-1830* (New York, 1941).

For Paris see Robert Burnand, *La Vie quotidienne en France en 1830* (Paris, 1943); Bernand Gavoty, *Deux Capitales romantiques: Vienne, Paris* (Paris, 1954); Louis Maigron, *Le Romantisme et la mode* (Paris, 1911); and A.-D. Tolédano, *La Vie de famille sous la Restauration et la Juillet-Monarchie* (Paris, 1943).

For Vienna see Max von Boehn, *Die Mode* (Munich, 1924); Otto Brunner, "Das Wiener Bürgertum", *Monatsblatt des Vereines für Geschichte der Stadt Wien*, XV (1933), pp. 220-31; Ann Tizia Leitich, *Wiener Biedermeir* (Bielefeld, 1941); and Eilhard Erich Pauls, *Der Beginn der bürgerlichen Zeit* (Lübeck, 1924).

13. The History of Musical Life

Two journalists have shown the way toward the systematic study of the social history of music: Arthur Loesser, *Men, Women, and Pianos* (New York, 1951), and Henry Raynor, *A Social History of Music* (New York, 1972). While their methodology may at points displease the social scientist, they bring to their works a healthy respect for the most worldly aspects of musical life. The renowned Theodor W. Adorno did, of course, spearhead social analysis of music — see his *Einleitung in die Musiksoziologie* (Frankfurt, 1962) — but kept intellectual and artistic problems as the focus of his work. For two broad-ranging works, see Wilfred Mellers, *Music and Society* (New York, 1950) and Wilfred Dumwell, *Music and the European Mind* (London, 1962). A more basic work can be found in Eric Mackerness, *A Social History of English Music* (London, 1964). The main studies of music during our period are Alfred Einstein, *Music in the Romantic Era* (New York, 1947) and Georg Knepler, *Musikgeschichte des 19 Jahrhunderts* (Berlin, 1961).

The history of musical life in London includes several helpful general studies: Adam Carse, *The Orchestra in the Eighteenth Century* (Cambridge, 1948); Robert Elkin, *Old Concert Rooms of London*

(London, 1955); and Reginald Nettel, *The Orchestra in England* (London, 1948), *The Englishman Makes Music* (London, 1952), and "The Influence of the Industrial Revolution on English Music", *Publications of the Royal Musicological Association,* LXXII (1945-46), pp. 23-40. See also M. B. Foster, *History of the Philharmonic Society of London* (London, 1912); Francis Hueffer, *Half a Century of Music in England* (London, 1889); John Ravell, "John Ella", *Music and Letters,* XXXIV (1953), pp. 93-105; Adam Carse, *Life of Jullien* (Cambridge, 1951); A. W. Ganz, *Berlioz in London* (London, 1950); and Christopher Pulling, *They Were Singing* (London, 1952).

Work on concerts in Paris is more erratic in its coverage. Jacques Barzun's *Berlioz and the Romantic Century* (New York, 1950) has brought the composer deserved recognition but is limited in its portrayal of musical life. The study of the Conservatory Concerts before mid-cent has been weak; see Jean Cordey, *La Société du Conservatoire* (Paris, 1941), A. Dandelot, *La Société des Concerts du Conservatoire* (Paris, 1897), and A. Elwart and E. Deldevez, *Histoire de la Société des Concerts du Conservatoire* (Paris, 1888). For general works on music and culture, see Léon Guichard, *La Musique et les lettres au temps du romantisme* (Paris, 1955), Claude Laforet, *La Vie musicale au temps romantique* (Paris, 1929) and Leo Schrade, *Beethoven in France* (New Haven, 1942). For closer examination of the concert public see A. Julien, *Paris dilettante au commencement du siècle* (Paris, 1884) and L. La Laurencie. *Le Goût musical en France* (Paris, 1905).

The study of Viennese concerts profits from one of the best books in the social history of music: Eduard Hanslick's detailed and perceptive *Geschichte des Concertwesens in Wien* (Vienna, 1869). But apart from this the intensive study of the life of Beethoven has not yet broadened into examination of musical life after his time. General works of interest include David Ewen, *Musical Vienna* (New York, 1939); K. Kobald, *Alt-Wiener Musikstätten* (Vienna, 1923); Alfred Orel, ed. *Musikstadt Wien* (Vienna, 1953); E. Preussner, *Die bürgerliche Musikkultur* (Hamburg, 1935); Leopold Sailer, "Wohltätigkeitskonzerte in Wien vor hundert Jahren", *Monatsblatt des Vereins fur Geschichte der Stadt Wien,* XV (1953), pp 63-66; Arnold Schering, "Die Frühjahre der Neuromantiker", *Jahrbuch Peters,* XXIV (1899), pp 44-72; and Alexander Witeschnik, *Musik aus Wien* (Vienna, 1949). For material on institutions see Heinrich Kralik, *Das Grosses Orchester* (Vienna, 1952); E. Mittag, *Aus der Geschi Wiener Philharmoniker* (Vienna, 1950); Richard von Perger, *Geschichte der k.k. Gesellschaft der Musikfreunde in Wien* (Vienna, 1912); C. F. Pohl, "Zur Geschichte der Gründung und Entwicklung der Gesells der Musikfreunde in Wien", *Jahres-Bericht des Conservatoriums der Gesellschaft der Musikfreunde* (Vienna 1869), and *Philharmonische*

Concerts in Wien (Vienna, 1885); Christl Schönfeldt, *Die Wiener Philharmoniker* (Vienna, 1956); *Wiener Philharmoniker, 1842-1942* (Vienna, 1942).

For discussion of leading musicians in Vienna, see Ernst Decsey, *Johann Strauss* (Stuttgart, 1922); *Joseph Hellmesberger* (Vienna, 1877); Hans Jäger-Sustenau, *Johann Strauss* (Vienna, 1965); Erick Schenck, "Robert Schumann und Peter Lindpainter in Wien", *Festschrift Joseph Schmidt-Görg zum 60. Geburstag* (Bonn, 1957), pp. 267-83; Franz Zagiba, *Chopin und Wien* (Vienna, 1951), Georg Kruse, *Otto Nicholai* (Berlin, 1911); Hertha Ibl, *Studien zu Johann Vesque von Puttlingens Leben und Opernschaffen*, Dissertation, University of Vienna, 1949; J. Hoven, ed., *Johann Vesque von Puttlingen, eine Lebensskizze* (Vienna, 1887).

Abbreviations of Periodical Titles Used in Footnotes

AMA	*Allgemeine Musikalische Anzeiger* (1831-39)
AMZL	*Allgemeine Musikzeitung* (Leipzig, 1798-1848)
AMZV	*Allgemeine Musikzeitung* (Vienna, 1817-24)
AT	*Athenaeum* (1830-48)
CO	*Connoisseur* (London, 1845-46)
CT	*Courrier des Théâtres* (1826-27)
DI	*Dilettante*
DMR	*Dramatic and Musical Review* (1842-46)
DO	*Domino* (Vienna, 1845-46)
EN	*Entr'acte* (1835-43)
FI	*Figaro* (1830-48)
FM	*France Musicale* (1837-48)
GE	*Gegenwart* (1845-48)
GM	*Gazette Musicale* (1834-35)
GR	*Grenzboten* (Leipzig, 1842-48)
HJ	*Neue komische Briefe des Hans-Jürgels von Gumpoldskirchen* (1830-48)
HN	*Harmonicon* (1828-35)
JD	*Journal des Dames* (1845-46)
JE	*Journal des Débats* (1830-48)
LT	*The London Times* (1830-48)
ME	*Musical Examiner* (1842-44)
MEN	*Ménestrel* (1836-48)
MM	*Music Magazine* (1835)
MP	*Morning Post* (1830-48)
MR	*Musical Record* (1845-48)
MT	*Mercure des Théâtres* (1843-46)
MW	*Musical World* (1836-48)
NZM	*Neue Zeitschrift für Musik* (Leipzig, 1834-48)
OC	*Oesterreichische Courrier* (1846-47)
OM	*Oesterreichische Morgenblatt* (1845-46)
PI	*Pianiste* (1834-35)
QMM	*Quarterly Music Magazine and Review* (1818-29)
RGM	*Revue et Gazette Musicale* (1835-48)
RGT	*Revue et Gazette des Théâtres* (1829-48)
RM	*Revue Musicale* (1827-35)
RMR	*Revue de la Musique Réligieuse* (1845-48)
SAM	*Sammler* (1830-46)
SB	*Wiener Sonntagsblätter* (1845-48)
SI	*Siecle* (1845-48)
SP	*Spectator* (1830-48)
TZ	*Theaterzeitung* (1830-48)
WAN	*Wanderer* (1830-48)
WMZ	*Allgemeine Wiener Musikzeitung* (1841-48)
WZ	*Wiener Zeitung* (1830-48)
ZU	*Wiener Zuschauer* (1843-48)

NOTES

Chapter 1

1. Introduction

1. Henry Raynor's *A Social History of Music* (London, 1972) provides an excellent overview of the development of musical institutions until the late eighteenth century.
2. Quoted in Robert Elkin, *The Old Concert Rooms of London* (London, 1955), p. 67.
3. Reginald Nette, *The Orchestra in England* (London, 1946), pp. 20-25.
4. Elkin, pp. 83-103; Percy Scholes, *The Great Doctor Burney* (London, 1948), II, p. 168; C. F. Phol, *Haydn und Mozart in London* (Vienna, 1867); Hugh Arthur Scott, "London's Earliest Public Concerts", *Musical Quarterly*, XXII (1936), pp. 446-457.
5. *QMM*, Vol. 1, No. 3, p. 342.
6. John Lough, *Paris Theater Audiences in the Seventeenth and Eighteenth Centuries* (London, 1957), pp. 186-87, 207-08.
7. Michel Brenet, *Les Concerts sous l'ancien régime* (Paris, 1900); Louis Striffling, *Esquisse d'une histoire du goût musical en France au 18ième siècle* (Paris, 1912); Théodore Fleischmann, *Napoléon et la musique* (Paris, 1965); J. G. Prodhomme, "La Musique à Paris, 1753-57", *Sammelbände der Internationalen Musik-Gesellschaft*, VI (1904-05), pp. 569-82.
8. For an engrossing discussion of this problem see David Bien, "The Ancien Regime in France", *Perspectives in the European Past*, ed. Norman Cantor (New York, 1971), Vol. II, pp. 3-26.
9. Hanslick, I, 3-137; Franz Farga, *Die Wiener Oper von ihren Anfängen bis 1938* (Vienna, 1947); Robert Haas, *Gluck und Durazzo im Burgtheater* (Vienna, 1925).
10. Jeanne Singer-Kérel, *Le Coût de la vie à Paris de 1840 à 1954* (Paris, 1961), pp. 98, 212; G. M. Young, *Early Victorian England* (London, 1934), Vol. I, p. 107; Richard Tilly, *Financial Institutions and Industrialization in the Rhineland, 1815-1871* (Madison, 1961), pp. 141-42.
11. Arthur Loesser, *Men, Women, and Pianos* (New York, 1954), pp. 132-35, 185-228, 251-67.
12. The chief periodicals useful for concert life in the period are *AMZL, AMZV, LT, MP, QMM, TZ, FI,* and *CT*. See also the tabulation of numbers of concerts for the season 1826-1827 in Table 1.
13. For Vienna, see Hanslick, I, pp. 375-433, II, *passim*. For London, see John E. Cox, *Musical Recollections of the Last Half-Century* (London, 1972), Vol. II; John A. Fuller-Maitland, *Music in the Nineteenth Century*, Vol. I. For Paris, see John Ella, *Musical Sketches* (London, 1878); Jacques Barzun, *Berlioz and the Romantic Century* (Boston, 1950), Vol. II; A. Elwart, *Histoire des concerts populaires* (Paris, 1864).
14. David H. Pinkney, "The Myth of the French Revolution of 1830",

Festschrift for Frederick B. Artz, ed. David H. Pinkney and
Theodore Rabb (Durham, 1964), pp. 52-71; Patrick L.-R. Higonnet and
Trevor B. Higonnet, "Class, Corruption, and Politics in the French
Chamber of Deputies", *French Historical Studies,* V (1967),
pp. 204-24.

15. Adéline Daumard, *La Bourgeoisie parisienne, 1815-1848* (Paris,
1963), pp. 28-29, 316; Andre-Jean Tudesq, *Les Grands notables en
France, 1840-1849* (Paris, 1964), Vol. I, p. 123.

16. "The Role of the Aristocracy in Late Nineteenth-Century England",
Victorian Studies, IV (1960), pp. 55-64.

17. Franklin Ford, "The Revolutionary-Napoleonic Era: How Much of a
Watershed?", *American Historical Review,* LXIX (1963), pp. 18-29;
Daumard, pp. 649-50.

18. *Ibid.,* p. 29; Johannes Nordmann, *Briefe aus Wien von einem
Eingebornen* (Hamburg, 1844), Vol. I, p. 70; Eduard Bauernfeld, *Ein Buch
von uns Wienern* (Leipzig, 1858), p. 316.

19. "The Middle Class in Western History, 1815-1848", *American
Historical Review,* LXXI (1966), pp. 826-40, and "The 'Middle Class'
Reconsidered", *French Historical Studies,* V (1967), pp. 53-56;
Alfred Cobban, "The 'Middle Class' in France, 1815-1848", *Ibid.,*
pp. 41-53.

20: The well-spring of this work is, of course, Philippe Ariès' *Centuries
of Childhood: A Social History of Family Life,* tr. Robert Baldick
(New York, 1961). Important contrasting views by a number of
sociologists can be found in *The Family and Change,* ed. John N.
Edwards (New York, 1969), especially "The Isolated Nuclear Family
Hypothesis: A Reanalysis," by Alfred M. Mirande. The main work on
the family during the first half of the nineteenth century is the
anecdotal *La Vie de famille sous la Restauration et la Juillet-Monarchie*
(Paris, 1943) of A. D. Tolédano.

21. For two productive attempts at unearthing the social bases of cultural
publics see Lough, *Paris Theatre Audiences,* and Daniel Roche,
"Milieux académiques et provinciaux et la société des lumières,"
in *Lettres et société dans la France de XVIIIe siècle* (Paris,
1965), pp. 93-184.

22. While the relationships between social class and high and popular
culture have received little conceptual attention, John G. Cawelti has
provided a useful set of aesthetic definitions in "Notes Toward an
Aesthetic of Popular Culture", *Journal of Popular Culture,* V
(1971), pp. 255-68.

23. Discussion of similar trends in other artistic fields is now
extensive: see Harrison C. White and Cynthia A. White, *Canvases
and Careers: Institutional Change in the French Painting World*
(New York, 1965); Cesar Grana, *Bohemian versus Bourgeois* (New
York, 1964); Ernest K. Bramsted, *Aristocracy and the Middle-Classes
in Germany* (Chicago, 1964), Part II; and Robert Darnton, "The
High Enlightenment and the Low-Life of Literature in Pre-Revolutionary
France", *Past and Present,* No. 51 (1971), pp. 81-116.

24. See Appendix I, p. 128.

25. The main histories of the cities are Francis Sheppard, *London,
1808-1870: The Infernal Wen* (Berkeley, 1971); Charles Simon,
Paris de 1800 à 1900 (Paris, 1900); M. Poëte, *Histoire de
Paris* (Paris, 1925); Heinrich Srbik, *Geschichte der Stadt*

Wiens (Vienna, 1962); and Rudolf Lachner, *Geschichte der Stadt Wiens* (Vienna, 2nd edition, 1883).

26. E. H. Wrigley, "A Simple Model of London's Importance in Changing English Society and Economics, 1650-1750", *Past and Present*, XXXVII (1967) pp. 44-70.

27. John Fisher Murray, *The World of London* (London, 1843), p. 194.

28. Lady Blessington, *Victims of Society* (London, 1842), II, pp. 161-227; Marianne Spencer, *Almack's* (London, 1826), III pp. 121- 25.

29. Tudesq, I, pp. 348-51.

30. Daumard, pp. 289-91, 305-06.

31. Victor de Balabine, *Journal, 1842-1847*, ed. Ernest Daudet (Paris, 1914), p. 119; *RGM*, March 27, 1842, p. 126.

32. Lachner, II, pp. 199-223; Josef Karl Mayr, *Wien im Zeitalter Napoleons* (Vienna, 1940), pp. 88-89.

Chapter II

1. A wide variety of periodicals were used for each city. The most important in London were: *LT, MP, MW, DMR, SP, AT, HN and QMM*. Those for Paris: *FI, SI, RM, RGM, CT, FM, MT, MEN and JE*. Those for Vienna: *TZ, WZ, SAM, ZU, WAN, GE, OM, WMZ and GR*. In many cases the periodicals were of assistance for more than one city. Only in London do records remain of concert licences, but they (found in the Theatre Collection of the Public Record Office) are less complete and much less informative than periodicals. For Tables, see pp. 159-68; for abbreviations of periodicals, see p. 138.

2. *CO*, January 1846, p. 7. For a similar comment in Paris see *Les Français peints par eux-même* (Paris, 1841), I, p. 172.

3. *FM*, January 25, 1839, p. 45.

4. Harriet Grote, *Personal Life of George Grote* (London, 1873), pp. 172-73.

5. In London the licence tax was challenged and effectively eliminated about 1837: see *SP*, April 30, 1836. In Paris the tax on entertainment businesses ("le droit des pauvres") continued to operate, but most concerts had to pay only ten per cent of their gross and many seem to have avoided even that. See Edmond Klein "Le Droit des pauvres", Dissertation, University of Algiers, 1911, pp. 141-61; Pierrefitte, *Etude historique sur le droit des pauvres du théâtre* (Paris, 1892), pp. 20-22; for some interesting (but difficult to interpret) data on the tax see *Obsérvations sur le mémoire de MM. les directeurs des théâtres tendant à une modification du droit des indigents sur les spectacles*, 1849, Library of the Hôtel de Ville. In Vienna a licence was required but no information is available about its procedures.

6. "Music in the culture of the Renaissance", *Journal of the History of Ideas*, XV (1954), pp. 509-53.

7. For the main musical study of the period, see Alfred Einstein, *Music in the Romantic Era* (New York, 1947).

8. For an admirable study of musical life during the period in political context see Robert M. Isherwood, *Music in Service of the King*

(Ithaca, 1973).

9. For several passages where the term appeared see: *SP*, January 14, 1837, p. 33; *MW*, November 6, 1844, pp. 534-35, *RM*, May 19, 1832, p. 125; *AMA*, Marck 9, 1847, p. 48; *TZ*, December 9, 1834, p. 976.
10. *MR*, March 11, 1845, p. 2.
11. *ZU*, June 10, 1846, pp. 733-34.
12. *MM*, April 30, 1846, pp. 2-3.
13. Several such composers who held concerts during the season were Hector Berlioz, Ferdinand David, Ignaz Moscheles, and Karl Nicholai.
14. *AMZL*, August 30, 1826, p. 573, October 22, 1800, p. 65. See also *AMZV*, March 14, 1821, pp. 163-64.
15. Vicomte de Launay (pseud.) [Mme. Emile de Girardin], *Lettres parisiennes* (Paris, 1856), I, p. 67 (March 15, 1837).
16. *HN*, November 1829, p. 279.
17. *Oeuvres* (Paris, 1873), IV, p. 35.
18. *MW*, June 13, 1844, p. 196.
19. *Gesammelte Schriften*, ed. F. Gustav Jansen (Leipzig, 1891), II, p. 122.
20. *Ibid.*, I, p. 293.
21. C. S. Peel. "Homes and Habits", *Early Victorian England*, ed. G. M. Young (London, 1934), I, p. 105; *HJ*, 1844, Vol. XII, No. 6, pp. 30-33. An Englishman who was much impressed, probably to excess, by the intense theater-going in Paris estimated that a lower-middle class gentleman might easily spend between 2.5 and 3 per cent of his 4000 fr. on the theater; see James Grant, *Paris and its People* (Paris, 1844), p. 223.
22. Though information on Viennese incomes is skimpy, one can estimate such a number from the 300-400 fl. earned by the starting shop attendant who generally earned the same amount. See Anton Langer, "Die Wiener Handlungsdiener", *Lebensbilder aus Oesterreich*, ed. Andreas Schumacher (Vienna, 1843), p. 19.
23. John Fisher Murray, *World of London* (London, 1843), I, pp. 118-19; R. Dudley Baxter, *National Income* (London, 1868), pp. 36-42, 88-95.
24. *Journal of the Statistical Society of London*, XV (1848), p. 297.
25. Peel, p. 107; Murray, I, p. 95; Count Edouard de Melfort, *Impressions of England* (London, 1836), pp. 78-79; F. Musgrove, "Middle-class Education and Employment in the Nineteenth Century", *Economic Historical Review*, XII (1959), p. 99.
26. Grant, II, pp. 36-37.
27. Wilhelm Christian Müller, *Briefe an deutsche Freunde* (Altona, 1824), I, pp. 76-77. A civil servant of the same upper-middle class status, however, earned only about 4,800 fl.; see Adolph Carl Naske, *Wiener Kanzlei-Zustände aus den Memoiren eines oesterreichischen Staatsbeamten* (Leipzig, 1846), p. 149.
28. *Subscribers to the Philharmonic Concerts*, 1830, British Museum.
29. Adolf Bäuerle, *Wien vor zwanzig Jahren* (Vienna, 1855), II, pp. 125-26. Bauerle was editor of *TZ*.
30. Comprehensive examination of concert advertisements in periodicals supports this conclusion. For comments on the early years of reserved seats, see *HJ*, 1840, Vol. I, p. 24; Rosamunde Brunel Gotch, ed., *Mendelssohn and his Frends in Kensington: Letters from Fanny and*

Sophie Horsley, *1833-1836* (London, 1934), pp 211-20; Moscheles, I,
pp. 103, 264; Prefect of Police, "Ordonnance concernant l'intérieure des
théâtres de la capitale", March 30, 1844, Archives Nationales, F21 1045.

31.   *MW*, September 11, 1845, pp. 438-39.

Chapter III

1.   *Men, Women, and Pianos* (New York, 1951).
2.   Gotch, p. 61.
3.   *TZ*, April 16, 1846, p. 364.
4.   Moscheles, II. p. 8.
5.   *CO*, January 1846, p. 7.
6.   Albert Cler, *Physiologie du musicien* (Paris, 1842), p. 60.
7.   *MR*, March 26, 1845, p. 2. See also *MW,* July 1, 1836, p. 52.
8.   *AMZL*, October 22, 1800, pp. 66-67.
9.   *MR*, April 19, 1845, p. 23; *QMM*, X (1828), pp. 88-89; *RGM*,
      May 31, 1846, p. 171; *Journal des Dames,* February 5, 1846, p. 73;
      TZ, December 19, 1836, p. 1014; *SAM*, January 7, 1834; de
      Launay, II, pp. 93-94.
10.   *RM*, IV (1833), pp. 515-16. See also *RGM*, February 8,
      1846, p. 46.
11.   *GM,* March 15, 1840, p. 110. See also de Launay, II, p. 93.
      HJ, 1835, Vol. 1, No. 2, p. 24; Lady Marguerite Blessington,
      Lottery of Life, (London, 1842), III, p. 9; *MW*, May 20,
      1841, p. 325.
12.   Julian Chownitz, *Moderne Wiener Perspectiven* (Leipzig,   1843),
      p. 164.
13.   *FM*, March 15, 1840, p. 110. See also de Launay, II, 93.
14.   *Salons célèbres* (Paris, 1837), pp. 233-34.
15.   Franz Wiest, *Geist, Witz, und Satyre* (Leipzig, 1847), p. 198.
16.   *QMM*, VII (1826), p. 299. See also: *Satirist,* July 13,
      1834, p. 222; Charles Kenney, *Memoir of Michael Balfe* (London,
      1875), p. 46.
17.   Rees Howell Gronow, *Reminiscences of Captain Gronow* (London,
      1892), I, pp. 132-34.
18.   *Der Deutsche in Paris* (Altona, 1838), II, p. 56; L. Rellstab,
      Paris in 1843 (Leipzig, 1844), I, p. 95; Maréchale de Castellane,
      Journal, 1804-1862 (Paris, 1896), II, p. 487.
19.   *RGM,* January 12, 1843, p. 51.
20.   Moscheles, I, pp. 16-18, 129; Trollope, *Vienna,* II, p. 380; *DO*, I,
      (1847), pp. 29-30; Hügel, II, pp. 104-05; Nordmann, I, pp. 70-72; Ann Tizia
      Leitich, *Wiener Biedermeier* (Leipzig, 1941), pp. 106-14.
21.   Matthias Koch, *Wien und die Wiener* (Karlsruhe, 1842), p. 366.
22.   *SAM,* I (1847), p. 103.
23.   *RGM,* December 31, 1843, pp. 440-41.
24.   Chownitz, pp. 1-14, 19, 62-77, 152-54.
25.   *PI*, July 5, 1835, p. 138.
26.   *Erinnerungen aus dessen Leben und Wirken* (Vienna, 1866),
      pp. 239-40.
27.   *RGM,* November 2, 1845, pp. 361-62.

28. *RM,* VII (1833), p. 7; *GM,* June 12 1836, p. 202; *MT,*
March 24, 1844, p. 24; *MP,* May 19, 1827, p. 3, *HJ,* 1839,
Vol. I, No. 5, p. 8; *LT,* July 8, 1845, p. 5.
29. *PI,* January 30, 1835, p. 48.
30. *RGM,* December 31, 1843, pp. 440-41.
31. *Caprice,* February 28, 1846, p. 41.
32. *HJ,* 1840, Vol. I, No. 2, p. 26. For a vivid description of Liszt
in Paris, see Heinrich Heine, *Lutèce* (Paris, 1872), April 22,
1844, p. 396.
33. *Souvenirs et portraits,* ed. Pierre de Sacretelle (Paris, 1956),
pp. 183-84.
34. *GR,* 1845, Vol. IV, pp. 269-70. See also Koch, p. 367.
35. Société Académique des Enfants d'Apollon, *Discours et tableaux
des membres,* 1847, p. 9, Bibliothèque Nationale.
36. *SP,* November 21, 1829, p. 313; May 26, 1838, p. 491; *MW,*
May 1, 1845, p. 208; *DMR,* May 30, 1846, p. 255.
37. Heine, April 20, 1841, p. 189.
38. *AMZV,* May 23, 1845, p. 240; *RGM,* March 8, 1846, p. 76;
MW, June 7, 1845, pp. 293-94.
39. *DMR,* August 16, 1845, p. 423, July 26, 1845, p. 383, August 2,
1845, p. 397; *MW,* January 2, 1842, p. 9.
40. *Mes Souvenirs, 1806-1833* (Paris, 1877), pp. 303-04.
41. *QMM,* VI (1824), pp. 224-32. See also VII (1825), pp. 209-10, 299.
42. *Ibid.,* IX (1828), pp. 90-94.
43. Daumard, p. 29; Ludwig Rellstab, *Aus meinem Leben* (Berlin, 1861),
II, pp. 275-78.
44. Balabine, p. 119.
45. *RGM,* March 27, 1842, p. 126. See also: *Ibid.,* April 17,
1842, p. 168, and Pierre-Sebastien Laurentie, *Souvenirs,* ed.
J. Laurentie (Paris, n.d.), pp. 135-37.
46. *WMZ,* January 21, 1823, pp. 51-52.
47. *TZ,* December 1, 1836, p. 991, November 22, 1839, p. 935.
48. *AMA,* May 10, 1838, p. 76; *HU,* April 21. 1838, p. 253;
TZ, May 1, 1838, p. 383, March 14, 1846, p. 251; Bauernfeld,
Ein Buch, p. 192.
49. *WMZ,* November 10, 1841, p. 544; Ferdinand Ritter von Seyfried,
Rückschau in das Theaterleben Wiens (Vienna, 1864), pp. 284-87;
Hügel and Grosshoffinger, I, p. 21.
50. *TZ,* October 25, 1845, p. 1026. See also: *Ibid.,* November
24, 1845, p. 1131, December 10, 1845, p. 1186, March 19, 1846, p. 268;
HJ, May 1839, pp. 5-6.
51. Francis Wey, "L'Ami des artistes", *Français,* I, pp. 233-45.
52. *Musée Danton* (Paris, 1838), p. 116.
53. *MW,* August 19, 1836, p. 149.
54. *MW,* May 12, 1839, p. 139, March 21, 1845, p. 136, May 13, 1836,
p. 142, July 11, 1842, p. 321; C. G. Carus, *The King of Saxony's
Journey through England and Scotland* (London, 1846), p. 93;
James Grant, *The Great Metropolis* (London, 1838), I,
p. 30; Eduard Hanslick, *Aus Meinem Leben* (Berlin, 1894), I, p. 119;
ZU, April 1, 1846, p. 415; *TZ,* February 27, 1846, p. 92.
55. *FM,* March 8, 1846, p. 77.
56. *Ibid.,* March 15, 1840, p. 116. See also de Launay, II, p. 93.
57. *Iris,* July 8, 1831, p. 108. The same thing happened to Thalberg

once in Vienna (*MW*, March 28, 1846, p. 144).

58. *Ibid.*, June 7, 1845, pp. 293-94. See also: *GE*, February
    22, 1846, p. 222; *Observations*, pp. 11-12; *PI*, September
    20, 1835, p. 176.
59. Miscellaneous Papers of Hector Berlioz, 14, Bibliothèque Nationale.
60. Alfred Shaw to Joseph Fischhof, April 24, 1839, Fischhof Nachlass,
    Vienna City Library. See also Theodore Lürtz to Fischhof, n.d.
    and Karl Holz to Fischhof, April 1835.
61. *MW*, June 7, 1845, pp. 293-94; *RGM*, April 16, 1844, p. 132.
62. *FM*, January 17, 1839, p. 33.
63. Lord William Lennox, *Story of My Life* (London, 1857), II, pp. 154-55.
64. *HN*, June 7, 1845, pp. 293-94.
65. *TZ*, November 8, 1845, p. 1075; *GE*, February 26, 1846,
    p. 222; *PI*, September 20, 1835, p. 176; *FI*, April 17,
    1827, p. 359.
66. *GR*, 1845, Vol. IV, p. 430.
67. *AMA*, May 10, 1838.
68. Koch, p. 370; [Gottfried Wilhelm Becker], *Meine grosse Reise von
    Leipzig nach Oesterreich* (Leipzig, 1835), II, pp. 55-58.
69. Mathilde Feldern-Rolf, "Ein Frühlingstag einer eleganten Wiener
    Dame", *Lebensbilder aus Oesterreich*, ed. Andreas Schumacher
    (Vienna, 1843), p. 147.
70. Hanslick, *Aus meinem Leben*, I, p. 83.
71. March 24, 1845, p. 1.
72. Moscheles, I, pp. 179, 224; II, p. 80.
73. *SP*, April 27, 1838, p. 389; C. L. Gruneison, *The Opera and
    the Press* (London, 1869), p. 4; Lord Lamington, *In the Days of
    the Dandies* (London, 1890), pp. 19-20; Spencer, *Almack's.*
74. Moscheles, II, pp. 20-31.
75. *RGM*, August 11, 1839, p. 297 (article by Hector Berlioz), July 4,
    1843, p. 218; *HN*, November 1829, p. 297 (article by F. J. Fétis).
76. *RGM*, July 12, 1846, p. 221.
77. *HN*, November 1830, p. 479.
78. *Ibid.*, May 1833, p. 110.
79. Lemercher de Longpré, Baron d'Haussez, *Grande-Bretagne en 1833*
    (Brusselles, 1838), pp. 93-94.
80. Count Edouard de Melfort, *Impressions of England* (London, 1836),
    pp. 66-68. See also: John Timbs, *Clubs and Club Life in London*
    (London, 1872), p. 214; Gronow, pp. 33-34; Murray, I, 44-45.
81. Alice Mangold Diehl, *Musical Sketches* (London, 1878), p. 40.
82. *FM*, January 17, 1839, p. 33.
83. Amedée Pommier, *Colères* (Paris, 1844), p. 31.
84. *FM*, February 14, 1839, p. 95; *RM*, February 14, 1839, p. 56;
    EN, January 6, 1835, p. 1.
85. *RGM*, November 2, 1845, pp. 361-62; Vicomte de Beaumont-Vassy,
    Les Salons de Paris sous Louis-Philippe (Paris, 1866), p. 127.
    The salons of the Comtesse de Merlin and the Comtesse de Belgioso had
    comparable standing; see *Ibid.*, p. 127, and Gay, p. 226.
86. de Launay, II, p. 65 (January 17, 1840).
87. d'Agoult, p. 344; Lina Ramann, *Franz Liszt* (Leipzig, 1880),
    I, p. 315.
88. Balabine, p. 88; *Cécile*, February 10, 1845, p. 1; Charles Bocher,
    Mémoires (Paris, n.d.), I, 368.

89. *Souvenirs*, p. 181. See also his *Ethel* (Paris, 1839),
     I, pp. 308-09.
90. *FM*, May 6, 1838, p. 7.
91. *RGT*, April 13, 1837, p. 2; *FM*, February 7, 1841, p. 43;
     CT, January 8, 1839, p. 2.
92. See Hanslick's *Wiener Concertwesen*, I, pp. 349-52, 422-24 for a
     detailed enumeration of use of instruments.
93. *Dwight's Journal of Music*, XIX (1866), p. 112 (reprinted from
     Viennese magazine *Recensionen*). See also Hanslick, I, pp. 426-27.
94. Scott, pp. 42, 51-59; William Thackeray, *Miscellanies* (London,
     1856, pp. 354-55; Raymond Mander, *British Music Hall* (London,
     1965), pp. 9-12; Marc-Constantin, *Histoires des cafés de Paris*
     (Paris, 1857); André Ibels, "Deux siècles de Caf'-Conc' ", *Touche
     à Tort*, July 1892, pp. 47-51; Adelbert von Bornstedt, *Pariser
     Silhouetten* (Leipzig, 1836), p. 60.
95. *Paris actuel* (Paris, 1842), p. 75.
96. *RGM*, January 11, 1846, p. 12.
97. *TZ*, October 25, 1845, p. 1026 (Heinrich Adami). See also *MW*,
     November 6, 1845, p. 535; *Musical Herald*, August 1, 1846, p. 31;
     MP, February 4, 1845, p. 6; *Charivari*, May 3, 1846, p. 4;
     FM, November 1, 1840, p. 389; *HJ*, 1842, Vol. 5, p. 14;
     DO, I, 31-32; *ZU*, May 27, 1846, pp. 669-71.
98. *TZ*, May 8, 1828, p. 223.
99. *MEN*, April 3, 1836, p. 4.

Chapter IV

1. Introduction

1. *MR*, June 24, 1845, pp. 53-54.
2. *The Classical Style* (New York, 1971), pp. 379-80.
3. *MR*, March 28, 1848, pp. 1-2. The magazine was program notes for
    the concerts and included a membership list at the start of each season.
4. Brochure, "La Société des Concerts de Musique Vocale", Bibliothèque
    Nationale.
5. *Subscribers to the Philharmonic Concerts*, 1813-1848. Papers of
    the Philharmonic Society and the Papers of Sir George Smart, British
    Museum.
6. *La Presse*, April 25, 1837, pp. 3-4 (article of Sophie Gay);
    RM, May 19, 1832, p. 125.
7. Concerts of Ancient Music, Concert Programs, 1810-1848, British
    Museum (membership lists in the first program of each season). Directories
    used included: *Boyle's Fashionable Court and Country Guide*, 1830,
    1848; *Clayton's Court Guide*, 1830; *Post Office London
    Directory*, 1830, 1848; *Robson's British Court and Parliamentary
    Guide*, 1832; *Royal Blue Book or Fashionable Directory*, 1829;
    Dictionary of National Biography. Identification of occupation for
    members of all London societies was made only under the following
    conditions. Persons were counted only if a) a professional title was

included in their citation or b) at least one forename or two initials were cited both on the list and in a directory. If the name were a common one (i.e., Smith, Thompson) at least a forename and an initial were required. The citation of married women with the forenames of their husbands permitted their inclusion; the listing of unmarried women immediately following a parent did so as well.

8. *MR*, March 28, 1848, pp. 1-2.
9. *Subscribers*, 1830, 1848. Circumstances prevented inclusion of women in the 1830 tabulation; their distribution occupationally in 1848, however, showed no differences from that of the men.
10. *Verzeichnisse der Mitglieder der Gesellschaft der Musikfreunde*, 1813-1848, Archive of the Society (hereafter to be designated as GMF). The lists cited occupations with remarkably precise terminology; those not identified were primarily titled persons. Likewise, the list of the subscribers to the magazine *Wiener Zuschauer* in 1846 (Vol. III, i-xxxi) included among the 301 identified (out of 350 total) twenty-nine per cent from the bureaucracy, twenty-three per cent from the liberal professions, and thirty per cent from the economic professions.
11. See Chapter IV, Section 4, note 8.
12. Planque, *Agenda musical* (Paris, 1837), III, pp. 218-19; *Annuaire musical* (Paris, 1845), pp. 313-24. Directories used included: *Almanach-Bottin du commerce de Paris*, 1845; *Almanach général parisien*, 1837; *Almanach des 25,000 principaux habitants de Paris*, 1845; *Les premières addresses de Paris*, 1845. Citation of addresses in the musical directories ensured the accuracy of identification. French provincial Academies of the eighteenth century had a similar over-representation of men from the liberal professions; see Roche, pp. 93-185.
13. *Premières addresse*.
14. Daumard, p. 138.
15. *FM*, March 8, 1846, p. 77.
16. *Souvenirs d'un journaliste* (Paris, 1859), pp. 127, 144 (entry of June 27, 1835).
17. "The Middle Class in Western History", *passim*.
18. For further discussion of the tastes of occupational groups see Gronow, I, pp. 132-4; *Satirist*, July 13, 1834, p. 122; "l'Avoué", *Français*, I, pp. 157-58; *Paris im Jahre 1836* (Stuttgart, 1836), p. 43; Honoré de Balzac, *Physiologie de l'employé* (Paris, 1841), pp. 84-86 and *passim;* "La Bureaucracie", *Tableau de Paris* (Paris, 1842), VII, p. 307; *TZ*, January 1, 1831, p. 1; Leitich, p. 106.
19. *WMZ*, November 10, 1846, p. 544.
20. *RM*, December 28, 1833, p. 403.
21. *HN*, September 1829, pp. 219-20; *RGM*, June 21, 1846, pp. 196-97; *Der Adler*, March 19, 1842, p. 283.
22. *FM*, January 29, 1839, p. 50.
23. Chownitz, pp. 152-53.
24. *Ibid.*, p. 154.
25. *MW*, August 8, 1837, p. 145.
26. *Monthly Musical and Literary Magazine*, 1830, p. 87; *SB*, March 27, 1842, pp. 223-26.
27. April 14, 1846, p. 354.

28. *Vienna*, I, 372.
29. Daumard, pp. 378-87.

2. **London**

1. *HN,* April 1830, p. 171.
2. de Longpré, I, pp. 197-200; John Ravell, "John Ella, 1802-1888", *Music and letters*, XXXIV (1953), pp. 99-100.
3. See Chapter IV, Section 1, Note 7.
4. Cox, II, p. 44.
5. Concert Programs, British Museum.
6. *HN,* June 1833, p. 136.
7. Spring, *passim.*
8. Moscheles, II, pp. 22-23.
9. *GM,* March 27, 1837, pp. 106-07. The Directors also frowned upon the performance of the far-too-witty music of Franz Josef Haydn (*SP,* June 28, 1834, p. 612).
10. *MP,* May 4, 1827, p. 3. For criticism of the concerts, see *HN,* April 1829, p. 90; *MW,* March 18, 1836, p. 6.
11. *DMR,* August 26, 1843, p. 412. See also *CO,* August 1846, p. 162.
12. *SP,* January 14, 1837, p. 33.
13. *Subscribers to the Philharmonic Concerts, 1813-1848.*
14. *Ibid.;* see Chapter IV, Section 1, Note 7.
15. *MW,* November 14, 1839, pp. 448-49.
16. Concert Programs, 1848.
17. Quoted in A. W. Ganz, *Berlioz in London* (London, 1950), pp. 50-51.
18. *HN,* April 1830, pp. 156, 171; *MM,* March 1835, p. 38; *MW,* March 25, 1836, p. 126, February 27, 1840, pp. 121-22; *ME,* February 25, 1843, pp. 117-18.
19. For example, see Minutes of Directors' meetings, May 22, 1831, March 11, 1832, March 17, 1833. In 1835 the Society grudgingly allowed occasional transfer between members of a family of the same sex but sharply restricted the practice (see Brochure, December 1, 1836, Miscellaneous Official Papers).
20. Minutes of Directors' Meetings, August 15, 1841; *LT,* February 21, 1843, p. 1, February 18, 1844, p. 1.
21. Account Book, Miscellaneous Papers.
22. *Ibid.*
23. *MR,* March 28, 1848, pp. 1-2.
24. *Ibid.* Four members of the lower nobility, however, had the very lowest title (given to younger sons) of "Honorable".
25. Royal Society of Musicians, Program, 1834, p. 5, London Museum.
26. *MR,* March 31, 1846, p. 31. The rule was stated on each program.
27. Diehl, pp. 113-17. The committee members and the audience included the most accomplished serious amateur performers in the city's elites. See *MP,* March 12, 1845, p. 5, May 14, 1845, p. 5; *MR* March 11, 1845, p. 5.
28. Ella, p. 91. Though autobiographies are generally not to be trusted for self-serving comments such as this one, the structure of the concerts bears him out.
29. *DMR,* December 13, 1846, p. 636.
30. *MM,* November 1835, p. 169; *MW,* January 20, 1836, p. 79, February 16, 1838, p. 105. Ella also held private chamber-music

concerts in his home during the decade.

31. "The Intellectual Aristocracy", *Studies in Social History,* ed.
J. H. Plumb (London, 1955), pp. 241-87.
32. William Kuhe, *My Musical Recollections* (London, 1896), p. 76.
33. *MW,* June 5, 1845, p. 265, June 26, 1845, p. 301.
34. Moscheles, II, pp. 19-20; 38, 100; Annan, p. 258, A number of prominent
people from this same milieu attended the Concerts of Ancient Music
and the Philharmonic Concerts.
35. *MW,* June 12, 1845, p. 280; *SP,* July 8, 1848, p. 656,
April 24, 1852, p. 39; E. L. Blanchard, *Life and Reminiscences,*
eds. Clement Scott and Cecil Howard (London, 1891), I, p. 51, n. 1.

3. Paris

1. *RM,* January 1827, p. 37. Another sign of the readiness for a new
classical style was the large and highly prestigious audiences which
the choral conductor Alexander Choron drew to several concerts of
sixteenth-century music in 1827. See *Erinnerungen aus Paris,
1817-1848* (Berlin, 1851), pp. 171-72.
2. A. Elwart, *Histoire de la Société des Concerts du Convervatoire*
(Paris, 1860), pp. 61-79.
3. *NZM,* July 5, 1836, p. 6.
4. *RGM,* January 22, 1837, p. 30.
5. *Paris in 1843,* I, 92-93. The cost of seats was the leading
example of underpriced classical-music tickets, for the rates went
from 2 fr. (in the lower price bracket) to 9 fr. (in the middle bracket).
See Elwart, pp. 115-17.
6. *Ibid.,* p. 114. For other evidence of the status of the public
see *RGM,* January 8, 1843, p. 15, January 18, 1846, p. 19;
GM, January 3, 1836, p. 5, January 22, 1837, p. 30; Charles de
Boigne, *Petits mémoires de l'opéra* (Paris, 1857), p. 297.
7. A. Dandelot, *La Société des Concerts du Conservatoire* (Paris,
1897), p. 14; M. Murland, "A. F. Habeneck", *Allgemeine
Musikzeitung* (Berlin), XXVII (1910), p. 1177. The latter claims that she
called the events "my concerts".
8. Balabine, p. 297; Rellstab, II, pp. 275-78; Ernest Legouvé, *Soixante ans
de souvenirs* (Paris, 1887), II, p. 120; Anton Schindler, *Tagebuch
aus den Jahren 1841-1843* (Frankfurt, 1939), pp. 55-56, 61-62;
FM, March 31, 1839, p. 207; Beaumont-Vassy, pp. 127-30.
9. Charles Dancla, *Notes et souvenirs* (Paris, 1893), p. 38; Schindler,
Beethoven in Paris (Vienna, 1841), pp. 78-79.
10. Joseph d'Ortigue, *Du Théâtre-Italien* (Paris, 1840), pp. 343-44.
Liszt said the same thing; see *RM,* August 30, 1835, p. 288.
11. Eugene Delacrois, *Journal* (Paris, 1895), I, p. 294; Antoine
Fontaney, *Journal intime,* ed. Rene Jasinski (Paris, 1925) pp. 163-64;
Léon Guichard, *La Musique et les lettres au temps du romantisme*
(Paris, 1955), pp. 106-07.
12. *Europe Littéraire,* May 13, 1833, p. 130.
13. *NZM,* July 5, 1836, p. 7.
14. *GM,* April 30, 1837, p. 152.
15. *RGM,* January 22, 1837, p. 30. Rellstab hinted at this as well
(III, p. 33).

16. *Annuaire*, p. 25.
17. M. Lassabathie, *Histoire du Conservatoire* (Paris, 1860), p. 64.
18. Balabine, p. 183 (January 12, 1845).
19. Leo Schrade, *Beethoven in France* (New Haven, 1942), *passim.*
20. *RGM*, August 16, 1846, p. 258.
21. Joseph d'Ortigue, *Palin-génésie* (Paris, 1833), pp. 18, 20; *RM*, January 28, 1831, p. 409.
22. Schindler, *Tagebuch*, p. 60. For further discussion of these events, see: Dancla, pp. 38, 45-47; Paul Landormy, "La Musique du chambre en France de 1850 à 1871", *Sammelbände der Internationalen Musik-Gesellschaft*, XIV (1911-1912), pp. 39, 46; *FM*, November 11, 1838, p. 1; *RGM*, September 25, 1843, p. 306, March 5, 1837, p. 81; Henry Chorley, *Thirty Years' Recollections* (London, 1862), III, 71n.
23. Brochure, p. 6.
24. *Ibid.*, p. 6. For further discussion of these events, see *RGM*, November 2, 1845, p. 362; *FM*, March 8, 1846, p. 75; Rellstab, II, pp. 275-78; *Annuaire*, pp. 34-38; *Revue des Deux Mondes*, XIV (1846), p. 150.

4. Vienna

1. *Vienna*, I, p. 372. See also II, pp. 379-80.
2. Schumann to Zuccalmaglio, October 19, 1837, II, p. 122.
3. *Vienna*, I, p. 372. For further discussion of the taste situation, see Sealsfield, p. 203; Müller, I, pp. 131-35, 143; Moritz Hartmann, *Briefe aus dem Vormärz*, ed. Otto Wittner (Prague, 1910), I. p. 47, 172-73; Koch, p. 374.
4. Leopold von Sonnleithner, "Musikalische Skizzen aus Alt-Wien", *Recensionen und Mittheilungen über Theater und Musik*, VII (1861), p. 838.
5. *GR*, 1845, Vol. 1, pp. 436-37; *AMZV*, April 18, 1818, pp. 136-37, May 2, 1818, p. 153.
6. Moscheles, I, p. 60; Gustave Schilling, *Das Musikalische Europa* (Speyer, 1842), p. 155; C. F. Pohl, "Zur Geschichte der Gründung und Entwicklung der Gesellschaft der Musikfreunde in Wien", *Jahres-Bericht des Conservatoriums der Gesellschaft der Musikfreunde* (Vienna, 1869), p. 4.
7. GMF, *Monatbericht*, January 1830, pp. 2, 15.
8. *Ibid.*, November 1829, p. 113, January 1830. pp. 2, 15; Schilling, pp. 151-358; Prokesch von Osten, *Tagebücher* (Vienna, 1909), p. 53; Ignaz Castelli, *Memoiren meines Lebens* (Munich, 1914), I, pp. 92-93, II, p. 242; Auguste Schmidt, *Denksteine* (Vienna, 1848), pp. 55, 207-10; Carl Löwe, *Selbstbiographie* (Berlin, 1870), p. 341; Hertha Ibl, *Studien zu Johann Vesque von Puttlingens Leben und Opernschaffen*, Dissertation, University of Vienna, 1949; Franz Gräffer, *Zur Stadt Wien* (Vienna, 1849), pp. 136-38; *Mittheilungen aus Wien*, I (1835), pp. 196-98; Franz Bockh, *Wiens Lebende Schriftsteller, Künstler, und Dilettanten im Kunstfache* (Vienna, 1822), pp. 364-83; *HJ*, 1842, Vol. II, pp. 22-26; Pohl, p. 4; Richard von Perger, *Geschichte der K.K. Gesellschaft der Musikfreunde in Wien* (Vienna, 1912); I, 49-59; Anton Ziegler, *Addressen-Buch von Tonkünstlern und Dilettanten in Wien* (Vienna,

1823), *passim;* Constant von Wurzbach, *Biographisches Lexicon des Kaisertum Oesterreichs* (Vienna, 1856-1890), 26 vols.

9. *Monatbericht,* January 1830, pp. 2. 2, 15; Schmidt, p. 61.

10. Pohl, p. 4.

11. Perger, I, pp. 12-22. Hanslick, *Geschichte,* I, pp. 185-88.

12. *Mitglieder Verzeichnisse,* 1847.

13. February 25, 1846, p. 440.

14. Chownitz, pp. 151-52. "Man muss ja! Es gehört *quasi* zum 'Ton'." The idiom "gehören zum Ton" was used conventionally to indicate a prestigious audience. On the status of the public see also *TZ,* February 28, 1846, p. 203, March 5, 1838, p. 195; *SB,* March 27, 1842, p. 224.

15. Sonnleithner, pp. 753-7; Prokesch-Osten, p. 22; Herbert Kleinlercher, *Josef Fischof, Leben und Werk,* Dissertation, University of Vienna, 1948, pp. 16-21. This series and the various choral concerts in Paris discussed before show the persistence of interest in Renaissance and Baroque music during the nineteenth century.

16. *WMZ,* April 1, 1845, p. 154; *TZ,* March 27, 1846, p. 295; Program Brochure, "Die Soiréen von Carl Haslinger, 1844", Archive of GMF. Another host was Baron Pasqualati, Professor of Analytical Chemistry at the Polytechnic Institute; see *TZ,* July 31, 1846, p. 728; Löwe, p. 356.

17. Schumann to Clara Wieck, October 8, 1838, II, p. 291. See also Schumann to family, October 13, 1838, II, p. 119. Many of the older members of the leadership group lived in their memories of friendship with Beethoven. A young classical-music fan wrote in the middle of the 1840s that the scene was burdened by the "monopolists" of Beethoven's music (the eminent piano teacher Carl Czerny particularly) who did not have the musical technique or imagination to perform it adequately. See *GE,* March 27, 1847, p. 331.

18. *Vesque von Puttlingen,* ed. J. Hoven (Vienna, 1871), pp. 42-43.

19. *WZ,* May 15, 1838, pp. 426-27. See also: *GE,* March 17, 1847, pp. 287-88; *SB,* December 11, 1842, p. 894; *AMA,* November 22, 1838, p. 188; *TZ,* December 5, 1833, p. 780.

20. *AMA,* February 7, 1839. Signed by "F.G.", the article was most likely written by the writer and civil servant Franz Grillparzer.

21. *TZ,* January 31, 1833, p. 90, January 7, 1833, p. 20; January 14, 1833, p. 38, January 15, 1833, p. 42, May 17, 1834, pp. 591, 593-94; Auguste Schmidt, "Selbstbiographie", *Wiener Männergesangverein,* ed. Rudolf Hofmann (Vienna, 1893), p. xiii; Heinrich Kralik, *Das Grosse Orchester* (Vienna, 1952), p. 15.

22. *Statistik der Oesterreichischen Kaisertum,* 1847, Table 31. The breadth of bureaucratic employees in the census is stated in Jäck and Heller, *Wien und dessen Umgebungen* (Weimar, 1822), p. 296, n. 2.

23. *TZ,* January 1, 1831, pp. 1-2.

24. *GR,* 1847, Vol. I, p. 285.

25. A. J. Gross-Hoffinger, *Wien wie es ist* (Leipzig, 1847), IV, pp. 36-37. "Wo ist die gute Zeit/ Wo uns Allmächtigkeit/ Den Lebensweg gebant?/ Wo's Amt gab den Verstand—/ Kein Mensch darnach gefragt,/ Wenn wir das Volk geplagt?"

26. Some used musical life for upward social mobility. The civil servant, singer, and composer Vesque von Puttlingen, for example, went up the bureaucratic ladder with the help of his musical abilities, ending up

as an assistant to Prince Metternich. See Ibl, pp. 12-13, 28, 68. Kiesewetter, on the other hand, lent his early successes in the civil service a wider prestige through musical activities. See Sonnleithner, pp. 753-77 and Moscheles, I, pp. 55, 60, 74-75.

27. Victor Andrian-Warburg, *Oesterreich und dessen Zukunft* (Hamburg, 1843), I, pp. 63-65; Adolph Carl Naske, *Wiener Kanzlei-Zustande aus den Memoiren eines oesterreichischen Staatsbeamten* (Leipzig, 1846), pp. 66-67, 106-12; Franz Grillparzer, *Selbstbiographie* (Vienna, 1872), p. 218; Adolf Glassbrenner, *Bilber und Traüme aus Wien* (Leipzig, 1836), I, p. 80.

28. *Die Kaiserstadt, Licht- und Schattenseiten* (Vienna, 1847), I, p. 215; II, p. 318.

29. Hanslick, *Aus meinem Leben*, I, pp. 100-01, 113-14; Julius Chownitz, "Wiener Genrebilder", *Oesterreichische Daguerreotypen* (Leipzig, 1841), pp. 55-69.

30. Hanslick, *Aus meinem Leben*, I, 108-14; Frankl, p. 266-79; Castelli, II, pp. 13-16, 54; Schmidt, pp. xiii-xv; Bauernfeld, *Ein Buch*, p. 317.

31. Hanslick, *Aus meinem Leben*, I, p. 108; Koch, p. 395; *GR*, 1845, Vol. 1, p. 138.

32. *SB*, March 27, 1842, pp. 223-26. A large number of its leading members died during the 1830s; see Perger, I, 47. See also *TZ*, February 8, 1845, p. 66.

33. *Wiener Zeitschrift*, March 9, 1846, p. 195.

34. For discussion of its management, see Schmidt, "Selbstbiographie", pp. xi-xii; *Musikalische Reise-Momente* (Hamburg, 1846), pp. 305-07.

35. C. F. Pohl, *Festschrift aus Anlass der Feier des 25-jährigen ununtergebrochenen Bestandes der im Jahre 1842 gegründeten Philharmonische Concerte in Wien* (Vienna, 1885), pp. 1-9; *Vesque von Puttlingen*, pp. 87-88.

36. Christl Schönfeldt, *Die Wiener Philharmoniker* (Vienna, 1956), p. 7; Pohl *Festschrift*, p. 9.

37. Joseph Sulzer, *Ernstes und Heiteres aus den Erinnerungen eines Wiener Philharmonikers* (Vienna, 1910), pp. 70-72.

38. Schonfeldt, p. 43.

39. January 7, 1846, p. 45. "Mit Freudigen Gefühlen konnen wir daher die Ansicht aussprechen, dass es zum guten Tone gegenwärtig zu gehören scheint, die Philharmonischen Concerten zu besuchen."

40. *GR*, 1845, Vol. 1, p. 523.

41. Schönfeldt, pp. 8-9

42. *WZ*, April 1, 1846, p. 735.

43. Schönfeldt, p. 35.

44. *WZ*, April 1, 1846, p. 735.

45. *TZ*, November 2, 1845, p. 1052.

Chapter V

1. Introduction

1. Paul de Kock, "Les concerts d'amateurs", *Nouveau Tableau de Paris*

(Paris, 1835), VII, p. 178; *HJ*, 1837, Vol. II, No. 1, p. 47; *DI*,
November 10, 1833, p. 1.

2. Daumard, pp. 60-67; J. A. Banks, *Prosperity and Parenthood* (London, 1957), pp. 85, 101, 111-12.
3. *Aus meinem Leben* (Berlin, 1894), I, p. 95, 97.
4. Daumard, pp. 249-57.
5. *ME*, December 21, 1844, pp. 89-90; *FM*, January 14, 1838, pp. 7-8.
6. Daumard, pp. 637-38, 645-46.
7. The main sources for low-status concerts are: *DMR, EN, FM, HJ, ME, MEN, MT* and *RGT*.
8. Paul Meuriot, *Des agglomérations urbaines dans l'Europe contemporaine* (Paris, 1897), pp. 253-54, 273. London covered almost ten times as large an area as Paris, 31,000 as opposed to 3,437 hectares); because of the peculiarities of municipal boundaries, Vienna was larger in size than Paris (5,534 hectares). See also D. A. Reeder, "A Theater of suburbs: Some Patterns of Development in West London, 1801-1911", *The Study of Urban History*, ed. H. J. Dyos (New York, 1968), pp. 253-71; Francis Sheppard, *London*, pp. 83-117.

2. Orchestral and Chamber-Music Concerts

1. Elkin, pp. 13-29, and *passim;* Brenet, pp. 159-62, 228-31; Hanslick, *Geschichte*, I, pp. 56-77.
2. M. Lassabathie, *Histoire du Conservatoire* (Paris, 1860), p. 64; *CT*, April 29, 1827, p. 3; *GM*, March 10, 1839, p. 151.
3. *RM*, May 19, 1832, p. 123-24, May 20, 1832, p. 5; *GM*, June 4, 1837, p. 193; *Dilettante*, November 5, 1833, pp. 4-5, January 8, 1834, p. 2; Planque, *Agenda musical* (Paris, 3 Vols., 1836-1837), II, pp. 72-74.
4. Planque, I, pp. 181-89; *Almanach-Bottin du Commerce de Paris* (Paris, 1845); *Almanach général parisien* (Paris, 1837); *l'Almanach des 25,000 addresses des principaux habitants de Paris (Paris, 1845).*
5. *MEN*, February 8, 1846, p. 3.
6. *Annuaire musical* (Paris, 1845), pp. 44-45, 102-08.
7. Planque, I, pp. 39-43; *Annuaire*, pp. 44-45, 102-08; directories cited in footnote 4. Citation of the addresses of all members ensured the accuracy of the tabulation.
8. *RGM*, February 1, 1846, p. 44.
9. *Annuaire*, pp. 61-94.
10. *RMR*, I (1845), pp. 281-84; *Paris im Jahre 1836* (Stuttgart, 1836), p. 138; Augustin Challamel, *Souvenirs* (Paris, 1885), pp. 318-19.
11. Cler, p. 74; E. Destouches, *Physiologie des barrières et des musiciens de Paris* (Paris, 1842), p. 83.
12. *l'Almanach des 25,000 addresses;* Planque, I, pp. 181-89; *Annuaire*, pp. 44-45, 102-08.
13. *Annuaire*, pp. 313-36; Planque, III, pp. 218-29.
14. *HN*, April 1830, p. 175; May 1830, p. 217, June 1830, pp. 264-65.
15. *ME*, February 4, 1843, p. 97; *MM*, March 1835, pp. 41-43; *HN*, April 1830, p. 175; *SP*, March 14, 1835, p. 257.
16. *Ibid.*, May 27, 1835, p. 489.
17. *ME*, February 4, 1843, p. 97; January 28, 1843, p. 86; *GM*, June 4, 1837, p. 193; *RM*, July 28, 1832, p. 208, May 19, 1832,

p. 123; *DI*, November 5, 1833, p. 4-5, December 15, 1833, pp. 3-4.

18. *MW*, November 20, 1845, p. 560; *DMR*, September 27, 1845, p. 493, October 4, 1845, p. 504.

19. The most informative periodicals for these concerts are *ME*, *MW*, and *DMR*. See especially *DMR*, March 2, 1844, p. 109, January 11, 1845, p. 21, July 19, 1845, p. 373; *MW*, January 2, 1847, pp. 4-5, November 5, 1840, p. 298; *ME*, January 28, 1842, p. 87.

20. *DMR*, January 13, 1844, p. 19, January 17, 1846, pp. 25-27, June 13, 1846, p. 281, November 22, 1845, p. 595; *MW*, January 6, 1842, p. 4, February 2, 1838, p. 73.

21. Richard Altick, *English Common Reader* (Chicago, 1957), pp. 188-94; James W. Hudson, *History of Adult Education* (London, 1851), pp. 49-52, 169-73, 212-13. While Altick has rightly warned against exaggerating the working-class base of the institutes, Hudson does show that a substantial minority of artisans did remain in the societies.

22. *DMR*, January 17, 1846, pp. 25-27, June 13, 1846, p. 281.

23. *DMR*, September 27, 1845, p. 493.

24. *HJ*, 1842, Vol. I, no. 1, pp. 27-31; *AMA*, February 7, 1846, p. 39; Richard Perger, *Geschihte der k.k. Gesellschaft der Musikfreunde in Wien* (Vienna, 1912), I, p. 64.

25. *TZ*, February 7, 1828, p. 12; *GE*, February 26, 1846, p. 223.

26. For interesting social sketches of informal lower-middle class gatherings see August Schilling, *Satyrisch-komische Wiener Skizzen* (Vienna, 1841), pp. 1-3, and *HJ*, 1837, Vol. II, No. 1, p. 47.

27. Charles Sealsfield, *Austria As It Is* (London, 1828), p. 202.

28. *Parlour Review* (London), February 17, 1838, p. 4.

29. *HJ*, 1840, Vol. III, No. 1, p. 60.

30. *SP*, January 4, 1834, p. 13.

31. *Ibid.*, June 23, 1832, p. 588.

32. *QMM*, Vol. VI (1822), p. 166.

33. Society of British Musicians: *MM*, February 1835, pp. 19-21, March 1835, p. 432, November 1835, p. 169; *MW*, April 30, 1840, pp. 265-66, June 11, 1840, p. 364; *RM*, May 17, 1835, p. 167. Vocal Society: *HN*, February 1833, p. 35, March 1833, p. 83.

34. *SP*, February 24, 1838, p. 179, February 10, 1844, p. 138; *AT*, April 23, 1836, p. 291, November 9, 1844, p. 1028; *MW*, November 3, 1842, p. 349, February 22, 1844, p. 57; John Fisher Murray, *World of London* (London, 1843), II, pp. 152, 154. John Ravell states incorrectly that the chamber-music concerts did not last more than a season, in "John Ella", *Music and Letters*, XXXIV (1953), p. 101.

35. *SP*, April 30, 1836, p. 353.

36. *MW*, November 3, 1842, p. 349.

37. *MW*, January 2, 1840, p. 5.

38. *MEN*, September 13, 1845, p. 1.

39. *NZM*, April 14, 1835, p. 1. For other such comments see *FM*, April 15, 1838, p. 7; *RGT*, April 19, 1838, p. 55; *NZM*, July 5, 1836, p. 6; and *RGM*, January 22, 1837, p. 30.

40. *MEN*, August 9, 1835, p. 4, September 13, 1835, p. 1, October 4, 1835, p. 4, October 23, 1835, p. 4, December 20, 1835, p. 1; *PI*, December 5, 1835, p. 23, December 20, 1835, p. 4; *GM*, May 31, 1835, p. 184; Armand Pinguet to Minister of the Interior, April 2, 1837, Archives Nationales F21 1038.

41. *PI*, December 5, 1834, p. 23; Planque, I, pp. 55-56; *EN*, January 31,

1840, p. 3; *FM*, January 14, 1838, pp. 7-8; Anton Schindler,
Beethoven in Paris (Vienna, 1841), pp. 57, 60; Schindler, *Tagebuch
aus den Jahren 1841-1843* (Frankfurt, 1939), pp. 47, 122.
42. Robert Hirschfeld, "Konzerte in Wien", *Zeitschrift der Internationalen
Musik-Gesellschaft*, I, (May, 1900), p. 230; Hanslick, *Geschichte*, II
pp. 409-10.
43. Francis Hueffer, *Half A Century of Music in England, 1837-1887*
(London, 1889); E. D. Mackerness, *A Social History of English Musics*
(London, 1964), Reginald Nettel, *The Orchestra in England* (London,
1948). A. Elwart, *Histoire des concerts populaires* (Paris, 1864).

3.   Choral Concerts

1.   Sources on the tradition are fragmentary, but suggestive. For Paris see
le Caveau, XII (1846), p. iii; N. Brazier, "La Chanson et les
Societes Chantantes", *Paris ou le livre des cent-et-un*, VII,
pp. 90-126. For London: Erik Routley, *Hymns and Human Life* (London,
1952); Percy Scholes, *The Great Doctor Burney* (London, 1948), II,
pp. 169-74.
2.   Music and the Community, XXXVII (1842), p. 2. See also a similar remark
by the contemporary Comte de Rambuteau in his *Souvenirs* (Paris,
1905), p. 356.
3.   L. Couailhac, "Les Sociétés Chantantes", in Honoré de Balzac, ed.,
Nouveau Tableau de Paris (Paris, 1845), p. 256.
4.   Ludwig August Frankl, *Erinnerungen*, Stefan Kock, ed. (Prague, 1910),
p. 302.
5.   *AT*, July 4, 1846, p. 691; see also *MW*, June 7, 1845, p. 294.
6.   Sacred Harmonic Society, "Rules of the Society", 1832, Royal College
of Music, London; *SP*, July 5, 1834, pp. 635-36; [John E. Cox],
Musical Recollections of the Last Half-Century (London, 1872), II,
pp. 46-47.
7.   *SP*, October 19, 1850, p. 996; *ME*, December 21, 1844,
pp. 89-90.
8.   Annual Report, 1832, p. 27; Sixteenth Annual Report (1843-44), p. 8;
Similar remarks are found throughout the reports of the '40s.
9.   Membership Lists, Records of the Society, 1832-1834, 1848-1849, Royal
College of Music. Since the lists included street addresses of members,
the determination of occupations through city directories (which listed
artisans extensively) had a high degree of accuracy; *Post Office
London Directory* (1830, 1848); *Robson's London Directory*
(1828-1832, 1846-1848). The lists included only the male singers. Some
of the members not found in the directories were identified through
census records in the Public Record Office.
10.   Confirmation of this data is found in *SP*, November 15, 1834, p. 1090.
11.   *MW*, March 12, 1840, p. 154.
12.   Vincent Novello, *A Century and a Half in Soho: A Short History of the
House of Novello* (London, 1861), p. 28.
13.   *MW*, February 6, 1847, p. 81. The figure may have been somewhat
inflated by purchase of tickets simply as support for the organization.
Another newspaper report (*AT*, November 19, 1856, p. 1471) claimed
an average of over seven hundred per concert — still a healthy figure —
for the years 1836-56.
14.   *ME*, December 21, 1844, pp. 89-90; *Musical Recollections*, II, pp. 50-51.

15. *MW,* March 1, 1838, pp. 1237-38.
16. *MM,* December 1835, pp. 188-89; *DMR,* index of 1845-46.
17. *Ibid.,* October 20, 1842, p. 336, November 3, 1837, p. 127; Elkin, pp. 126-27.
18. *MM,* November 1835, p. 169; *DMR,* January 25, 1845, p. 45, April 18, 1846, p. 186, August 12, 1843, pp. 385-87.
19. Cox, II, pp. 52-53; *MW,* January 27, 1842, p. 225.
20. General information on the singing tradition can be found in Brazier, "La Chanson"; Couailhac, "Les Sociétés Chantantes"; *Le Caveau,* 1834-48; *Les Enfans du caveau,* 1834-?; Enfans d'Apollon, "Règlement", 1834, pp. 3-4, Bibliothéque Nationale.
21. Brazier, VII, pp. 90-115; Couailhac, pp. 246, 254; "l'Histoire de la musique en France", *Encyclopédie de la musique* (Paris, 1931), p. 3727; Henry-Abel Simon, *Histoire générale de l'institution orphéonique française* (Paris, 1909), pp. 33-35.
22. Only a few documents – few of them very informative – remain in the Archive de la Seine. The main sources on Wilhem and his program are: *Encyclopédie,* pp. 1315-30; Simon, pp. 25-32; *Annuaire musical,* pp. 96-98; Rambuteau, *Souvenirs,* pp. 355-56; letter of Wilhem to Rambuteau, Febraury 15, 1838, Archive de la Seine, AZ 315.
23. *RGM,* January 3, 1841, p. 6. See also *Ibid.,* December 7, 1845, p. 400, August 7, 1836, pp. 379-81; *SI,* May 16, 1846, p. 2: Princesse de Ligne, *Souvenirs* (Paris, 1922), p. 90; Enfans d'Apollon, *Discours,* 1847, p. 4.
24. *RGM,* December 7, 1845, p. 400.
25. *RMR,* I (1845), pp. 172-73.
26. *RGM,* December 7, 1845, p. 400. See also *MEN,* March 4, 1838, p. 4; Ligne, p. 90. Jean Orfila was one of the leading "courtesans" (*RGM,* November 2, 1845, p. 2).
27. Frank, p. 304-07; August Schmidt, "Selbstbiographie", in *Der Wiener Männergesangverein: Chronik der Jahre 1843 bis 1893* (Vienna, 1893), p. 26.
28. *Ibid.,* pp. 5, 13, 25, 41.
29. *Ibid.,* pp. 4, 9-10, 20-21, 180; Frankl, p. 301.
30. *Wiener Männergesangverein,* pp. 625-42. Like the membership lists of the Friends of Music, those of the Singing Society cited occupations in virtualy all cases.
31. *ZU,* February 24, 1847, p. 255; November 3, 1847, p. 1407; *WMZ,* May 25, 1844, p. 250, February 14, 1846, p. 79.
32. Ignaz Moschele to Friedrich Rochlitz, January 8, 1840, p. 4, Austrian National Library. See also *GR,* 1847, No. 4, p. 311; *WMZ,* October 16, 1845, p. 496; *HJ,* 1842, Vol. I, No. 1, pp. 32-33; Perger, pp. 54-59.
33. *HJ,* 1839, Vol. I, No. 3, p. 60.

4. Promenade Concerts

1. Matthias Koch, *Wien un die Wiener* (Karlsruhe, 1842), pp. 344-45; Hügel and Gross-Hoffinger, II, pp. 88-89. Much the same was reported of the Champs Elysées at this time; see Frances Trollope, *Paris and the Parisians in 1835* (London, 1835), II, p. 348, and Victor Lang, *Paris wie es ist* (Heidelberg, 1835), pp. 300-01.
2. *WMZ,* March 30, 1844, p. 153; *RGM,* December 31, 1843, p. 441;

Charles Manby Smith, *Curiosities of London Life* (London, 1853), p. 4. London had an enormous realm of new "pleasure gardens" which attracted much the same public (though probably more artisans) as the promenades but were not considered part of the conventional musical world. See Harold Scott, *Early Doors: Origins of the Music Halls* (London, 1946).

3. *MP*, July 12, 1845, p. 5, November 16, 1844, p. 5; *CO*, November 27, 1845, p. 573; Trollope, *Vienna and the Austrians* (London, 1838), I, pp. 296-97; *RGM*, July 16, 1837, p. 546; Joint Commission representing the London County Council and the London Survey Committee, *Survey of London* (London, 1960), XXIX, Part I, p. 240.

4. *PI*, November 5, 1834, pp. 4-5; *Paris chez Musard* (Paris, 1857), pp. 18-26; Adam Carse, *The Orchestra in the Eighteenth Century* (Cambridge, 1940), pp. 39-40, 54.

5. *GE*, March 13, 1847, p. 279. See also Enfans d'Apollon, *Discours*, (1847), p. 5.

6. *MW*, April 3, 1845, pp. 160-61.

7. *Mittheilungen aus Wien*, 1837, Vol. I, p. 22. For other comments on this group see: *RGM*, May 30, 1839, p. 178, January 3, 1841, p. 6; Paul Duval, "l'Employé français", *Francais peints par eux-même* (Paris, 1847), I, p. 302; *Intellectual Guide or How to Live in Paris* (London, 1835), pp. 59-60; Anton Langer, "Die Wiener Handlungsdiener", Andreas Schumacher, ed., *Lebensbilder aus Oesterreich* (Vienna, 1843), p. 21; *Mittheilungen*, 1834, II, pp. 192-93; Moscheles, II, p. 95; Carse, pp. 49-50; *Punch*, XXVII (1845), p. 255.

8. *MW*, December 3, 1840, p. 353; *Paris chez Musard*, p. 27.

9. Elwart, p. 55; *MP*, November 16, 1844, p. 5.

10. John Sanderson, *An American in Paris* (Phildelphia, 1839), II, p. 145; *MEN*, May 15, 1836, p. 4.

11. Baüerle, p. 162.

12. Enfans d'Apollon, p. 6.

13. Maréchale de Castellane, *Journal, 1804-1862* (Paris, 1896), p. 87.

14. Prefect of Police to Minister of Interior, May 29, 1843, pp. 1-3, Archives Nationales, F21 1038.

15. *FM*, January 6, 1839, p. 14. Similarly, an English travel guide to Paris warned its countrymen about the weaker deference to social station found in the French capital (*Intellectual Guide*, pp. 21-24).

16. *Mittheilungen*, pp. 192-93. See also *GE*, March 13, 1847, p. 279, and *Europäische Geheimnisse einer Mediatisirten* (Hamburg, 1836), p. 31.

17. Hügel and Gross-Hoffinger, II, p. 40.

18. *EN*, May 11, 1834, p. 3, May 22, 1834, p. 2; *MEN*, June 7, 1835, p. 4, June 14, 1835, p. 4, May 15, 1836, p. 1; *RGM*, June 18, 1837, p. 214.

19. *Paris chez Musard;* Trollope, *Paris*, I, p. 81; Elwart, pp. 55-56; *FM*, June 10, 1838, p. 7; Sanderson, II, p. 145; *MEN*, March 22, 1846, p. 1; *JT*, January 24, 1846, p. 4; *RGM*, December 29, 1839, p. 587, May 17, 1840, p. 309.

20. Adam Carse, *Life of Jullien* (Cambridge, 1951); Warwick Wroth, *London Pleasure Gardens of the Eighteenth Century* (London, 1896), pp. 83-89; Boleyne Reeves, *Sports and Pastimes in Town and Country* (London, 1841), pp. 191-92.

21. Marc-Constantin, *Histoire des café-concerts* (Paris, 1872) and

Histoires des cafés de Paris (Paris, 1857); Adelbert von Bornstedt, *Pariser Silhouetten* (Leipzig, 1836), p. 60; Caroline Pichler, *Denkwürdigkeiten aus meinem Leben* (Vienna, 1844), IV, pp. 164-66; *Die Kaiserstadt*, I, pp. 128, 143.

22. Raymond Mander, *The British Music Hall* (London, 1965), pp. 9-12; Warwick Wroth, *Cremorne and the later London Gardens* (London, 1907), p. vi.

23. *Paris chez Musard*, pp. 18-19.

24. Trollope, *Paris*, II, p. 349.

25. Bornstedt, p. 60; Marc-Constantin, *Histoires des cafés,* pp. 62-63.

26. Koch, pp. 369-70.

27. *WAN*, March 31, 1845, p. 307; *MW*, March 21, 1846, p. 132.

28. Baüerle, pp. 162-63; *HJ*, 1841, Vol. I., No. 1, p. 11.

5. Conclusion

1. For a recent such study, see Gareth Stedman Jones, "Working-Class Culture and Working-Class Politics In London, 1870-1900; Notes on the Remaking of a Working Class", *Journal of Social History*, VII (1974).

2. Daumard, pp. 249-89.

Chapter VI

1. For a useful recent discussion of modernization by an empirical historian, see E. A. Wrigley, "The Process of Modernization and the Industrial Revolution in England", *Journal of Interdisciplinary History,* III (1972), pp. 225-260.

2. For the most extreme interpretation of the family as a refuge, see Richard Sennett, *Families Against the City* (Cambridge, Mass., 1970).

3. "Working-Class Culture and Working-Class Politics in London 1870-1900; Notes on the Remaking of a Working Class", *Journal of Social History,* VII (1974).

4. "Class and Class-Consciousness in Early Nineteenth-Century England: Three Classes or Five?", *Class and Ideology in the Nineteenth Century* (London, 1972), pp. 15-41.

5. Peter N. Stearns, *1848: the Revolutionary Tide in Europe* (New York, 1947), pp. 99-103.

6. Charles Tilly, "The Changing Place of Collective Violence", *Essays in Theory and History: An Application to the Social Sciences,* ed. Melvin Richter (Cambridge, 1970), pp. 139-65.

7. "The Myth of the French Revolution", *Aspects of the French Revolution* (New York, 1968), pp. 90-112.

Appendix A

1. Daumard, pp. 11-30.

2. *Tafeln zur Statistik der Oesterreichischen Kaiserstadt* (Vienna, 1847), Table 31, pp. 2-3.

3. Great Britain, Office of the Census, *Census of 1841* (London, 1844), I, pp. 376-83.

4. F. Musgrove, "Middle-Class Education and Employment in the Nineteenth Century", *Economic History Review,* XII (1959), p. 100.

TABLES

Table 1

*The Numbers of concerts in London, Paris, and Vienna
during the seasons 1826-1827 and 1845-1846**

	London		Paris		Vienna	
	1826-1827	1845-1846	1826-1827	1845-1846	1826-1827	1845-1846
Benefit concerts	63	173	53	213	68	108
Groups of professionals	20	56	–	13	10	2
Theaters	12	3	7	2	1	1
Businesses	–	1	–	39	–	9
Educational institutions	13	6	10	4	2	7
Government occasions	–	2	–	8	–	–
Groups of amateurs	7	77	7	46	26	21
Cultural societies	1	58	1	25	–	–
Charity institutions	9	15	–	33	4	15
Total	**125**	**381**	**78**	**383**	**111**	**163**

* For Tables 1-10, see Chapter II, note 1.

Table 2

*Numbers of high- and low-status concerts and
divisions in taste during the season 1845-1846*

	London		Paris		Vienna	
Low-status concerts	161	42%	69	18%	24	15%
High-status concerts	220	58%	314	82%	139	85%
Total	**381**	**100%**	**383**	**100%**	**163**	**100%**
High-status concerts:						
Popular music	157	71%	239	76%	100	72%
Classical music	44	20%	25	8%	18	13%
Composers' benefit concerts	4	2%	20	6%	14	10%
Concerts with mixed programs	15	7%	30	9%	7	5%
(Total of last three categories)	(63	29%)	(75	23%)	(39	27%)
Total	**220**	**100%**	**315**	**99%**	**139**	**100%**

Table 3

Growth of the number of concerts

Seasons	London	Paris	Vienna
1826-1827	125	78	111
1845-1846	381	383	163
Percentage increase	305%	491%	˙47%

Table 4

Growth in the ratio of concerts to population

Seasons	London	Paris	Vienna
1826-1827	8	11	38
1845-1846	22	37	39
Percentage increase	175%	275%	3%

Table 5

Expense brackets of concert prices

Brackets	London	Paris	Vienna
Lower	1s.-5s.	1fr.-4fr.	10kr.-1fl.
Middle	5s.-10s. 6d.	4fr.-10fr.	1fl.-3fl.
Upper	10s. 6d.-21s.	10fr.-20fr.	3fl.-5fl.

Abbreviations and equivalencies:

d. = penny	21s. = 1 guinea
s. = shilling	20s. = £1
£. = pound	12d. = 1s.
kr. = kreutzer	60kr. = 1fl.
fl. = florin	1fl. = 1 gulden

Table 6

Lengths of price brackets (in francs)

Brackets	London	Paris	Vienna
Upper	13.10	10.00	5.07
Middle	6.90	6.00	5.07
Lower	5.00	3.00	2.06
Total	**25.00**	**19.00**	**12.20**

Table 7

Distribution of price settings by price brackets

Brackets	Upper		Middle		Lower		Total No. of Price Settings	Total converts with known prices
	No.	%	No.	%	No.	%		
Vienna	38	29	65	50	28	21	131	80
London	90	28	113	34	120	37	323	232

Table 8

Top prices of all concerts

Brackets	Upper		Middle		Lower		Total
	No.	%	No.	%	No.	%	
Vienna	38	48	33	41	9	11	80
London	90	39	88	38	54	23	232

Table 9

Base prices of all concerts

Brackets	Upper		Middle		Lower		Total
	No.	%	No.	%	No.	%	No.
Vienna	0	0	52	65	28	35	80
London	65	28	47	20	120	52	232

Table 10

Numbers of concerts whose prices overlapped brackets

Brackets	Upper & middle	Middle & lower	Upper, middle & lower	Total	% of concerts with known prices
Vienna	32	13	6	51	64%
London	24	65	1	90	39%

Table 11

Family occupations of subscribers to the Concerts of Ancient Music during the seasons of 1830 and 1848*

	1830		1848	
	Non-titled	Titled	Non-titled	Titled
Titled persons without known occupation	0	97	0	38
Gentry	29	0	19	0
Economic profs.	3	0	8	0
Law	2	0	18	0
Church	19	2	5	2
Medicine	0	0	1	0
"Doctor"	6	0	0	0
Bureaucracy	0	0	4	0
Journalism	0	0	1	0
Military	20	3	10	1
	79	102	66	41
Total identified		181		107
Total subscribers		519 35%		220 49%

* For Tables, 11-16, see Chapter IV, Section 1, Notes 3, 5, and 7.

Table 12

*Numbers of titled persons among the subscribers
to the Concerts of Ancient Music*

	Total subscribers	Total titled persons		Total peerage titles	% of titled persons	% of total subscribers
1808	576	158	25%	48	30%	8%
1820	683	214	31%	38	18%	6%
1830	519	102	20%	34	32%	7%
1840	340	53	13%	22	41%	6%
1848	220	41	18%	14	34%	6%

Table 13

*Numbers of titled persons among the subscribers
to the Concerts of the Philharmonic Society*

	Total subscribers	Titled subscribers		Subscribers with peerage titles	% of titled subscribers	% of total subscribers
1820	697	55	7.9%	15	27.2%	2.2%
1830	661	46	6.9%	9	19.0%	1.4%
1839	499	28	5.6%	4	14.2%	.8%
1843	314	20	6.3%	5	25.0%	1.6%
1848	439	22	5.0%	8	36.3%	1.8%

Table 14

Family occupations of subscribers to the concerts of the Philharmonic Society in 1830 and 1848

Male subscribers:	1830	1848
Titled persons without known occupation	30	19
Gentry	5	1
Rentiers	0	5
Liberal professions:	64	98
Law	23	14
Church	24	9
Medicine	6	4
Arts	11	69
Technical arts	0	2
Bureaucracy	5	3
Military	11	5
Economic professions:	61	32
Wholesale	12	3
Retail	21	16
Finance	7	3
Manufacture	11	10
Unidentified	10	0
Total	**176 of 417 (41%)**	**163 of 284 (57%)**

Table 15

Listings of concert subscribers in 1848 in Boyle's Court Guide

	Philharmonic Society	Concerts of Ancient Music	Musical Union
Present	27%	50%	71%
Absent	20%	13%	11%
Unascertainable	53%	37%	18%
	100%	100%	100%

Table 16.

*Family occupations of subscribers to the Musical Union
during the season of 1848*

Occupation	Non-titled persons		Titled persons
Titled persons without known occupation			110
Gentry	14		
Rentiers	3		
Liberal professions:	16		
Church		6	4
Law		3	
Medicine		4	
Journalism		1	
Academic professions		2	
Military	9		9
Bureaucracy	1		
Economic professions:	8		
Finance		4	1
Manufacture		4	
Total	51		124
Total identified			175
Total subscribers			312 56%

Table 17

*Occupations of members of the Viennese
amateur leadership group**

	Titled	Non-titled	Total
High aristocracy	2		2
Rentiers	1		1
Liberal professions	1	7	8
Economic professions	1	5	6
Bureaucracy	8	19	27
Unknown	1	4	5
Total	**14**	**35**	**49**

* For Tables 17-19, see Chapter IV, Section 1, notes 10 and 27, and Section 4, notes 4 and 8.

Table 18

Status levels of bureaucratic employees among the members of the Society of the Friends of Music in 1846

	Participating members		Supporting members	
High status	3	3%	53	28%
Middle status	34	38%	78	37%
Low status	14	16%	11	2%
Unascertainable	38	43%	44	23%

Table 19

Occupations of Members of the Society of the Friends of Music in 1846

	Participating members			Supporting members	
Liberal professions		34	18%		62	15%
Medicine	0			19		
Law	7			7		
Church	1			19		
Teaching	6			3		
University	1			3		
Arts	19			9		
Unascertainable	0			2		
Economic professions		39	21%		116	30%
Retail	7			38		
Wholesale	5			36		
Finance	0			1		
Manufacture	7			10		
Accountant	7			2		
Employee: high	4			5		
Employee: low	9			8		
Artisan	0			16		
Bureaucracy		89	48%		186	48%
High titles	0			28		
Low titles and Nontitled	89			158		
Military		1			7	2%
Rentier		21	12%		17	5%
Total		**184**	**99%**		**388**	**99%**
Total members		**225**	**(82%)**		**540**	**(72%)**

Table 20

Occupations of members of Parisian amateur orchestras*

	Société Philhar-monique	Société Bonnet	Société d'Emula-tion	Société du Lycée Musical	Total
Wholesale & finance	0	4	1	2	7
Retailing	3	3	0	5	11
Clerks	1	2	0	2	5
Liberal professions	8	5	2	5	20
Rentiers	1	2	0	0	3
Artisans	16	6	3	6	31
Musicians	56	15	0	14	85
Unidentified	35	35	23	21	114
Total	**120**	**72**	**29**	**55**	**276**

* See Chpater IV, Section 2, notes 4, 6 and 7.

Table 21

Occupations of members of the Sacred Harmonic Society during the seasons 1832-1834 and 1848-1849*

	1832-1834	1848-1849
Liberal professions	4	5
Economic professions:		
Wholesale	5	3
Retail	27	15
Artisanal	36	28
Employees	1	1
Total identified	**73**	**52**
Unidentified	**60**	**123**

* See Chapter IV, Section 3, note 9.

Table 22

Occupations of the members of the Men's Singing Society between 1843 and 1847*

	Participating		Supporting	Total	Titled persons	
Economic professions						
Employees	37		30		4	
Retail	22		84			
Wholesale	1		3		1	
Finance	1		2		2	
Manufacture	5	66	7	126	2	9
Liberal professions						
Law	12		5		1	
Medicine	6		13		3	
Arts	11		5			
Music	49		0			
Teaching	26		0			
Technical	9		8			
University	0		4			
Miscellaneous	0	113	2	27		4
Students	21	21		0		
Bureaucracy						
High nobles	0		2		2	
High posts	0		14		12	
Legal posts	1		18		3	
General	92	93	68	102	8	25
Military		0		8		3
Rentiers		4		23		2
Crafts		22		16		0
Unknown		39		10		0
Aristocrats without professions		0		28		28
Totals		358		350		71 (23%)

* See Chapter IV, Section 3, note 30.

INDEX

169

170